REAL PEOPLE

£12.99

34/50/99

-time opening hours:

Mon-Thurs: 9.00 - 8.00 p
Friday:

WITHDRAWN

REAL PEOPLE

*Personal Identity without Thought
Experiments*

KATHLEEN V. WILKES

CLARENDON PRESS · OXFORD

Oxford University Press, Walton Street, Oxford OX2 6DP

Oxford New York Toronto
Delhi Bombay Calcutta Madras Karachi
Kuala Lumpur Singapore Hong Kong Tokyo
Nairobi Dar es Salaam Cape Town
Melbourne Auckland Madrid

and associated companies in
Berlin Ibadan

Oxford is a trade mark of Oxford University Press

Published in the United States by
Oxford University Press Inc., New York

British Library Cataloguing in Publication Data
Wilkes, Kathleen V.
Real people: personal identity without
thought experiments.
1. Man. Identity—Philosophical
perspectives
I. Title
126
ISBN 0-19-824080-5 (pbk.)

Library of Congress Cataloging in Publication Data
Wilkes, Kathleen V.
Real people: personal identity without thought experiments/
Kathleen V. Wilkes.
Bibliography. Includes index.
1. Identity (Psychology). 2. Consciousness. 3. Psychology,
Pathological. 4. Psychology—Methodology. I. Title.
BF697.W4935 1988 155.2—dc19 88-5313
ISBN 0-19-824080-5 (pbk.)

1 3 5 7 9 10 8 6 4 2

Printed in Malta
by Interprint Ltd

For H.B.J.M.

PREFACE

The subject of Personal Identity is one of the most enjoyable—as well as the most perplexing—in philosophy. The quality of the literature about it is in general very high. So too is the quantity. Why then add another book to the list?

In the first chapter I try to explain why. Personal Identity has been the stamping-ground for bizarre, entertaining, confusing, and inconclusive thought experiments. To my mind, these alluring fictions have led discussion off on the wrong tracks; moreover, since they rely heavily on imagination and intuition, they lead to no solid or agreed conclusions, since intuitions vary and imaginations fail. What is more, I do not think that we need them, since there are so many actual puzzle-cases which defy the *imagination*, but which we none the less have to accept as facts. To clear the way for discussion of these, then, the first chapter questions the methodology of thought-experimentation, at least if it is deployed without very stringent controls.

Whatever else they may be, typical persons are rational, can use language, are Intentional systems, require certain kinds of treatment from others, are agents of responsible behaviour themselves, and seem to have some special kind of (self-)consciousness. Problems arise when any of these strands are missing. Thus the second chapter considers (normal and abnormal) infants and foetuses; we shall see here the paramount importance of the question of the treatment they should receive. The third chapter looks at the adult insane. Here again we have to examine the sort of moral and practical stance appropriate to take to them; evidently, too, the problem of spelling out what it is in which human rationality consists arises centrally.

In the fourth chapter we start off on a three-chapter examination of human (self-)consciousness, and the degree of 'unity' and 'continuity' of consciousness we expect to find. Chapter 4 looks at breakdowns in continuity suffered by those with fugue states, and breakdowns in both unity and continuity found in hypnotized individuals and cases of multiple personality. This last puzzle, I argue, is the one paradox which is completely intractable—the concept of a person cannot cope with full-blown cases. Chapter 5 examines the breakdown of unity shown by people with split brains—apparently two centres of consciousness in one body, working separately but simultaneously. This is argued to pose *no* difficulty for the concept of a person; it is a good example of something which is not 'imaginable' but which is nevertheless a fact. Here we need to go into the concept of 'a mind' at some length. Chapter 6 tries to take consciousness itself to bits, showing how it is not a notion that can be relied on to set, or solve, any of the questions that have been perplexing us.

The penultimate chapter is a somewhat self-indulgent sprint through interestingly different views of the person found in Homer, Aristotle, the post-Cartesians, and contemporary cognitive science with its so-called 'computer model of mind'. It ends by suggesting that, knowingly or not, we are returning to the Aristotelian model of the individual; and that we are right to be doing so. In the final chapter, the 'Epilogue', it is suggested that all 'persons' would have to be more or less human.

Far too many have assisted with various chapters of this book to make adequate acknowledgement possible. In particular, the first chapter (about which I was the most uncertain) went through numerous sea changes as a result of discussion; comments and objections were particularly vigorous in the philosophy departments of Warsaw, Uppsala, the Open University, Bristol, and St Andrews. Ancestor versions of each chapter, though, benefited greatly from such discussions at numerous universities, and it would be impossible to list them all. An invitation from the University of Minnesota allowed me time to complete a very early first draft of the whole. An antepenultimate version was given chapter by chapter to an Oxford graduate seminar, and I learned much from the ensuing criticisms.

Not chapters, but individual arguments (especially those touching on the philosophy of science), immersed in other papers, were presented to the Philosophy of Science course in Dubrovnik several years running, and I am particularly grateful to the Inter-university Centre there, and to the participants, for that opportunity.

Some chapters are (substantially rewritten) versions of papers published elsewhere. An ancestor of chapter 2 has appeared (in Polish translation) in *Etyka*. Earlier versions of much of chapters 4 and 6 appeared in the *British Journal for the Philosophy of Science*, and of much of chapter 5 in *Philosophy*. I am much indebted to the editors for allowing me to use (modified and updated) versions of the arguments first offered in their journals.

K.V.W.

CONTENTS

1

Thought Experiments

As I was sitting in my chair
I *knew* the bottom wasn't there,
Nor legs nor back, but I *just sat,*
Ignoring little things like that.

(Hughes Mearns)

1. INTRODUCTION

This book differs from other tracts on the same subject in that it abjures
the use of thought experiments. Instead, it concentrates upon the sorts
of things that can (really, actually) happen to the object we call a person,
and the implications that wait to be drawn from those things. The
immensely rich literature on the subject of Personal Identity—and have
no doubts: the literature is not only richly profuse but fun—is, however,
rich and fun at least in part precisely *because* of the centrality of thought
experiments; they amuse, provoke the imagination, and allow one to
reach splendidly revolutionary conclusions.

So that kind of fun will be missing from this book. It aims to use
science fact rather than science fiction or fantasy. My contention is that
the conclusions will be more plausible because based in the real world;
and also that what actually can and does happen is usually more
gripping than what the perfervid imagination dreams up from the
philosopher's armchair. However, I need to defend this policy, and so
the bulk of this (long) first chapter is devoted to explaining what
thought experiments are, and why I find them problematic in general
and, for this topic in particular, highly misleading as a philosophical
tool.

2. WHAT THOUGHT EXPERIMENTS ARE

Thought experiments are found both in science and in philosophy. In
science, as we shall see, they can be helpful; and they tend to be

relatively unproblematic. (The qualifying 'can be', and 'tend to be' are essential; many are neither useful nor clear.) In philosophy on the other hand, and in particular in the domain of the philosophy of mind, they can be—in fact they usually are—both problematic and positively misleading. Whether they prove useful, instructive, or illuminating depends (both in science and in philosophy) on the context of their deployment.

The central idea behind the thought-experimental method runs roughly as follows. Suppose that we want to test a claim made by some scientific theory (and hence to test the theory); suppose we want to see what might follow if certain theoretical claims were true; suppose we want to examine the plausibility of some philosophical theses or principles; suppose we want to examine the range and scope of a concept. It may be appropriate, in all these different domains, to ask a 'what if . . .?' question. Such a question typically postulates an imaginary state of affairs, something that does not in fact happen in the real world. Put another way, in the modern jargon, we imagine a 'possible world' in which the state of affairs *actually* occurs—a world like our own in all relevant respects except for the existence in that world of the imagined phenomenon. ('Relevance' is, unsurprisingly, going to require a lot of spelling out; we shall turn to examine it specifically a little later, in Section 4 of this chapter. For the time being I shall just assume a common-or-garden grip on the notion.) Then we try to draw out the implications—'what we would say if' that imagined set-up were to obtain; that is, if we inhabited that possible world. By such means (we shall come to examples soon) we may, perhaps, get weaker or stronger reasons for thinking a scientific claim to be true or false; for concluding that a philosophical thesis is plausible or implausible; or for claiming a discovery about the limitations and scope of one of our everyday concepts.

Both elements in the label 'thought experiment' are important. Such forays of the imagination are called *thought* experiments precisely because they are imaginary, they cannot be realized in the real world. (The force of this 'cannot' is, again, something that will require a lot of discussion shortly. At the moment I leave it vague; we will return to it in Section 5.) But they are none the less thought *experiments* because, to be of any value, they have to obey many of the constraints on experimentation. In particular, we must be clear just what (in the imaginary scenario) remains constant, and what has been altered in thought. This is, as we shall discover, a crucially important factor in their success or failure.

One point of clarification. Following Brown [1986]—on whose paper I shall rely for much of my discussion about thought experiments in physics—we should avoid unnecessary misunderstanding by excluding from discussion two related but importantly distinct methods of experimentation-in-thought. The first of these he calls 'merely imagined': those experiments which are not *in fact* carried out in practice, but which could be. For instance (his example): Galileo wondered what would happen if a cannon ball and a musket ball were dropped from the same height. He claimed, *contra* Aristotle, that they would fall at the same speed. This is 'merely imagined' because although Galileo (probably) did not try it out, he could easily have done so. Many examples in moral philosophy are like this, are 'merely imagined': asking people what they think they would do in certain circumstances that may be unlikely or exotic, but which might possibly occur. Consider for example the over-familiar thought experiment often used to attack utilitarianism: the sheriff in one of the Southern states of the USA who has to choose between hanging a black scapegoat, someone he knows to be innocent of the alleged rape of a white woman; or doing nothing, which would mean that a lynch mob would carry out its threat to massacre several equally innocent blacks. I gather that this example had in fact some slight basis in history; whether or not that is so, it is the sort of thing that *could* happen. I shall not primarily be concerned with 'merely imagined' thought experiments, although they will from time to time be relevant to the discussion.

The second class of cases to exclude from the argument are the kinds of experiment 'which take place in thought', where (Brown's example again) we engage in some form of introspection to find out whether a sentence such as 'colourless green ideas sleep furiously' is grammatical or not. These should be excluded because they are, after all, real experiments and not imaginary ones. Anyway, I have little quarrel with either of these, and shall not be discussing them.

Excluding these, then, let us now illustrate the thought-experimental technique with some examples. First, a couple from physics, both lifted shamelessly from Brown's paper.

Examples from physics

Einstein, contemplating Maxwell's electrodynamics, wondered what someone travelling beside the front of a beam of light would see. No individual could travel at this speed—the experiment could not be performed. But *if* he did, then, according to Maxwell's theory, he should see something that could not exist: a stationary oscillatory field. Hence, from this thought experiment alone, there are *at least* serious difficulties with Maxwell's theory. The imaginary state of affairs is an individual travelling at the speed of light; the implication drawn, that the theory is inconsistent.

Simon Stevin gives us a second thought experiment, concerning the properties of an inclined plane, as shown in Fig. 1. The argument is admirably simple and decisive. The imaginary state of affairs is of two perfectly frictionless planes (which never exist in the real world) joined at an angle so that there is one steep, and one less steep, incline down. Would a chain draped over such a plane remain put, or would gravity pull it down one side or the other? On one side there are fewer links but a steeper slope, on the other a shallower slope but a greater number of links. The answer is obvious the minute one makes the chain circular (joining the two ends under each bottom edge of the planes); for, if it is to slide at all, it would evidently have to slide for ever. Given that there are no perpetual motion machines, the chain in the original thought experiment would, clearly, have to remain in equilibrium. The imaginary state of affairs is the perfect lack of friction; the conclusion (if we assume the absence of perpetual motion), conclusive.

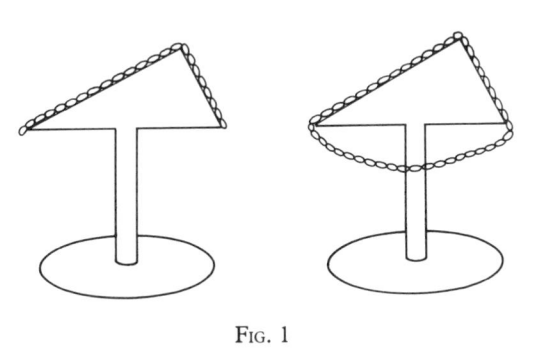

Fig. 1

Let us turn next to consider philosophical theses and concepts, and the use of thought experiments in moral philosophy, epistemology, and the philosophy of mind.

Examples from philosophy

We can begin with an example from moral philosophy. As all know, there are several theories about the basis of morality—that it is ultimately for self-interested reasons that we are moral; or that morality derives from natural emotions of love, fellow-feeling, generosity, pity, etc.; or that it is based upon rationality; or that it is the result of a fictional social contract; or that it is inevitable, given what we know about sociology and human psychology. One test suggested to discover the fundamentality of morality is to ask 'what if we all had a Gyges' ring to make us invisible at will?' As we know, no humans are actually invisible, so we cannot try the experiment and see. So we imagine a possible world in which people have such rings, but which is in other respects just like ours. If it seems that in such circumstances nobody would remain moral (i.e. if we think that when we could guarantee getting away with it, we would not bother with moral standards), then, crudely, it looks as though morality is based rather on self-interest than on anything grander. The imaginary state of affairs is the invisibility; one conclusion *may* be that morality must be based ultimately on self-interest.

A second familiar *philosophical* example, this time taken from epistemology, tests the scope and range of a concept rather than the truth of a thesis. 'What if we found a substance that looked, tasted, behaved, reacted, and was used exactly like water, but which was not H_2O? Would we still call that *water*?' The imaginary state of affairs here, which we believe not to obtain in the real world, is of course that we should come across something like water in the relevant respects. In such a case, if we think we would say it was *not* water, then we discover that we hold it as a necessary truth about water that it is H_2O—there is no possible world in which water is not H_2O—so we would count nothing as water unless it *was* H_2O. Hence by thus stretching a concept into the unknown one may find out more precisely what it is to which we are committed; we see its scope and extent more easily than we could if we merely observed how the term was actually used in normal circumstances. If the concept fractures under the strain—if, that is, we would not know *what* to say in the hypothesized circumstances—then too the scope and limitations of the term's range and extent become clearer. We learn much about a concept by finding where its remit ends.

Such a method of filling out the content of a term may seem particularly well suited to the examination of our intuitions concerning ordinary-language terms; and now of course we are getting closer to our central theme of personal identity. For there are relatively few everyday terms which have crisp and tidy definitions; how many of us, for example, would be willing to produce a set of necessary and sufficient conditions for something to be a table, a game, or an ornament? (The biggest mistake made by some interpreters of so-called 'ordinary-language philosophy' is to assume that one has to start with the prescription 'Define your terms!' Such a strategy is generally vastly misleading.) But even if we reject the possibility, or the desirability, of characterizing a concept by resort to a comprehensive definition, we can, it seems, none the less learn much about its meaning by appeal to variations on these 'what if . . .?' questions.

The subject of personal identity—and 'person' is paradigmatically a term of the vernacular—has probably exploited the method more than has any other problem area in philosophy. Many of the examples are familiar: Descartes, for instance, imagining away his body to help him reach the conclusion 'sum res cogitans'; Locke testing 'what we would say if' the soul of a cobbler migrated into the body of a prince, or if the Mayor of Queinborough awoke one day with all of Socrates' memories. Then, as now, we find further flights of fantasy. There are statues that come to life (today, more commonly, we tend rather to postulate robots with many or most of our distinctively human characteristics); non-human animals with human intelligence; people who split like amoebae or fuse like clouds; brain transplants; mind transplants (i.e. wiping the 'program' out of the hardware of one brain and programming a 'blank' brain with it); transplants of the left and right hemispheres of the brain into two different bodies; and so on and so forth. None of these circumstances, we need scarcely add, occur in the world as we have it; we need to describe possible worlds in which they do.

All this is of course great fun; and it has fostered a range of often startling conclusions. But there are drawbacks to the method, and I shall be arguing in this chapter that the armchair theoretician is bound by constraints upon his use of thought-experimentation that are as stringent as are the constraints that restrict the laboratory researcher. These constraints, we shall find, should generally force philosophers back from fiction and fantasy into something much closer to the sober exploration of science fact—to the study of 'what actually happens when . . .', rather than of 'what might happen if . . .'.

3. FIRST DIFFICULTY: THE BACKGROUND

There is a striking difference between thought experiments in science, and those in the philosophy of mind, or ethics. (The difference may be one of degree rather than of kind; but I have never understood why people discussing differences of degree feel compelled to add the qualifier 'only'. There are 'only' differences of degree between the bumps in my lawn and the Himalayas.) The difference harks back to the fact that thought experiments are indeed *experiments*, in one central sense at least, and subject to many of the same constraints as normal ones.

One vital constraint is this. The experimenter—any experimenter, in thought or in actuality—needs to give us the background conditions against which he sets his experiment. If he does not, the results of his experiment will be inconclusive. The reason for that is simple and obvious: experiments, typically, set out to show what difference some factor makes; in order to test this, other relevant conditions must be held constant, and the problematic factor juggled against that constant background. If several factors were all fluctuating, then we would not know which of them (or which combination of them) to hold responsible for the outcome.

Now these stable relevant conditions may be taken for granted, or they may be explicitly stated; but they cannot be left wholly amorphous. For instance, the psychologist studying aggression in rats will not bother to say that the rats of his experimental and control groups are normal and healthy, that he was sober throughout the procedure, his computer efficient, the temperature of the cages and the laboratory roughly normal. All these are relevant to the success of the experiment, but tend to go without saying. By contrast, he may however need to state explicitly that all his rats were (or were not) of the same sex, or were all of the species *rattus Norvegicus*; and he will typically describe the apparatus he uses. As far as is possible, then, the relevant *ceteris paribus* conditions are either stated, or assumed. Many background conditions will be irrelevant (or thought to be so)—such as the average length of the rats' whiskers or the day of the week on which each was born. The general point is that we know, or can assume, that we have before us everything that is thought to be relevant for assessing the outcome of the experiment. It cannot be stressed too strongly that all experiments (in real life and in thought) are for a *particular* purpose, testing a *particular* factor, and 'relevance' is relative to this.

The thought experiments in physics that we have mentioned so far conform to this canon. We are asked to suspend belief in one feature, and to suppose *that* Einstein could travel at the speed of light, or *that* Stevin has found perfectly frictionless planes and chains. That is all;

everything else remains as it was, conforming to the laws we know and trust. Put another way, the 'possible world' is *our* world, the world described by our sciences, except for one distinguishing difference. So we know or can assume everything else that it is relevant to know, in order to assess that thought experiment. The fact that Einstein would not survive such an experience, were it to be possible, is true but not relevant. It is not relevant because the experiment, note, is *not* aimed at illustrating human tolerances and capacities (if it were, it would of course be highly relevant), but at an implication of Maxwell's theory concerning the properties of light. Only one factor is juggled, and its impossibility is not relevant to the conclusion; the relevant remainder stay constant.

It is because the background is adequately described in such thought experiments as these, I think, that Brown [1986] can say:

Thesis I: The burden of any thought experiment rests on the establishment (in the imagination) of a phenomenon. Once the phenomenon is established, *the inference to a theory is fairly unproblematic*; that is, the jump from data to theory is relatively small . . . (p. 4).

. . . if we got the phenomenon right *then the theory followed more or less automatically* (p. 13; italics mine).

Note the last clauses: the jump from the imaginary data is small, and follows readily. This, I suggest, is precisely because the relevant background is adequately fixed, so that the result of the imagined state of affairs is immediately clear. Were it not so, the inference could not be 'unproblematic'. By contrast, when we have thought experiments in philosophy, there are as we shall see problems in making the inference—precisely because of the ambiguous uncertainty concerning the relevant background conditions, leaving it unclear whether we have indeed 'established a phenomenon'. This means that our intuitions run awry, and the inferences are not only problematic, but the 'jump' from the phenomenon to the conclusion is made the larger because of the further need to imagine just what these backing conditions, under the imagined circumstances, would be. The 'possible world' is inadequately described.

To bolster this point, let us consider one more thought experiment in physics which—according at least to Niels Bohr—went wrong precisely because the relevant background was not, and could not be, fixed precisely enough for the purposes of the thought experiment; where the jump from data to theory originally *looked* small, but where further consideration of the background forestalled the inference; where the phenomenon could not really be 'established'. Einstein in 1930 imagined a box with a hole in its side, suspended on a spring balance with a pointer reading its position on a scale fixed to the balance support (thus: the box hangs from a spring; a pointer sticks out of one side measuring the rise or fall of the box against a scale attached to the supporting structure; on the other side of the box is a hole). The hole in the side of the box could be closed by a shutter which was moved by a clock inside the box. If the box contained some radiation and the clock was set to open the shutter for a tiny interval, a single photon could be released through the hole at a moment precisely specified. But also, by weighing the box before and after the event, one could measure the energy of the photon, by exploiting the famous formula $E = mc^2$. This would have been 'in definite contradiction to the reciprocal indeterminacy of time and energy quantities in quantum mechanics' (Bohr [1959], p. 226). However, *when general relativity theory is taken into account*, any 'use of the apparatus as a means of accurately measuring the energy of the photon will prevent us from controlling the moment of its escape' (Bohr [1959], p. 228): one can either time it, or measure the amount of energy—but not both at the same time. The thought experiment thus cannot be carried through to reach the desired conclusion. There is no possible world in which this phenomenon could be 'established'.

Both the 'clock in a box' and the 'speed of light' thought experiments involved impossibilities. As noted above, the sort of possibility and impossibility in question needs, and will receive, fuller discussion; for the moment, though, we need to be clear about why one impossibility matters—is 'relevant'—and why the other does not. The reason is this: when deriving the conclusion about time and energy quantities in quantum mechanics, general relativity theory (which blocks the original inference) is central to the theory in question, central to the argument, and cannot be ignored. But arguments about Maxwell's theory of electrodynamics are entirely independent of human capacities and tolerances. One impossibility nullifies the thought experiment, the other is merely heuristic and does not. Evidently it will often be very unclear when an impossibility 'matters': we will not always have such neat contrasts. But these two thought experiments illustrate the two extremes and can serve as touchstones.

The general moral is clear: just as with real experiments, thought experiments presuppose that all relevant background conditions are included and specified.

Before turning to contrast some thought experiments in philosophy of mind, or ethics, with the examples from physics, let us look at a different but interestingly analogous enterprise: fiction, especially the fantasies of familiar children's stories. Tolkien, Milne, or Lewis Carroll ask us to suspend disbelief wildly and extensively: hobbits in hats, girls who walk through mirrors unscathed, slithy toves, tigers cohabiting amicably with piglets. This is prima facie as unlike Einstein's whooshing along with a light beam as could be. But there is a crucial point of resemblance: *in so far as it is relevant*, the background to all the propositions in which one is asked to suspend belief is supplied, and is as consistent as it needs to be for the purpose in hand (entertainment). Thus, after the original suspension of belief, the rest is 'believable'; and we can assess the extent to which the purpose of entertaining successfully has been achieved. The background to Einstein's travel is, but for his celerity, our normal world. But Carroll and Tolkien, and to a lesser extent Milne, take pains to create an entire (and fundamentally different) world, with its own principles of operation and, *where relevant*, the differences from the real world indicated. If you like wearing hats, it is plausible to suppose you are likely to talk too. A world in which one can walk through mirrors is, as explicitly indicated, a world of a dream; in such a world mushrooms can make one grow or shrink, a shop can turn into a boat, Queens can believe six impossible things before breakfast. For such fantasy, we have another world sketched for us, against the background of which the events are intelligible. These fantasies borrow what they want from the real world (Alice fell down the hole because that is what gravity does to you); but they add their own dreamlike assumptions too: eggs can talk. Against that mixed real/fantastical background, the events make sense. Were we to quibble that the fantastical and the actual would often *in fact* collide, we would have missed the point of fiction: it is the *relevant* background that is assumed or sketched, and what counts as 'relevant' is in part a function, as we have already seen, of the purpose of the enterprise. (Consideration of function is not enough to determine 'relevance'; but it helps. As promised, we shall shortly discuss 'relevance' explicitly.) The purpose of fantasy, after all, is to entertain; not to bolster or test our theories or concepts.

Another way of putting this point is to contrast fantasy with the sort of fiction found in detective stories. Sherlock Holmes may have learned much from the dog that did not bark in the night; but we would not accept the story if a bloodhound had sat opposite him in an armchair describing the scents of the butler and the baron. Conan Doyle, that is, sets his stories explicitly against our real world. Tolkien and Carroll set out to describe a quite different world, and the condition for success is that all *relevant* details are provided. The fact that some such details may *in fact* conflict with accepted physical laws is no more relevant—unless it is!—than the fact that travelling as fast as light conflicts with our present understanding of human capacity. We must always look to the point of the enterprise, the goal of the imaginary endeavour.

Let us turn now to thought experiments in philosophy. Consider first Gyges' ring: before we can make sense of this thought experiment, several points press to be answered—there are relevant background conditions that need to be known before we can draw any conclusion(s) from the imagined phenomenon. We need more information than we yet have about this 'possible world'. For instance, is the owner of the ring to be intangible as well as invisible? That makes a substantial difference *to the issue at issue*: if he is not intangible, he might by mistake bump up against, and get arrested by, a policeman, or get his hand slammed shut in the till-drawer. Thus a potential criminal may yet have self-interested reasons for staying within the bounds of morality. Is there anything that would count as 'punishment' for an invisible and intangible agent? If so, what—and how unpleasant would it be? If you are both invisible and intangible, could prison walls hold you? And if they could not, could *you* hold a gun, or a caseful of banknotes? Again, would others know that one owned such a ring? If so, then there might be extra reasons for *remaining* moral: viz., that unsolved crimes might otherwise be ascribed to you. The point is that the purpose of the thought experiment cannot be met unless such questions are answered: they are deeply relevant. The background is inadequately described, and the results therefore inconclusive.

Consider next one of the familiar thought experiments to do with personal identity: that we might all split like amoebae. It is obviously and essentially relevant *to the purposes of this thought experiment* to know such things as: how often? Is it predictable? Or sometimes predictable and sometimes not, like dying? Can it be induced, or prevented? Just as obviously, the background society, against which we set the phenomenon, is now mysterious. Does it have such institutions as marriage? How would that work? Or universities? It would be difficult, to say the least, if universities doubled in size every few days, or weeks, or years. Are pregnant women debarred from splitting? The *entire* background here is incomprehensible. When we ask what *we* would say if this happened, who, now, are 'we'?

The point here is, I think, central. Thought experiments are, like all experiments, undertaken for a specific purpose. Thought experiments to do with personal identity have, as their official ambition, the job of revealing the heart of our *current, present*, notions of what it is to be a person. But the only one discussed so far—the amoeba-style split— seems to lack the capacity to do any such thing, and for this reason: *in* a world where we split like amoebae, everything else is going to be so unimaginably different that we do not know what concepts would remain 'fixed', part of the background; we have not filled out the relevant details of this 'possible world', except that we know it cannot be much like ours. But if we cannot know that, then we cannot assess, or derive conclusions from, the thought experiment.

4. PARENTHESIS: RELEVANCE AND NATURAL KINDS[1]

Throughout the foregoing we have been assuming that what counts as 'relevant' to a particular experiment, or thought experiment, will by and large be something scrutable by common sense. Often, of course, it may be. Few would think that the day of the week on which an experimental rat was born made any difference at all to experiments involving mature rats; the colour of an agent's car would rarely be relevant to thought experiments in moral philosophy. We are helped, too, by consideration of the *function* of an experiment (whether real or imaginary), as we have seen already. Since the job of Einstein's thought experiment was to explore some properties of light, the impossibility of travelling at that speed seems not to infect the conclusion: it is impossible, sure, but not relevantly so. By contrast, general relativity theory is essentially and destructively relevant to the 'clock in a box' thought experiment.

Thus we need to ensure that what is imagined could be realized in some possible world; or that if it could not be, this impossibility is not 'relevant' to the derivation of the conclusion. Not only that, of course; as we have seen, further factors belonging to the 'background' may, or may not, be 'relevant' to conclusions based on the thought experiment. Common sense, aided by a consideration of the purpose or function of the experiment or thought experiment will often—as we have seen— give us enough to determine 'relevance', especially in the tightly defined world of science. What we can conclude so far, then, on the basis of this

[1] I am very grateful to Eric James (who has helped improve this chapter at several places) for convincing me of the utility of the line of argument developed in this section.

and the previous section, is that every fruitful thought experiment, or indeed 'real' scientific experiment, presupposes that the background, the general context, has been adequately described.

In science we often have a supporting background of theory, and experiments conducted against fixed physical parameters; thus in many cases the situation is indeed adequately described, and relevance or irrelevance can be determined with fair safety. When we move away from the relative security of the mature sciences to the rich and glorious chaos of common sense—which is the domain in which most philosophical thought experiments romp around—this is missing. This is in large part because, as claimed already, few everyday terms have crisp and tidy definitions. Whereas the sciences on the one hand aim for clarity, economy, and the absence of ambiguity in their conceptual apparatus, common sense on the other revels in the riot of Roget's *Thesaurus*. Thus ascriptions of common-sense terms have conceptual *links, suggestions, mutual involvements*—but few clear *entailments*. (For instance, to call someone 'prejudiced' suggests that his prejudice is false. But it does not entail this; it is just for the most part true that prejudiced people have false beliefs. Saying that *A* hates *B* may suggest that *A* does not love *B*; but that too might be false.)

The difference in 'tightness' between the implications held by statements of science and those of common sense is, again, one of degree—and none the worse for that. Many statements of science only weakly imply certain other statements, and doubtless many of our common-sense assertions have clear and sharp entailments (for instance, boringly: if Smith is watching a squirrel, then Smith is looking at a squirrel). I am the last to want to criticize (*pace* both P. M. Churchland [1984] and P. S. Churchland [1986]) the splendidly flexible vocabulary of common sense, flexible in the main precisely because it does *not* aim at the austerity, economy, and generality of science: it has too many non-scientific jobs to do. The point is that whereas science is aiming to find a taxonomy such that systematic generalizations can be distilled from it—and hence such that relatively sharp implications and entailments can be derived—common sense aims for no such thing; and this point could be expressed by saying that science, but not common sense, is concerned to discover and explore 'natural kinds'.

'Natural kinds' is an expression which has often come under fire—indicted for vagueness, obscurity, hand-waving. This is a mistake. Whatever the difficulties, for any and all sciences, of homing in on 'true' natural kinds; whatever the difficulties in saying which of them are 'fundamental' and which derivative; even if the whole notion of a natural kind is shorthand for the idea of a class of phenomena which more advanced scientific theories will explain in due course in more fundamental terms; despite all that, they serve a useful purpose, even if only to pick out groups of things which science finds it useful, profitable, convenient to isolate. They are useful because natural-kind terms provide, in the main, the central *explananda* and *explanantia* for systematic study: they are the terms for which, and with which, the laws and generalizations of science are framed. Hence 'water', 'mass', and 'tiger' are natural-kind terms; 'fence', 'ashtray', and 'ornament' are not.

If this is acceptable—and I have deliberately attempted to put the point as uncontentiously as possible—then it would be unsurprising if both experiments and thought experiments in science, *inasmuch as* they are primarily concerned with natural-kind *explananda* and *explanantia*, tend to give us what we need to determine 'relevance'. The reason is that natural kinds, since they are the sorts of things about which we have laws and generalizations, are therefore and thereby the sorts of things whose presuppositions and implications we know (to a greater or lesser extent, of course). We know under what conditions a particle may be affected by *only* electromagnetic forces, and we know what follows if these circumstances obtain. We know too, albeit with less precision, what happens if it is affected by both electromagnetic and gravitational forces. Our discussion and description of electromagnetic force comes along with a relatively clear insight into what *ceteris paribus* (or perhaps rather *ceteris absentibus*) clauses are needed (i.e. what is 'relevant'), and what it is that we need to include and exclude in order to focus upon this natural-kind phenomenon. The ramifications of manipulating natural kinds in thought experiments (in possible worlds) can relatively easily be charted. In sum, the more we explore natural kinds—discovering the laws and generalizations that hold true of them—the more we know about what will be 'relevant' in both experimental and thought-experimental contexts.

We lack this with terms that do not pick out natural kinds, where we have to rest content—unavoidably—with *explananda* about which we have few if any laws and generalizations, and hence where we have less security when trying to work out what *ceteris paribus* conditions are relevant to the matter in hand. Common-sense assertions have implications, certainly; but they are irreducibly context dependent, nuance ridden, purpose, speaker, and audience dependent. This, as I have suggested already, is not in any sense a criticism of the common-sense conceptual framework; but it may be something which thought-experimenters in philosophy have cause to regret, just because it makes it so much harder to spell out what background conditions are relevant to the thought experiment and which are not. In particular, it is difficult to be sure that the 'impossibility' of the imagined scenario is not destructively relevant to the derivation of the conclusion (cf. the 'clock in a box' example).

This helps to explain why thought experiments in physics have generally been effective and substantial (as Brown claims); why thought experiments in philosophy that pick on natural-kind terms, such as 'gold' or 'water', seem conclusive (as many claim); and why other thought experiments in philosophy in general, and those concerning personal identity in particular, are not (or so I shall claim). For it is improbable that 'person' is in any legitimate sense a term that can usefully be construed as a 'natural kind' (this is something which needs argument—but the bulk of the book provides that); whereas 'human being' seems to be just that: humans belong to the biological species *homo sapiens*, a natural kind in the broad sense characterized above. The moral of this section is thus to suggest that, whenever we are examining the ranges of concepts that do *not* pick on natural kinds, the problem of deciding what is or what is not 'relevant' to the success of the thought experiment is *yet more problematic* than the same question as it arises in science; and, unlike the scientific problem, it may not even have an answer 'in principle'.

5. SECOND DIFFICULTY: IMAGINATION AND 'POSSIBILITY'

Imagination and intuition, we may say, are to the thought-experimenter what observation and measurement are to the experimenting scientist. We need to be able to trust our imaginative forays; to appeal to *agreed* intuitions about 'what we would say if' the imagined situation were to come about. In the two first examples borrowed from physics, there was little difficulty after the phenomenon is clearly established: the conditions under which the imaginary situation would obtain were specified, and then backing physical theories make the conclusion to be drawn a matter of simple inference or deduction. Scientists who share a given theory can be presumed to have the same intuitions—if indeed it is in place to call them 'intuitions' at all, since they seem rather to be straightforward inductive or deductive inferences—about what would follow from Einstein's 'speed of light' observation, or Stevin's linked chain on frictionless planes. (Only a scientist obstinately believing in the possibility of perpetual motion machines could dispute the conclusion of the Stevin thought experiment.)

In science, then, because of the firm backing theories, our 'intuitions' (if we rather misleadingly call them that) are usually unproblematic. But when we are dealing with the rich and riotous chaos of common-sense concepts, we are dealing with terms that generally do not pick out natural kinds, and so there is no body of explicit theory or shared and agreed generalizations about them; we are rather dealing with implicit and partial, rough-and-ready, common-sense assumptions. Hence the importance of intuition grows in direct proportion to its precariousness. We must deploy it; for we must (as we have seen) have some way of agreeing about the relevant background to the thought experiment in question. But when is intuition reliable?

We find on the one hand those like Kripke, who will come out solidly in defence of intuition:

Of course, some philosophers think that something's having intuitive content is very inconclusive evidence in favor of it. I think it is very heavy evidence in favor of anything, myself. I really don't know in a way what more conclusive evidence one can have about anything, ultimately speaking (Kripke [1972], pp. 265-6).

That is clear enough; and Kripke is by no means alone in maintaining such a view. Yet on the other hand we find those like Rorty, who argues in much of his later writings (see, for example, his [1980]) that what you know and believe determines what you do, or do not, find imaginable, so that one man's intuitive certainty may be another's falsehood. (And see also Quine [1972], pp. 489 f.)

In support of the scepticism there is of course the brute fact that intuitions can and do clash, and nowhere more so than in the interesting— in other words the difficult—cases. Thus, if I say that I have succeeded in imagining some possible state of affairs, thereby 'establishing the phenomenon', your retort might be that I only *think* that I have succeeded, and that if I thought the matter through more carefully I would realize that I have not. There are clear examples of this in the literature on personal identity. For example: to many, at least at first sight, it seems readily imaginable that they might have been born of parents other than their actual ones. Yet, if one follows Kripke ([1972], especially pp. 312–14), this is not after all a coherent supposition: 'anything coming from a different origin would not be this object' (p. 314). So is it impossible to imagine this? To adapt Leibniz's familiar challenge, are you instead imagining a world in which you fail to exist, but in which a new and quite different person does exist? The two imagined cases seem, and of course are, utterly different; it is at least odd to say to someone that he may think he has imagined the first, but has in fact—whether he realizes it or not—imagined the second. Just what has he imagined? At this point, notoriously, opinions diverge sharply and the strength of intuitions on each side, being equally balanced, helps not at all.[2]

The thought-experimental technique, in fact, may all too often rely upon an inchoate and confused assumption or belief that is, although highly questionable, rarely questioned enough. That is, if something is imaginable, *or* conceivable, *or* describable, then it is logically, *or* theoretically (= 'in principle') possible.[3] There is, in other words, a 'possible world' in which the imaginary situation *does* obtain. (Remember of course that impossibilities are acceptable in thought experiments—so long as they are not 'relevant'. The impossibility of humans travelling at the speed of light did *not* contaminate Einstein's thought experiment.) The content and the status of this thought need examination.

It may seem that what counts as *logical* possibility is clear enough: something is logically possible if it is not ruled out by the laws of logic. So although it is not a logical possibility that $2 + 2 = 5$, or that anything is both a man and not a man, it is logically possible that gold does not have atomic number 79, that water is not H_2O, that whales are fish, that iron bars can float on water, that rabbits are carnivorous,[4] that one might have seven-league boots.[5] Now there could of course be fairy stories in which all these logical possibilities occurred as actualities. There is a sense, as we have seen, in which the stories of someone like Tolkien or Lewis Carroll are representations of coherently describable states of affairs, *given* the purpose for which they are written. As with all fiction, we are required to suspend disbelief—and the suspension-cable may need to be more or less stout: one assumes that Kripke, for example, or a physicist, would find it harder than the rest of us to swallow a story in which gold proved to have the wrong atomic number.

---

[2] Williams [1966/1973] has a sensitive and important discussion of the problems of using the imagination to reach conclusions concerning personal identity. (I am not of course suggesting that this means that he would be sympathetic to the arguments of this chapter more generally.)

[3] Few would deny that the converse fails to hold—in other words, few would claim that *un*imaginability implies *im*possibility. Results from spacetime physics, non-Euclidean geometry, and quantum mechanics show this conclusively. 'I see no necessity that intelligibility to a human understanding should be necessary to the truth or existence of a thing', Boyle [1672/1772], vol. iv, p. 450.

[4] This example and the preceding example are taken from Seddon [1972].

[5] I owe this example to Andrew Harrison.

However that may be, though, bare logical possibility is presumably not the focus of our interest. It certainly tells us nothing about what *might* or *could* happen. We know—at least those of us who have any sympathy at all towards the idea that there are necessary truths that are not clearly analytically true or true a priori—that anything which is a fish cannot be a whale; put another way, that we cannot believe in the existence of something that is indisputably a whale but which is also a fish. So also for water not being H_2O, gold with a different atomic number, and the rest. There is, we can say, no possible world in which these states of affairs obtain. In sum, even if by reliance on the willing suspension of disbelief we are prepared to say that logical possibilities such as these *are* imaginable, in the sense that a Tolkien could write a story in which they all occurred, or in the sense that we can all form mental images of whale-like fish, we also know that most or all of these things *could not happen*: are, in short, impossible. The point is this: what is fine in literary fantasy (where the ambition is to entertain) is not necessarily enough to 'establish a phenomenon' (from which the ambition is to draw conclusions).

So we should look rather to the 'theoretical', or 'in principle' possibility of the *relevant* background conditions—the conditions we need to specify before we can be sure both that the imagined scenario is adequately described, and that the inference from the imagined state of affairs to the conclusion can be made. This would be the test of validity for a thought experiment. This we can characterize as a matter of what could or could not happen given our backing scientific knowledge: what our theories allow to be possible or not. So, for example, gold could not, possibly, have had a different atomic number. Again, iron bars cannot, possibly, float on water—nothing which is iron, i.e. which has a specific gravity within the range 7.3—7.8, can float, i.e. have also a specific gravity of less than 1 (see Seddon [1972]). Once we describe the situation adequately, once we hand ourselves the backing theory of metals, then the (relevant) impossibilities appear—indeed, in the case of the iron bars the theory turns the impossibility into a logical one: nothing can both have and not have a specific gravity of less than 1. Similarly, again following Seddon, theory rules out firmly the possibility of carnivorous rabbits on Mars.

But is theoretical possibility/impossibility a clear enough notion? We know full well that scientists are fallible, and that theories come and go. How is it that we can rely on our present theories as tests of theoretical possibility and impossibility, when these theories will probably prove to be as treacherous or inaccurate as earlier ones? In fact we might find ourselves in one of at least five different positions:

(*a*) The first position is the one most favourable for my argument. Suppose that there is a theory T_1 which is strong, well supported by the evidence, universally accepted, and without serious rivals. This theory tells us, let us suppose, that the Martian atmosphere cannot sustain animal life.

Where we have such a theory, few would claim any merit for philosophical thought experiments that require rabbits on Mars, still less carnivorous ones (but see (*e*) below). It would be as if we postulated that gold had atomic number 69, or if we ignored the general theory of relativity when discussing time and energy quantities in quantum mechanics.

(*b*) But perhaps T_1, although indeed well supported by the evidence, has a rival T_2 whose credentials seem equally impressive. T_2 denies what T_1 says about the Martian atmosphere, and allows for the possibility of animal life there. Scientists are roughly divided between the two schools of thought; so far no experiments have been found, nor observations made, which could decide the issue between them.

When a situation like this obtains, then we surely do not know what to say about the thought experiment that there might be rabbits on Mars. This is because we do not know how to describe the background adequately—we do not know what factors are or are not relevant to any thought experiment based on it.

(*c*) Alternatively, there is only one theory, T_1. It is well backed, accepted by the scientific community, and rules out animal life on Mars—but it is not known outside scientific circles. The layman's beliefs about Mars stem solely from (say) science fiction.

In this case the layman might believe that he has succeeded in 'establishing a phenomenon' (rabbits on Mars) in thought, but he might be wrong; it might be like imagining iron bars floating on water. Mental pictures, yes; an 'established phenomenon' in a possible world, no. This state of affairs is particularly pertinent to thought experiments concerning personal identity, precisely because most of the thought-experimenters know little (and unfortunately care less) about biology and physiology. Thus the background is not adequately described, and relevant obstacles to the derivation of the conclusion (compare the way that general relativity blocked the 'clock in a box' thought experiment) will be ignored.

(*d*) Again, there might be a single theory T_1 about the Martian climate, and another theory T_3 about lagomorphs; but both at present in a very sketchy state. It is not yet determined whether the Martian atmosphere can sustain animal life, nor precisely what air is needed by rabbits' lungs.

As with (*c*) above, in examples such as this we would not be able to tell whether we have successfully 'established a phenomenon' or merely framed a mental picture; the relevant background features of the possible world are insufficiently known. Since the brain and behavioural sciences are largely in a very sketchy state, (*d*) too is likely to hold true of many thought experiments in personal identity; we do not yet know enough about what can and cannot happen to people.

(*e*) Finally, we might have a single theory T_1 which is again strong, well backed, universally accepted—but which is in fact largely false. It rules out the possibility of rabbits surviving the Martian climate, but does so mistakenly; rabbits can and do live and breed there. The judgements made of the climatological and atmospheric conditions were erroneous, just a product of faulty space-probe equipment.

In such a case, we might wrongly have ruled out or rejected the thought experiment in question. The history of science abounds with examples of scientists rejecting conjectures and 'what if . . .' suggestions because their trusted theories, subsequently falsified, excluded their possibility. Consider Kelvin's rejection of the electromagnetic theory of light; alternatively, could an ancient Greek have accepted the possibility of sunspots? He thought that the sun was divine, and deities tend not to be spotty.

It is clear that the possibilities (*b*) to (*e*) do not legitimize the use of thought experiments; (*b*), (*c*), and (*d*) appeal to our ignorance of theory, and only license the judgement that we do not know that the hypothesized state of affairs is *im*possible—which is, or ought to be, a far cry from saying that it is possible. Ignorance is a poor *justification* for any experiment, scientific or philosophical; for what we are ignorant about is what we most need—an adequate description of the relevant background conditions. Only when we have that do we know what the imagined scenario *is*, only then have we 'established' it, so that we can derive interesting conclusions from it. (*e*) points out that our judgements about theories (and hence about theoretical (im)possibilities) are not immune from error. It does not permit the random rejection, or imagined suspension, of a law (but remember: we are talking of laws *relevant* to the purpose of the thought experiment) selected from one of those theories. We cannot move from (*e*) to build a case on the basis of the assumption that what we now think to be theoretically impossible might prove possible after all.

In sum, then, although we can *in a sense* imagine all sorts of things—anything, in fact, that is not a logical impossibility—this kind of imaginability does not validate thought experiments built up upon it. The fact that a Carroll or a Tolkien can exploit even theoretical impossibilities in their fantasies, the fact that one can enjoy associated mental pictures (of someone walking through a mirror, say) is not enough of a basis upon which to build conclusions about what we would say if such things *did* happen: we firmly believe that they cannot happen in any possible world. (Later, in Section 8, we shall find further reasons for this conclusion.) The notion of imaginability that is needed for genuine thought experiments will presuppose attention to the relevant backing theories.

6. CONDITIONS OF PERSONHOOD

We shall soon return to exploit this line of argument. Meanwhile, let us look more directly at the problem of personal identity. In this book I shall be concerned with the two pre-eminent aspects of the question: that of identification, and that of reidentification.[6]

The first, the issue of *identification*, concerns what it is, or what it takes, to be a person. We ask, for example, whether, and to what extent, the classes of persons and of humans coincide and why they do so; whether other entities, be they non-human animals (like hyperintelligent chimpanzees or dolphins), alien species from Mars, artefacts, or disembodied spirits, should now or some time soon get included in the class of persons; whether savagely retarded, psychopathic, or senile humans, or newborn children, should be counted; or whether we should all (following Puccetti [1973]) regard all humans as really being two persons in one body. The second issue, that of *reidentification*, is the problem of how to decide when *A* is the same person as *B*. *A* and *B*

---

[6] Rorty ([1976], pp. 1–2) suggests that there are several questions here, and not just two. However, the two I emphasize seem the most general, and many of the other questions she lists will be touched upon, at least, in the course of the book.

may be separated by time (when, say, A is eight, B eighty); what makes A and B one and the same person? Alternatively, there might be puzzle-cases set up by brain or body swaps; half-brain transplants; reincarnation; *doppelgänger* or replica creation; and 'mind' transplants (the re-programming of A's brain with the memories etc. of B's). Perhaps also A and B might divide like amoebae or fuse together like clouds or raindrops. More realistically, we might consider the actually existing oddities revealed by commissurotomy[7] and other kinds of brain section or injury, the various forms of dissociation that range from hysteria to multiple personality, and the difficulty of fitting into any account individuals with ailments like senile dementia or sweeping amnesia.

In this chapter neither side of the problem of personal identity will be taken far; that is the task of succeeding chapters. In so far as I sketch conditions (as I shall) on what it takes to be a person, these will be drawn so vaguely and generously that they should excite no comment; unhelpful as the bland imprecision of this set of conditions would be if we were at this moment *examining* the identification and reidentification of persons, we shall find it adequate for the present aim. For the present aim is to try to discover what constraints, if any, we can impose on the method of thought-experimentation when it is applied to the concept of a person. And for that we shall need only an outline sketch, so drawn as to provoke the minimum of disagreement, of what it takes to be one.

What is surely not in serious dispute (except perhaps by Puccetti, whose arguments [1973, 1981] will be considered in the course of a later chapter) is that as things now stand there is *at least* a very substantial intersection between the class of persons and the class of human beings. Most single human beings just are, unproblematically, single persons. Conversely, we know of no *non*-humans such that any significant number of people regard them as true persons. I am here making the obvious and trivial point that the normal human being is our sole paradigm of personhood ('personhood' is an ugly word, but one that is unfortunately too convenient to reject); the normal human is the one entity whose right to that title is granted without comment. If it were *not* granted without comment, then it is unclear that the concept of a person could remain coherent, for we would have no other sample or standard to use instead. One could, I suppose, tell a long and elaborate story, describing various dramatic changes taking place over

---

[7] Commissurotomy is the surgical bisection of the corpus callosum, which is the great band of fibres connecting the two halves of the cerebral cortex. We shall be discussing commissurotomy in some detail in ch. 5.

time in ourselves, in society, and in the environment, such that we might reach the point where the thoroughly altered humans now seemed *not* to qualify as persons. But such a story would need to be very far-fetched and fantastical.[8] What we cannot consistently do is to question *now* the assertion that all normal humans are persons.

Since this is so, it will clearly be useful as a first move to examine our unchallenged persons, to find out what makes them so. We can be reasonably expeditious here, since much of the work has been done already and we can for present purposes merely borrow the conclusions. Dennett [1976] has usefully summarized six 'conditions of personhood'. He, of course, goes on to discuss them in detail, but the overview is all we need at the moment; they are all familiar enough from the literature. Although there are various logical relationships between them—some of the conditions are presupposed by others—it will not matter if we simply state them as though they were separate and independent. The list runs as follows: (1) persons are rational. (2) they are the subjects of Intentional ascriptions. (3) a certain stance or attitude must be taken towards them, a point that introduces the idea that persons are, *inter alia*, moral objects. (4) they can reciprocate when such a stance is taken, which similarly introduces the idea that they are, *inter alia*, moral agents. (5) they are language-users. Finally, (6) they have a special kind of consciousness, perhaps self-consciousness; and this goes along, according to Frankfurt [1971] and others, with the ability to form 'second-order' states (e.g. beliefs and desires about beliefs and desires) and hence with one version of freedom of will.

I am tempted to add a seventh condition, but will not exploit it in the remainder of the book (because I need to think more about it). That would be the human ability to construct and use tools. It seems to me that this is just as significant as language-use (point (5) above), and for the same reason. Both probably developed together in a chicken-and-egg manner, and each fostered t'other. It is likely that each capacity calls upon roughly complementary areas of the brain. It is certain that each makes massive demands upon our cognitive capacity and ability. In short: both are alike examples of *extremely sophisticated* behaviour; there is no reason whatsoever, or so it seems to me, to single out *verbal* behaviour as particularly, uniquely, outstanding. Maybe we are the only species spontaneously to have developed a language (supposing, probably chauvinistically, that the dolphins' clicks and whistles are not

---

[8] Consider how elaborate is the story, devised by Putnam [1962], to show how the statement 'all bachelors are unmarried' might come to be regarded as not invariably true.

forms of language, and supposing we reject the bees' dance as 'language'). But, equally, we are the only species to have an extensive— indeed a totally dependent—relationship to our own artefacts. Chimpanzees whittle sticks to help them catch ants; but no non-human species deploys anything even so relatively simple as a wheelbarrow. Tool-using has been unduly neglected by philosophers, certainly; this is partly a product, and partly a cause, of the fact that we like to separate 'cognition' sharply from 'sensori-motor control' (some reasons why we like to do this are explored in Chapter 7). This separation urgently needs defence, which I do not believe will in the long run prove adequate. Certainly no such distinction ever *receives* any defence.

However, since I do not make much, in what follows, of the fact that persons alone use language in a sophisticated manner, it will not perhaps matter too much that I also neglect the fact that we alone invent, construct, and use tools to a significant degree. For I consider the two as being roughly on a par, and thus of approximately equal and parallel significance. So, in what follows, when I talk of 'the six con- ditions', the reader should tacitly include 'artefact construction and use' along with 'linguistic behaviour'.[9]

Few, I hope, would wish to challenge any of these conditions; as yet they are too broadly stated to merit dispute. Some of them will be discussed in the bulk of the book, and there disagreement may well arise. In particular, (1), the rationality condition, will be examined at some length; as will (3) and (4), the conditions about the stance or attitude that is taken by or to persons, and the extent to which they can reciprocate such attitudes; and (6), the consciousness condition, will with its implications absorb three chapters. The Intentionality condition (2) will be frequently mentioned, but not scrutinized: so many non-persons (non-human animals, computers) are subjects of Intentional ascriptions that this does not help us distinguish 'real persons'.[10] Condition (5), that persons can use language, is—perhaps surprisingly—not particularly helpful for the problems of personal identity. Both apes and computers can, *to some extent*, use language; but in both cases their ability, when compared with that of humans,

---

[9] I am much indebted to Srđan Lelas for first convincing me of the importance of artefact production and use—in this and in other connections.

[10] Evidently here it would be question-begging to substitute for 'intentional predicate' Strawson's [1958] 'P (person) predicates'—intentional predicates which are the 'predicates we apply to persons'. We have yet to discover what these are. (But one of Strawson's 'P-predicates' is 'is in pain', which seems not obviously restricted to persons . . . and so I am not entirely clear if, or how, 'P-predicates' are in fact any different from 'intentional predicates' generally.)

is much contested. Moreover, the weight of this condition is in fact carried by the first condition (rationality) and to some extent the last (consciousness). Anyway, these last few remarks are merely promissory: for the immediate purposes of this chapter we need only regard all six conditions as maximally hospitable, and give the most extensive and tolerant reasonable reading to all the problematical terms.

Already we can see how most if not all non-human animals will be excluded from the category of persons. They have rationality (even if in low degree), and are the subjects of quite a bunch of Intentional ascriptions; we need to treat them as moral objects, inasmuch as most of them are clearly capable of feeling pain and of having interests, emotions, likes, and dislikes. But on the other side of the scale they cannot reciprocate the treatment they receive, so they are not moral agents; and probably only in the hotly disputed case of chimpanzees do we find much of an approximation to a developed language (we are too ignorant about the dolphins' clicks and whistles to use them for or against these claims).[11] Rarely and fleetingly do we find behaviour that is best explained by ascribing self-consciousness or second-order states; Frankfurt [1971] nicely describes non-human animals as 'wantons', driven to action by first-order desires and hence by whatever desire is phenomenologically the strongest—therefore such animals are 'slaves to their passions', and must lack any substantial freedom of the will.[12] If it is indeed true that the capacity to form second-order beliefs and desires is essential for free action, we can see again why non-human animals cannot be moral agents, since they cannot be held responsible for what they do.[13] It seems plausible to suppose, too, that such a 'second-order'

---

[11] Some might want to argue that there are kinds of behaviour, such as the bees' dance, which transmit information in a manner sufficient to allow for the description 'language'. Bennett [1964] seems to me to have adequately rebutted this claim, but we need not deny it here—and should not, since we have explicitly undertaken to use a maximally hospitable construal of all six conditions. Bees fail to qualify on virtually all the other counts, so exclude themselves anyway.

[12] But Milton made the point first, in *Paradise Lost*, VIII, l. 635-7: 'Take heed lest passion sway/Thy judgement to do aught, which else free will/Would not admit.'

[13] Evans [1906/1987], in a splendid and fascinating book (to which a review by Julian Barnes in the *Observer* of 21 June 1987, p. 25, drew my attention), describes medieval trials of animals: a cock which committed the 'heinous and unnatural crime' of laying an egg was tried and sentenced to be burnt at the stake; a pig was hanged for having sacrilegiously eaten a consecrated wafer (but it was first given a qualified defence counsel); serious consideration was given to whether a mad dog could plead insanity, or whether locusts had the right to a priest. Hard to grasp this; but perhaps, as Barnes suggests, it had something to do with an idea that the natural and social order (particularly the subordinate place of non-human animals in the God-given hierarchy) must be sustained, and violations punished.

capacity is required for reciprocation—it may be that in order to respond appropriately to someone else's attitude, that attitude has to be recognized and acknowledged, which would introduce the second-order level that non-human animals typically lack. (We see at this point how several of the six conditions interlock.) This is conjectural; what is not conjectural is that animals fail three of the conditions, and thus none of them is regarded as a person.

What prevents non-human animals from being counted as persons is primarily an intellectual matter, a failure of sapience rather than of sentience. With present-day computers, however, it seems to be the other way about—at least at first sight. For, first, there is a perfectly intelligible sense in which they can be said to use language. Second, they can be programmed to report upon their own information-bearing states in a manner that might permit us to talk of 'beliefs about beliefs', which gives them one of the elements of self-consciousness (or at least something that looks closely analogous to it; and remember, we are for the moment deliberately interpreting the six conditions as leniently as possible). Third, their rationality is, so to speak, built in. And fourth, one cannot handle sophisticated computers effectively without resorting to Intentional ascriptions (see Dennett [1971]).

No doubt there are conspicuous, and perhaps crucial, differences between computer and human sapience with respect to all these features. Nevertheless, the lax application of the six conditions which we are allowing ourselves at present might permit us to say that computers could qualify as far as these four marks of personhood are concerned. (Later, however, I shall withdraw this concession.) But on the other hand, as soon as we turn to (4) and (5), the 'stance' and 'reciprocation' conditions, all existing computers are decisively ruled out. They have no dignity, no title to respect and consideration; it is we and not they who are upset when rough handling damages or disrupts their performance. Nor are they bothered by human pleasure or dismay at their output—indeed, they are not even indifferent to it. If (4) and (5) are to hold, we would need not only the cognitive capacity which, as we have just seen, is required for (5), the ability to reciprocate; but also we must be able to ascribe sentience: pains, moods, feelings, emotions, dispositions, attitudes. It will surely be agreed that no *actual* computers are sentient, have feelings or attitudes; and for the moment we are thinking only of present-day machines. In sum, then, animals do better on the 'sentient' side of things, computers, it may seem, on the 'sapient'.

7. THE IDENTIFICATION ISSUE: LAWS AND THEORETICAL IMPOSSIBILITIES

It is reasonably clear, then, why humans have no rivals to the title of 'person' as yet. At this point, of course, the thought-experimenter wants to chip in. What if, he asks,[14] computer technology developed even more rapidly, so that computers became sentient too? Dennett [1978a] has already sketched the outlines of a pain-perception flow chart, and perhaps, as he suggests, one should hesitate before kicking a robot endowed with such a program. Moreover, there are plenty of 'good' and 'bad' robots in plausible-seeming science fiction. Alternatively, what if Washoe or her descendants, stimulated by the expansiveness of the horizons open to language-users, started rapidly to catch up with us?

To deal with this challenge, we need to look back at the six conditions; and shall shortly want to exploit the remarks made earlier about theoretical possibilities. The six conditions, note, are all such that no *normal* human being can lack any—there is a sense in which they are all necessary to him. For instance, the psychopath is perhaps stunted with respect to (5), the reciprocation condition, but he is abnormal and impaired. The savagely retarded human vegetable may be less rational than a chimpanzee, but he is drastically impaired. All six marks will one day distinguish the infant, even though few do so in his early days. Those reared by animals in the wild may find it hard to reciprocate humane treatment, but theirs is a grossly aberrant upbringing for any human; man is, as Aristotle puts it (*Nicomachean Ethics*, i. 7. 1097^{b}11), *by nature* a social animal,[15] and the society he meant was the society of man's own kind. Anthropoids far enough back in our evolutionary ancestry to rank in intelligence with today's apes were not yet persons. In sum, no healthy adult living in society is without any of the six features. Put another way, none is culture relative or race relative. Even if one were to be a relativist about rationality (as I am not), still each culture will require that its members have (their own kind of) rationality. To adapt a simile from

---

[14] Throughout this book the reader will find that I take it for granted that 'man' embraces 'woman'. It is a brute fact that the converse does not hold. I realize that my acceptance of this convention will annoy some; but, for my part, I am annoyed by the clumsiness of 'he or she', '(s)he', 's/he', and their ilk. The use of 'she' in place of 'he' strikes me as misleading ('woman' does not embrace 'man') ; and is, to my ear, distractingly precious and political. Anyone who thinks that language helps determine sexual attitudes should contemplate Turkish.

[15] The term Aristotle uses—*phusei*, which I have translated as 'by nature'—could equally well be translated 'essentially'. For him man's social nature was no merely contingent truth or historical product.

Dennett [1971], which he found in a short story by MacDonald Harris, a *society* of, say, psychopaths would have the survival potential of a soluble fish. These six cannot be detached from the normal human.

Now if that is so, we could have reached the same list by a different route. A tally of characteristics that would include our six features—and many more besides, such as being bipedal and mammalian—could be derived from biological, sociological, evolutionary, anthropological, and psychological theories concerning the natural-kind species *homo sapiens*. In other words, philosophy and science would converge; the conceptual analysis of personhood and the theoretical and empirical analysis of the human would agree upon at least these points. Put another way, we can bring to bear the (relative) clarity of a natural-kind term—*homo sapiens*—on to the puzzling intricacy of the everyday notion 'person'. As we have seen already, the implications and entailments of statements concerning natural kinds tend to be easier to map than those of statements about entities that are not (known to be) natural kinds. This means that the physical, psychological, and sociological theories of the nature of man can be expected, or at least asked, to explain why the typical human must have these marks of personhood—how it is, for example, that he is rational, able to learn and use a language, capable of self-consciousness. Equally, of course, theory and research could be asked to explain why chimpanzees and dolphins do *not* qualify.

The class of human beings, then, is a natural kind (in the broad sense sketched earlier). However, we do not necessarily want, and assuredly do not need, to commit ourselves to any strong version of essentialism about natural kinds and insist, implausibly, that every member of kind *X* necessarily has all the properties characteristic of *X*s. Certainly all biological kinds (at least) have abnormal members. We need something between stringent essentialism and loose conventionalism, something that will allow us to insist, as we want to insist, that the human species is a kind governed by law, while not denying that some of these laws may fail to hold of individual members of the species. What we need, in fact, is something between logical possibility on the one hand and 'merely practical' possibility on the other—none other than our old friend, theoretical possibility.

We can get this if we make two claims, one of which is by now very familiar. *First*, we can say, as many have indeed said, that a lot of kind terms, and in particular the terms that pick out biological kinds, are 'law-cluster concepts' with a more or less determinate heart of 'core facts'. (See for example Putnam [1975].) Only a small subset of the laws defining the kind, and a tiny subset of the laws describing the core facts, can fail to hold if something is indeed to be included in that species. So it is this cluster of laws that can be exploited to restrict the range of what is or is not theoretically possible—because it will help us determine what presuppositions and implications are 'relevant' to the hypotheses we play with. However, this argument, although surely correct, gets but a short distance on its own. For all the real work of identifying in each case the relevant law cluster and the core facts is evidently an affair for experiment and theory; in other words, for the scientist.

But we can add a *second* claim, one that is less often emphasized. Scientific laws—certainly the laws describing biological kinds—are not disjoint and independent, detachable from one another like beads on a string. They are interrelated, to varying degrees of course, in at least three ways.

(*a*) The phenomena governed by one set of laws will frequently interact with phenomena governed by another set.

Thus, for instance, a full psychophysiological account of the processes of human perception must at some stage link up with part at least of the explanation of linguistic ability; for we very typically see things under a certain description, and that description may be a very sophisticated one (cf. 'I see the cloud chamber').

(*b*) Any given law must itself be amenable to explanation at a deeper level, where 'deeper' usually means either 'more theoretical' or 'microstructural', or both.

We expect there to be an explanation for the fact that all, or n per cent, of As are Bs. But deeper explanation often serves to unify (or conversely to distinguish) things that seem disparate (or conversely similar) on the higher level. One familiar example here is that of Newton's laws of motion, which unified phenomena that seemed to be unrelated—e.g. the movement of the tides and the paths of projectiles. Conversely, biological theory taught us that the apparently close relationship between wolf *canis* and the Tasmanian wolf is misleading. Examples from the brain and behavioural sciences are just as easy to find, however. The set of disabilities called 'Gerstmann's syndrome' (Gerstmann [1931], Benson and Geschwind [1969a]) shows how a single underlying explanation can account for four (or perhaps five) failures that might prima facie seem unrelated: finger agnosia, right–left disorientation, agraphia (the inability to write), acalculia (the inability to calculate), and, perhaps, constructional apraxia. This same example equally shows how abilities that are apparently closely related may be more distinct than intuition would suppose, for such patients, although they cannot write, often have well-preserved reading capacity.[16] Similarly, the striking disability of pure alexia also illustrates both halves of the coin: the patient with pure alexia cannot read but *can* write. However, he typically fails to match seen colours to spoken words—even though the rest of his visual competence, including his ability to match and sort colours, may be well preserved. As with Gerstmann's syndrome, there is again a single underlying explanation for this peculiar distribution of retained and disrupted capacity—see Benson and Geschwind [1969b].[17] (We shall return in Chapter 5 to discuss pure alexia more fully, in a different connection.)

(*c*) The laws of two theories in different domains should be consistent with one another.

This is in fact no more than an extension of the first point above, but it extends the requirement of consistency within any one theory to hold between distinct theories. We could illustrate the point with astronomy, astrology, and psychology; the claims of astrologers flout, and are not compatible with, what we are told by astronomers and psychologists.

All in all, we can conclude that it will be rare that we find an *isolated* breach of a single law. It is far more likely that such a violation will have consequential effects upon other laws, where such laws are either at the same sort of level (in the same or a different theory), or where they are more fundamental laws that describe the operations and the limitations of such higher-level laws as the law we are supposing to be violated. The physical, just as much as the psychological, is holistic—with laws arranged in a systematic hierarchy of mutual dependence and involvement. To press the point home, *contrast* here Stevin's 'frictionless

---

[16] It should be admitted that many writers would deny that there is such a phenomenon as Gerstmann's syndrome. Since many reputable scientists think that there is such a thing, though, and since the role of the example is purely heuristic, I leave it in.

[17] Pure alexia seems to be due to the combination of damage to the left occipital lobe—so that all that is seen derives from input to the right hemisphere's visual cortex—combined with damage to the splenium, which connects the right hemisphere visual areas with the left hemisphere. Thus what is seen cannot be reported, *unless* by an indirect route. Letters normally have no associations with touch, sound, smell, or taste, and nor do colours; thus the stimulus from the optic centre in the right hemisphere would not evoke any response in, say, the motor cortex or the auditory cortex, from whence it might travel by intact pathways to the language centre in the left hemisphere. By contrast, a hammer, for example, would be easily recognized and named since the optical stimulus would have many connections with non-visual regions elsewhere in the right hemisphere. As promised, we shall see more of pure alexia in ch. 5.

planes' thought experiment. The world as we know it does not allow for perfectly frictionless planes; but they would be a limiting case of the frictionlessness that we can achieve. Postulating pure frictionlessness does not therefore have unwanted implications for other laws relevant to the purposes of the experiment.

What all this means is that we can no longer *simply* say 'what if Washoe had a vocabulary ten times the size, if she started to ask questions,[18] to read, if she had an IQ of Mensa standard . . .?' This is about as silly as the similar question whose pointlessness is exposed by Seddon [1972], 'what if there were carnivorous rabbits on Mars?' For either of these imagined scenarios to come about, vast numbers of other transformations must also have occurred; and we need to make sure that these other transformations are theoretically possible. That is, we have to fill out much more of the background in the possible world we are supposing. In Washoe's case, we would need to reject or adapt laws governing, say, the proportion of cortical to subcortical tissue, cellular and dendritic growth, decay, and development, the production and proportion of neurotransmitter substances, the potential for expansion in the skull-case . . . and doubtless a lot more besides. We have no reason at all for thinking that the sum and total of the laws governing Washoe as she actually is (a chimpanzee) would permit such a development—a development into something that would no longer clearly *be* a chimpanzee (not that this fact would matter). Quite the contrary: we have excellent reason to believe that they would not permit it. But if the sum of these laws will not allow such drastic changes, then the impossibility is not 'merely practical', but is as 'hard' as are any of the impossibilities urged on us by the essentialists, such as gold having a different atomic number. The fact that we may not have identified all the relevant laws makes no difference, except to mislead: since we are largely ignorant of them and of their interconnections, it of course *seems* easy to imagine the transformation; the obstructive facts are not there to obtrude. However, as we saw earlier, ignorance is a poor foundation for thought experiments, because, if ignorant, all we can say is that we do not know whether the state of affairs is theoretically possible or not; and that is a long way from saying that it is possible. We do not know

---

[18] It seems that Washoe, although she knew about questions in the sense that she knew that she had to answer them, never herself asked one. This is a curious discovery, but of course it may be untrue—it cannot always be easy to distinguish, in a monkey's use of AMESLAN (American sign language), the interrogative from the indicative or imperative moods. Nor are the furry performatives of monkeys unambiguously detectable in their furry faces.

whether we have successfully sketched a possible world: it has not been adequately described. We have fairy stories at this point, not genuine thought experiments.

I do not want this argument to mislead, or to be taken too far. For what we can of course imagine—since it merely repeats a process that has occurred since life first began—is an evolution, even a dramatically rapid evolution (aided perhaps by modern technology and gene-juggling) of the chimpanzee species. But that is quite another, and a less difficult, thought experiment. It is less difficult because, by the time we had achieved such a result, the philosophical problems with which we are here concerned would have answered themselves (which does not of course mean that there might not be hefty legal and social problems: if racism, sexism, and slavery are hard to control, 'speciesism' would be yet more so).[19] Philosophically speaking, however, refusing to call such animals persons, if they met to our satisfaction the six conditions, would be just another form of prejudice.

So much for non-human animals, for the time being.

We should acknowledge, though, that thought-experimental challenges to the existing monopoly of personhood by humans have—at least recently—come rather from artefacts than from other animal species. Are *these* experiments legitimate?

The issue here is a little less clear-cut. At present, of course, it is just a brute fact that current artefacts are light-years away from meeting our six conditions; and, despite what was suggested earlier, they are as far away on the 'sapient' side as they are on the 'sentient'. Christopher Evans (see Berry [1979]) assessed the IQ level of the most sophisticated computers of 1979 as ranking approximately level to the earwig.[20] Now, no doubt some would quibble with many of the particular tests he devised to measure intelligence; and many more might quibble with the very attempt to measure intelligence not only across species, but also

---

[19] In this respect the problem would be just like that of racism, sexism, or bastardy. There are no respectable arguments to justify discrimination on grounds of race, sex, or parents' marital status, but, of course, there are problems with all three because people often do so discriminate. Philosophically, however, all these issues are immensely boring, and it will be a relief when they disappear from the pages of journals.

[20] Dennett (in conversation) has suggested that neither Evans nor I can really be serious in citing this finding. I cannot speak for Evans; I am perfectly serious. I emphasize: it does not matter in the slightest if Evans's findings are, in detail, askew when measured against tests which others would wish to apply; and see the next footnote. Present-day computers are *extremely stupid* when measured against what we would wish to call 'intelligence'; the paragraph following may help to explain why all should agree that this is so.

across 'intelligent systems' more generally.[21] However, we need not examine his method, or the detail of his results, to see that all contemporary machines *must* come very low on any IQ scale. We can see why by reflecting on the so-called 'frame problem'. Computers perform admirably so long as they are bounded in tightly defined 'micro-worlds' (see Dreyfus [1979])—as, for example, when they are programmed to play chess or backgammon. Already computers have beaten the world backgammon champion, and they can defeat all but the best at chess. But so far nobody has been able to imagine any way of loosening the 'frame', the constraints: of getting them to function well when the parameters within which they are asked to operate are vague, messy, or not fully known and specified. The result is that no chess-playing computer, even if equipped with a robotic arm, could at present even set the board; indeed, a shape-recognition program that enables a computer to distinguish cubes from pyramids leaves it helpless when it is asked to sort nuts and bolts.[22]

The point is that current artefacts can do one task, or a very restricted range of tasks, admirably—so long as the parameters are set and all the variables controlled; but this is precisely on a par with the ability of spiders to build webs, of migrating birds or eels to find their way across thousands of miles to a very specific place, or of the *idiots savants* who can perform prodigies of calculation at lightning speed while being unable to cope with even the simplest range of mundane non-mathematical tasks. The normal unaided human can do none of these things, but we are not tempted to call spiders, birds, eels, or *idiots savants* 'intelligent'. Descartes put precisely this point, 'Reason is a universal instrument that can serve for all contingencies'—not just for one (*Discourse on the Method* [1637/1967], vol. i, p. 116). No more are any present-day computers intelligent, and for just the same reasons. Flexibility and range, presupposed by anything that qualifies as intelligent, require—before they can come to be true of the computer—a solution to the frame problem, and that is just not forthcoming as yet.

[21] It would be easy to quibble. MacPhail [1982, 1986] claims that there is no solid evidence for any difference in cognitive capacity between any vertebrates (excluding man); the goldfish might be as intelligent as the chimpanzee. This is a startling thesis, and one shouting out to be supported or refuted.

[22] Perhaps PDP (parallel distributed processing) mechanisms will soon make a big difference; already these machines are more promising than the Von Neumann machines in the domains of pattern recognition and smooth three-dimensional movement. Equally, they may begin to solve simple instances of the frame problem. Since these models are strongly biologically constrained, and, unlike the traditional computer models, are capable of modelling plausibly some forms of learning, the prospects look better than for the Von Neumann machine models.

(Pessimists suggest that it could not be solved without so great a combinatorial explosion of variables that we might as well forget it; *perhaps* the problem will become more tractable with the new parallel distributed processing mechanisms, but their potential is only now being explored, and they have a long way to go.) Thus although it may seem easy to imagine a computer, or more likely a robot, that challenged human intelligence, this is again an imaginative possibility that relies on ignorance rather than upon a well-based judgement that there is a genuine theoretical possibility here. If the 'how' cannot be imagined, the 'that' thought-experimental conclusion becomes decidedly meagre. We have not 'established a phenomenon' in any possible world. The 'jump from data to theory' looms too large; and if there is any point in it at all, we might as well have stuck with genuine fairy tales of wooden Pinocchios and ice maidens in the first place.

None the less, in the abundant literature on the subject it has been rather machine *sentience* that gets disputed than machine *sapience*, so it would be as well to turn next to this.

Many have thought sentience to be non-programmable. In Gunderson's terms ([1971], pp. 73-4) features of sentience are 'program resistant' rather than 'program receptive', and he regards it as a 'methodological howler' (p. 73) to attempt to simulate pain perception (for example) on a computer. On the other hand, as we have already noted, Dennett [1978a] has written an outline sketch of a pain program. The boundary between the programmable and the non-programmable, what can and what cannot be mechanically simulated, what we can and what we cannot write a flow-chart diagram for, is challenged whenever it is drawn. It should be stressed that it is almost certainly an error to jump on just *one* crucial thing that computers will never be able to do. Such temerity usually meets its nemesis sooner or later. What we can argue, though, is that the challenge to personhood from computers is not yet something that we have the knowledge to imagine successfully— and that this is as true with respect to sentience as we found it to be with respect to sapience.

To see this, let us look a little more closely at one of the arguments that suggests that sentience might, one day, be programmable: that of Dennett [1978a]. I shall not recapitulate his whole argument, for only one small part of it is needed here.

Following Melzack and Wall (see e.g. their [1965] and [1982]), Dennett writes a program-sketch that features, *inter alia*, the operations which in the human are performed in the paleocortical limbic system, the operations ascribed to the 'aversive system', the 'motivational-affective processing pathway'. But this is too fast; it will not do as it stands. We need far more than this before we have an adequately described background—a grip on further factors that must be relevant to the supposition. For we cannot *just* put a program into a machine and call a bit of it 'aversive' or 'motivational'. If it is to merit the description, the system as a whole must be sensibly said to be averse to some range of stimuli, and to be motivated. So Dennett's robot could not have just the capacity—the capacity alone—to experience pain. We shall need also to ascribe some interests to it (so that it could be averse to what conflicts with or obstructs them), and probably also such things as emotions and attitudes (for these are among the most central motivating states). Otherwise we have not yet 'established the phenomenon' in the imagination upon which we can build a theory or hypothesis. For so far we have been offered no description of what would count as a robot having interests. It can, of course, be given goals, such as winning at chess; but it has so far no interest in the outcome. Consider one of our most fundamental interests, the interest in survival. A robot could perhaps be programmed to put the goal of its own physical safety above all, or almost all, other goals—but that is a far cry from saying that it would *mind* destruction or damage, that it has an interest in this goal. Interests, and perhaps emotions too, seem not to be a matter of ever-more-sophisticated programming; or, at minimum, nobody has yet hinted at any account of how they could be. It might be a question, as Gunderson ([1971], pp. 66-7) nicely puts it, not so much how the robot is programmed as how the program is roboted: a matter of hardware rather than of software. This would certainly be supported by the well-backed conjecture that there is a genetic basis to the organic drive for survival—a silicon chip, unlike (perhaps) a gene, cannot be said to be 'selfish'. But if that is so, then simulation of interests, and, inextricably involved with them, other psychological features such as pain, emotions, moods, attitudes, dispositions, etc. (all of which are pre-supposed by the 'stance' and 'reciprocation' conditions, (4) and (5), mentioned above), might require us to abandon silicon chips and turn instead to synthesized cells. We are as yet, however, very far from constructing artefacts from synthesized cells which have an interesting behavioural repertoire. So perhaps even the most imaginatively agile thought-experimenter would regard the hypothesis rather as science fantasy—a fairy story—than as a philosophically useful 'what if . . .?'

question, a theoretical possibility.[23] Thus I shall not pursue this line of thought any further.

In sum, then, all the challenges from thought experiments to the human monopoly of personhood can be fairly fought off.

8. THE REIDENTIFICATION ISSUE: MORE SCIENCE FANTASIES

It is, however, with the second strand of the personal identity debate—the 'reidentification' question—that thought experiments have really bloomed. Here too, I think, we shall find that we already have the materials for dismissing the more bizarre blossoms of the 'what if . . .?' hypothesis. For clearly, to take one familiar example, we can rule out absolutely the fission or fusion of humans; this is not theoretically possible. The total impact of the sum of laws that group us together as human beings (a natural-kind category) precludes our splitting into two (I postpone until a later chapter the apparent exception of brain bisection) or fusing with someone else. The phenomenon cannot be 'established' in thought. We can see this clearly if we ask ourselves to try to imagine, not merely the 'that', but also the 'how'—how this fission or fusion is to be supposed to occur, how we are to fit fission or fusion into the backing theory of the human species. We have such a theory; certainly large tracts of it need fuller development, but much has been secured. Amoeba-style fission, or fusion, between humans is at least as 'impossible', by this theory, as is the hypothesis that iron bars can float on water. Once we seriously accept that, the impossibility becomes immediately apparent. The impossibility, note, is directly relevant to the outcome or purpose of the thought experiment (compare the impossibility in the 'clock in a box' example, and contrast the non-relevant impossibility in the Einstein 'speed of light' example). Certainly amoebae divide (and we can explain how), but we are not amoebae (and we can describe the differences). Perhaps there are individuals on other galaxies who are persons but not humans, and who divide or fuse. The thought-experimenter can play with that notion for as long as he likes, but he has crossed the tenuous and amorphous line between philosophy and fairy story, and his play is not philosophy; for

[23] If we allow—just for the sake of the argument—that such an artefact might one day be created, then again, once the six conditions are satisfied, there would be no philosophical *problem* about its status as a person, although undoubtedly there would be social and legal knots to dissolve.

the original, and originally worrying, question was what we would say if *we* divided or fused. The philosophical problems of Alpha Centaurians must remain theirs until we meet them and construct a theory about them.

Other thought experiments may not be so evidently ruled out, but all must be transformed, and most lose much of their appeal. What we know and believe about natural-kind organisms determines the genuine theoretical possibilities. Perhaps, for example, the laws of human nature allow for brain-swaps. We should note, though, that the operation will be messier than once thought, since if we want to preserve minimal psychological competence, we should insist that it must be a brain-and-spinal-cord swap; neglected as it usually is, the spinal cord is centrally implicated in many psychological functions. I shall not deny, though, that this might count as a theoretical possibility; at least, scientists in the USA have already successfully carried through the unpleasant experiment of transplanting monkey heads from one to another. Half-brain transplants, however, become far more dubious. They became popular in the literature for two reasons. First, it was noted that individuals with either a left, or a right, hemispherectomy[24] were still, by any sensible criteria, the same persons as the persons they were before the operation—they were severely impaired, but there was no doubt about who they were. Thus it seemed that anyone could manage with only one hemisphere. Second, philosophers have recently become interested in the results of brain bisection, an operation which appeared to split the brain in two and generate two independent centres of consciousness; in short, it seemed again that either hemisphere alone could underpin consciousness and purpose. Philosophers talking about half-brain transplants needed to add the postulate that the two hemispheres were equipollent, in order to set up a clear and alarming puzzle—the puzzle that if *A*'s brain were first divided, and then the two halves put into *B*'s and *C*'s skulls, who then would wake up as *A*? Both *B* and *C* appeared to have an equally good title. Although it is of course not true that the hemispheres are equipollent, the hypothesis that they might be so is probably, just barely, legitimate, since human brains are almost indefinitely various in their distribution of capacities between the two hemispheres.

But matters are not that straightforward. They rarely are, for all that philosophers would like them to become so: as Austin said, oversimpli-

---

[24] A hemispherectomy is the surgical removal of the cerebral cortex of one hemisphere of the brain.

fication is something which 'one might be tempted to call the occu-
pational disease of philosophers if it were not their occupation' (Austin
[1962], p. 38). Hemispherectomies do not entail the removal of a whole
half-brain. Only half of the *cortex* is surgically eliminated. Commissurotomy does not split the brain in half. Only (parts of) the *cortex* are
divided. The subcortical regions are left intact and untouched in each
case, and these areas are crucial to all psychological functions. Indeed,
Dimond thinks that they are in a sense *more* important than is the
cerebral cortex:

From this perspective [from the inside] the brain appears more like a busy map
room or an operations room, where the most important actions take place right
at the very centre, whereas the surround is used to display the information and
to provide the back-up facilities. If we look at the brain from without, we tend to
think that the cortex is the most important structure and that the rest of the
brain becomes progressively less important in a gradient from there on. If,
alternatively, we adopt the perspective from within, not only do we re-evaluate
the centre structures at the very heart of the machine, but also the more
peripheral parts take on a different perspective more like the display facilities of
an operations room (Dimond [1980], p. 515).

We need not here, however, adjudge relative importance; all that
matters is that we should agree that the subcortical brain tissue is
completely indispensable.

Thus the thought-experimenter has to suppose that all the non-
cortical regions can be surgically sectioned too; *or* that the bits that
cannot be divided are not essential to an individual's adequate,
particular, and idiosyncratic modes of intellectual operation. These are
very large assumptions (and what are we supposed to do with the spinal
cord?). It is true that tumours or injury sometimes require the surgeon
to operate to remove part of one of the midbrain or paleocortical organs,
but then what remains afterwards usually cannot manage nearly so well;
we do not know and cannot say whether an individual could survive at
all with only half of *each* of these subcortical organs. Moreover, there is
no reason to suppose that the connections of, say, the left hemisphere
part of any midbrain organ, or of a paleocortical structure such as the
hippocampus, are solely, or even primarily, ipsilateral. If they were not
ipsilaterally connected—if, that is, their activities were directed either to
their own other half, or to different organs and regions in *either*
hemisphere—then no crude physical division down the middle would or
could produce the results envisaged. Indeed, there are good reasons to
suppose that subcortical structures are connected both ipsilaterally and

contralaterally thus indifferently. But that means that half-brain transplants are not a genuine theoretical possibility, that the problem is not, as Parfit suggests ([1984], p. 255), 'merely technical'. We know that we cannot take out a whole hemisphere, midbrain, paleocortex, and all. We are completely ignorant about what would happen if the detachable parts of two half-brains from one head were sewn on to the undetachable parts of the two different brains (death is certainly the most likely outcome); and thus no conclusions relevant to personal identity could be drawn, since, as I argued above, we cannot justify thought experiments by appeal to our ignorance of theory. To insist, 'But if this, this, and this, then that, that, and that' may be fun but is not helpful: the laws governing human development and function may, and in this case probably do, *forbid* 'this, this, and this' from obtaining under any circumstances. Not knowing whether the 'this' could hold, we have no justification in concluding any 'that'; thought experiments that are the product of ignorance simply mislead. We have failed to 'establish the phenomenon', to describe the relevant background adequately.

Memory swaps—rewiring brain B to give it the memories of brain A, treating brains like computer hardware and memories like the transferable software—also lose their original charm. Brief reflection on what the brain is actually like ensures this. An appalling number of cells decay each day, in anyone over (about) sixteen years old; on the other hand, cell dendrites sometimes grow and develop new connections—nothing is less static than cerebral hardware. Brains differ grossly in size: Turgenev's, at 2,012 grams, weighed almost twice that of Anatole France, at 1,017 grams (see Steele Russell [1979], p. 128). But even if we forget the *structural* plasticity of the brain, the complex plasticity of neural *function* is still intimidating. The cells of the average brain (opinions differ about the number: current conjectures range between 10^{10} and 10^{11}) are in ceaseless flux, each at any given time firing, resting, or inhibited, each with up to 2,000 synaptic links with others.

Imagine, as a simple and largely inadequate analogy, two 'crazy typewriters', in which every key is constantly jumping to different places on the keyboard. Where each jumps, and when, is a complex product of what the typist has typed in on all past occasions, and each typist uses only his own machine. Suppose next that simultaneously each typist types a string of letters and digits, and the keys that each presses are the same as far as their physical location on the keyboard is concerned—e.g. each at the same instant strikes first the third key from the left, bottom

row, then the seventh key from the right, second row, . . . etc. The two
resulting print-outs have, evidently, the remotest possible likelihood of
being identical, or even similar. Now if we suppose that each print-out
represents the 'memory trace' of the 'experience' which is represented
by the sequence of key-strikings, it becomes clear that nobody can take a
single memory from one brain and just rewire it into another, any more
than one could get the same print-out from the second typewriter as that
produced by the first just by pressing the keys in the same locations. To
get the same print-out on the second typewriter as the one achieved on
the first would require a long-term study of the key jumps of the second
so as to work out which keys would be where, and when. Moreover (and
here the analogy with the typewriters, never very strong, breaks down
completely) memories interlock with other memories, and interlock
with other psychological competences—with remembering how and
remembering where, with learned skills like driving and typing, with
capacities like perception and perceptual recognition, and even with
dispositional states like depression, euphoria, and especially attentive-
ness. As the jargon phrase has it, the mental is holistic; the set of
memories describable as 'rememberings that' cannot be isolated from
all else and transplanted or wired in *en bloc*. When we add the essentially
holistic nature of the mental to the fact that *which* cell-firings realize a
memory trace (of, say, the visual experience of seeing a python) is a
function of what those cells and others have been up to in the near and
remote past, then it is hard to see how one could rewire anything
without rewiring everything.[25]

Of course, thought-experimentalists have been willing to contemplate
even this radical degree of mind (= software) transplanting. We read of
the construction of *doppelgängers*, hyper-identical twins, with every
memory, thought, belief, disposition (etc., etc.) wired in. None, of
course, supposes this to be possible in practice. However, it is said to be
possible in principle, and on that basis one goes on to construct
problems for the reidentification of persons. But surely it is more than
just practically impossible. If we return for a moment to the crazy typewriters, then we can see that what print-out is secured when keys at
certain locations are hit is a product of what has been typed in the past,

---

[25] What is really wrong with this whole approach is that it treats memories (and
beliefs, thoughts, etc.) as if they were marbles in a bag: one can just 'take' one out of a
brain, they are discrete and isolable. Whatever else may be shown about memory, we can
be absolutely certain that this is a radically misleading model. In ch. 4, when discussing
fugue states, we shall see that 'memory' is *far* more complex than the 'marbles in a bag'
caricature.

since that—we supposed—determined the new locations of all the jumping keys. If each typewriter has a different owner with different literary, scholarly, or utilitarian tastes and interests, then the correlation of keys struck with print-out produced will be token-token; put another way, we cannot predict either what keys need to be struck to produce *this* word, nor what word would result from *these* keys being struck, unless we have kept a record of every key ever pressed.

In the brain the problem is the same, only infinitely worse. Cells are not only far more numerous than typewriter keys, but also we know that they are not as discrete and independent as are the keys of a typewriter, so they must be expected to have far more complicated interactions than anything we could model on any machine.

Now *some* psychological phenomena we could plot reasonably well. We might find, for instance, that some cells of a specific type and in a specific location are sensitive to light in the red wavelength, or that other individuatable groups of cells will fire when and only when there are vertical lines in the centre of the visual field; or, to take a more general example, we might find that this individual must have Wernicke's aphasia, because of damage to certain regions in part of the cortex (the posterior superior temporal area of the left hemisphere, to be technical). So also we might perhaps ('in principle') map on to brain *B* some of the *capacities* of brain *A*, ensuring, for example, that both are red-green colour blind, or have unusually acute auditory powers, or have constructional apraxia. In so doing, we would be examining systematically fruitful *explananda* and *explanantia*—in other words, 'natural kinds'. Given the arguments above, it is predictable that such capacities are suitable for systematic study.

By contrast, however, we will be unable to isolate the individual contents of individual mental states (beliefs that *p*, desires for *x*, expectations that *q*, and so forth) in *A*'s brain, let alone recreate them in *B*'s. The billion cells of the brain are in incessant flux—firing, resting, inhibited—and synaptic connections change over time; every cell will be implicated in dozens of different patterns, but may be replaced by another cell or set of cells if it is resting or if it decays; although cells do decay, axons sprout and dendrites grow to form new connections; changes in the amounts of the various neurotransmitters make great differences to cellular activity . . . and so on. Thus to sort out which sets and patterns of firings and inhibitions are engaged in realizing *this* thought about cameras rather than *that* thought about cuckoo clocks would presuppose that some general features of the brain's functioning go along with the former rather than the latter, and vice versa. But this we have no reason to suppose, any more than we have any reason to suppose that there are general features of atomic structure that correlate with ashtrays rather than saucers. Individual belief contents (etc.) may, as Davidson [1970] argues, be token-token identical with neurophysiological states;[26] but the anomalousness of this identity ensures that we can rarely if ever find out to *which* states they are identical. Note, though, that there is no reason whatsoever to suppose that such 'individual belief contents' are natural kinds, suitable for systematic scientific study; it will therefore be wholly *un*surprising to discover that they have as little systematic connection with brain states as fences have with descriptions of atomic lattices.

I suggest, then, that it is not theoretically possible to take one mature adult brain, inspect its contents, and map them on to another system. This would be impossible whether the other system is a 'washed' brain, or whether it is a brain created from scratch with synthesized cells; the reason is that we could never individuate its 'contents' and their neural basis.

What, though, of the thought experiment that it might be done from the other end, so to speak: that instead of starting from psychology and looking to find, and duplicate, the relevant hardware processes, we should ignore the 'software' completely and simply ('simply' is something of a misnomer) concentrate upon copying each and every atom and molecule? The underlying assumption is that of physical determination: if two systems are in *exactly* the same physical state, then exactly the same higher-order (here psychological) predicates must be true of them—apart, of course, from their relational properties. One problem here, though, is that the building would have to be completed in one instant, just because the model brain will not stay immobile while it is being copied (the thought-experimenter will presumably say that it might be frozen). Besides that, of course, no two atoms are going to behave in exactly the same way, since they too have complex internal economies; and thus the very notion of getting complete identity at the micro level is somewhat absurd. What is 'the "bottom", or "micro", level', anyway? Philosophers—generally blithely neglectful of neuroscientific facts—talk freely about cell-firings. For this thought experi-

---

[26] I do not, incidentally, go along with such a view. I have argued elsewhere [1983a, 1987] that most of the propositional attitudes that we ascribe to others should be construed *instrumentalistically*, and hence that there would not always be 'a belief' to be identified or not with a state of the brain. But this is a separate argument, which is not necessary for our present purposes.

ment, however, we are asked to go a bit more 'micro' than that, and to contemplate atoms and molecules. But neither molecules nor atoms are conspicuously 'micro'; as all know, below them lies the bewildering and terrifying complexity of subatomic physics. The alleged possibility here is no more than hand-waving, another fairy story.

I conclude then that the difficulties for the more *outré* versions of thought-experimentation are quite as serious when the method is applied to the question of reidentification as they are when identification is the problem at issue.

9. LOSING TOUCH WITH REALITY

I now return to pick up a point that was left half-developed earlier. I provided rather few arguments for the claim that fairy stories, merely logical possibilities, what Parfit calls 'deeply impossible' thought experiments, were of little use to us. We are now in a position to see more clearly why this is so.

Philosophers are fond of disputing the relevance of empirical data to their 'conceptual' conclusions. At the same time, as we have seen, they are not slow to jump on novel data—such as the findings from com-missurotomy—to support brand-new thought experiments. Whether or not split-brain patients are 'in two minds', philosophers at least seem to be, when they consider the role of facts in conceptual analysis. Kripke, for instance [1972], allows himself, and uses, the empirically established facts about the chemical constitution of water and the atomic number of gold to support 'philosophical' conclusions about meaning, reference, and necessity. Yet he attempts to refute the identity of pain with brain states by supposing that his opponent wants to claim that 'pain is identical with C-fibre firing'—although anyone who has skated through an introductory textbook in neurophysiology knows that such a claim is not only false, but is obviously so. (C-fibre firing is neither necessary nor sufficient for pain. It is typically an early member in the complex series of parallel and sequential cerebral processes required for pain experience.)

It seems that established and respectable theories—in chemistry and physics, say—can help determine philosophical ('conceptual') con-clusions; whereas underdeveloped theories and facts that are *relatively* unknown, or at least tend to be unknown to the non-specialist, can safely be ignored. But this position is indefensible. It would require one to defend the implausible position that thought experiments can indeed be based on ignorance, on an inadequately described background, where the 'relevant' factors, being unknown, are swept under the carpet. It runs head-on against Rorty's claim mentioned above—which the history of science and philosophy surely puts beyond all doubt— that what we know and believe determines what we do, and what we do not, find imaginable, possible, fruitful to explore. Maybe Mill was exaggerating when he defined philosophy as 'the scientific study of man'; but we do not, surely, want to return to the kinds of definition neatly satirized by Larmore:

Definitions of what counts as 'philosophical' are never very fruitful. Their usual intent is to exonerate the philosopher who makes them from having to learn anything about the areas of inquiry they exclude (Larmore [1980], p. 13; I am grateful to Eric James for this reference).

'Deeply impossible' thought experiments, in which scientific data are trampled underfoot, are inconclusive for several reasons.

First, we should ask the 'fantastical' thought-experimenter how he distinguishes what he does from what the writer of fairy stories does. Certainly the distinction will often be blurred and amorphous;[27] but is there any difference between the two—except in the purposes for which the two are written? Now he may of course cheerfully concede, even welcome, the conflation. He may argue that philosophers should, as a matter of professional duty, go to see *2001* and *The Return of the Jedi*. If the thought-experimenter does concede the conflation, though, then we should ask him why he needs Washoe, or the data from commissuro- tomy, or why he appeals to what computers can actually do. For in so far as he is abandoning theoretical possibility, he might as well have stuck with clear and agreed theoretical impossibilities, such as Pinocchio, Martians, or Galatea. There would be no difference as far as the heuristic value of the stories is concerned; and, most importantly, there would be far less danger of getting misled into the thought that one is dealing with anything other than bare logical possibility. *If* such experiments with bare logical possibilities are philosophically fruitful, then amoeba-like Martians are as good, in fact better, than half-brain transplants.

[27] A volume that treads the borderline and now falls on the 'philosophically useful' side and then on the 'enjoyable science fiction' side is Hofstadter and Dennett's [1981]. (I keep my own volume sometimes on the library shelves, sometimes as light reading by the guest bed.) Humphrey [1983] said of this book in his review: '[w]hat the book so cleverly demonstrates is that when people carry over their common-sense concepts about mind into the Wonderland of Science Fiction computers, teleclones and brain surgery, they can and do get those common-sense concepts in a twist' (p. 185).

But they cannot be fruitful. The reason we have seen already, in Section 3. Thought experiments deliberately compare themselves with scientific experiments. However, as we noted, experiments in science typically take place in an artificial, carefully designed, experimental context. The role of this artifice is to fix the *ceteris paribus/absentibus* conditions that surround *any* attempt to generalize from one sort of thing to another. To repeat: as far as is practically possible, the experimental set-up operates to identify all the potentially relevant factors, and then to exclude certain variables completely, and to hold others fixed. Generally speaking, too, such experiments take as *explananda* and *explanantia* natural-kind terms (in the broad sense given above). Thus, *and for these reasons*, the results of the experiment can be ascribed with greater or lesser security to the features that were deliberately varied for the purposes of the experiment. In short, the scenario has been adequately described. Correspondingly, legitimate thought experiments must spell out for us the (relevant) respects in which the 'possible world' does and does not differ from the actual world. In sharp contrast, what we find in the fantastical thought experiments we have been considering is a virtual abandonment of any attempt to identify, restrict, or fix the *ceteris paribus* conditions. These 'experiments' take us too far from the actual world, and from the 'other things' that hold roughly 'equal' here: 'Such facts as mostly do not strike us because of their generality' (Wittgenstein [1963], p. 230[e]). This means that we are left with no clue as to what has been varied in thought and what left (supposedly) untouched. A world in which half-brains could be transplanted, or in which *doppelgängers* could be created, is one *so* radically different from our own that no philosophically interesting conclusion can be drawn: even if we succeed in reaching some conclusion, we shall not know to which of the variable and varying factors to ascribe it.

Nor is it any good to reply to this objection that fantasy (such as *Star Trek*, or *Alice*) has made readily intelligible to us thought experiments that are even more radical than those we have been considering here. Such a reply is like arguing that Carroll had Alice walking through a mirror, and that *therefore* it is legitimate to wonder what would happen if we could do this too. *Alice*, and *Star Trek*, are all very well so long as we deliberately abandon or suspend belief in the rest of the world as we know it—and that means as our scientific theories allow us to know it. This is legitimate enough in fiction of that general type: for such fiction has a *different* purpose, that of entertaining. The author of a fantasy sets out for us a new framework within which the events taking place are (given a generous dollop of suspended belief) intelligible. He is not setting out to enable us to draw conclusions about our theories and our concepts.[28] But philosophical thought experiments are, in theory at least, intended to tell us what we *would* say if. . ., precisely *in* the world as we know it from our scientific theories—so that we can explore the ramifications of the concept in question. This has to be so; after all, if the world were indeed radically different, then practically nothing is left for us to rely on, and it is doubtful that any of our concepts would remain secure. Certainly we cannot claim that just the notion of a person alone would (or would not) need to vary.

In sum, we cannot extract philosophically interesting conclusions from fantastical thought experiments. We cannot do this because we have the following choice: either (*a*) we picture them against the world as we know it, or (*b*) we picture them against some quite different background. If we choose the first, then we picture them against a background that deems them impossible—that insists that hemisphere transplants (for instance) violate fundamental biological and physical laws. If we choose (*b*), then we have the realm of fantasy, and fantasy is fine to read; but it does not allow for philosophical conclusions to be drawn, because in a world indeterminately different we do not know what we would want to say about anything.

Put another way, intuition works reasonably well—mostly—when we are imagining real-life situations. We then have a platform (our ordinary background beliefs and assumptions) as a springboard from which we can make the imaginative and intuitive jump. Real-life situations, or so I shall argue, can probe and test our concepts, our intuitions about their scope. They can set up maddeningly puzzling paradoxes, far better than can thought experiments: just because with them we have available all the data we need. We have 'the background'; we may be unclear which features of it are relevant, and so we are not given on a plate the *relevant* background. But since the puzzling and probing phenomena have occurred in the real world, the quest for details that might or might not be relevant can be met. When we are puzzled about how to describe or explain the phenomenon before us—and we very often are, as I hope to show in Chapter 4—we cannot complain about lack of data: the back-

---

[28] *Star Trek* allows me to illustrate specifically the inconclusive nature of science fantasy. Captain Kirk, so the story goes, disintegrates at place *p* and reassembles at place *p**. But perhaps, instead, he dies at *p*, and a *doppelgänger* emerges at *p**. What is the difference? One way of illustrating the difference is to suppose there is an afterlife: a heaven, or hell, increasingly supplemented by yet more Captain Kirks all cursing the day they ever stepped into the molecular disintegrator.

ground can be described fully and adequately. But when we take an example like reincarnation, or half-brain transplants, or mind-swapping, then we have *no* such platform. We have deliberately, in fact, extracted the case from this surround, cut away the platform. The result is then that our intuitions become increasingly dubious, uncertain, and contestable. The 'jump from data to theory' gapes wide. We do not know what to say, and we should admit as much.

The argument is close to one offered by Hare in the context of moral reasoning:

it shows the lack of contact with reality of a system based on moral intuitions without critical thought, that it can go on churning out the same defences of liberty and democracy *whatever* assumptions are made about the state of the world or the preferences of its inhabitants. This should be remembered whenever some critic of utilitarianism, or of my own views, produces some bizarre example in which the doctrine he is attacking could condone slavery or condemn democracy. What we should be trying to find are moral principles which are acceptable for general use in the world as it actually is (Hare [1981], pp. 167 f.).

Hare is here (in my terms) offering an argument that applies as much to the 'merely imagined'—but in principle possible—thought experiments as to those with which I am primarily concerned: those that would not be possible in the world we actually inhabit. He is complaining that some moral theorists argue that the social and moral world might have been very different (as it indeed could have been) from the way it actually is, but that they fail to spell it out in detail; they ignore the need to describe the assumptions about 'the state of the world or the preferences of its inhabitants'. There is, however, a general point that applies both to the 'merely imagined', and to the 'actually impossible' thought experiments: *no* conclusions are worth anything unless the background is adequately described, and where the implications and presuppositions of the imaginary scenario are spelled out. The more bizarre and unrealistic the thought experiments, the less utility they can have. This is true both in moral reasoning and in the problems of personal identity.

It is of course true that if things *had* been radically different, then so would be our concepts. Wittgenstein argues in a well-known passage:

I am not saying: if such-and-such facts of nature were different people would have different concepts (in the sense of a hypothesis). But: if anyone believes that certain concepts are absolutely the correct ones, and that having different ones would mean not realizing something that we realize—then let him imagine certain very general facts of nature to be different from what we are used to, and the formation of concepts different from the usual ones will become intelligible to him (Wittgenstein [1963], p. 230ᵉ).

If we adopt this recommendation we can indeed understand how intelligent beings might have devised quite different concepts from our own. What we cannot do (and Wittgenstein never says that we can) is imagine what these concepts would look like; and this is absolutely crucial for the thought-experimenter. We cannot, that is, couch them in our own terms: there is no background common to the two worlds, since the 'very general facts of nature' are left indeterminate and undetermined. In a world where these general facts of nature were so unlike our own as to allow amoeba-like Martians to flourish, we just have no idea what we should say about it.

10. A PROMISSORY NOTE

This chapter has been a wet blanket which has poured cold water on a mare's nest of red herrings. But I hope too that it has acted as a new broom to sweep away deceptively beckoning culs-de-sac; for the fact is that we have a plethora of here and now actual puzzle-cases. These fulfil the same function of stretching the concept of a person to its limits and beyond, and correspondingly of stretching the philosophical imagination. They are ready to hand—waiting only to be dug out of the psychological, neuropsychological, medical, psychoanalytic, and anthropological literature. One of the few everyday proverbs that seems to me broadly correct is that truth is, almost invariably, stranger than fiction; and if we look at what can indeed happen to our subject-matter, the person, we shall reach more reliable results than if we stayed dreaming in the realms of fantasy. Perhaps there is no 'logic of discovery'. Perhaps, that is, inspiration can come from any or all sources: fantasy, shapes in the sand, the Delphic oracle. Nevertheless, basing our argument on actual cases allows us to check our imagination against the facts, and our intuitions get strengthened and rendered more trustworthy.

2

Infants and Foetuses

Children, behold the Chimpanzee:
He sits on the ancestral tree
From which we sprang in ages gone.
I'm glad we sprang: had we held on,
We might, for aught that I can say,
Be horrid Chimpanzees today.

(Oliver Herford)

1. INTRODUCTION

With Chapter 1 as a preamble, and an excuse, for the abandonment of thought experiments in favour of real-life conditions and occurrences, we turn now to start discussion of borderline—or apparently borderline—instances of persons. We will begin in this chapter with the not-yet-born, and the very young.

Not all individual members of the human species are 'paradigm persons', normal healthy adults; so much is trivial. This means, though, that some such members will not meet all the six conditions outlined in the preceding chapter, since, as we saw, these characterize the typical mature human being as such, as well as being conditions on what it is to be a person. In the present chapter we shall consider the status of those who may fall short of one or more of the conditions because of their immaturity: neonates and foetuses. We shall then examine what we need to say about impaired and retarded infants. It will soon become obvious that the important issues require above all scrutiny of the 'stance' condition mentioned in the preceding chapter: the attitude that we should take towards anything that is a person, and how far we should extend that attitude to the immature.

2. POTENTIALITIES AND INTERESTS

Potentiality

If a baby or foetus is normal then, at minimum, it is *potentially* a person. This, we shall see, is of the utmost importance. Unfortunately, though, 'potentiality' is an elusive and many-faceted notion, and the kind of potentiality here, and its relevance, needs to be spelled out carefully.

After all, the plurality of sperm and ovum (the pre-conception stage, in other words) might also be said to be potentially a person. Does the potentiality of the zygote, the fertilized cell, differ significantly from that of the gametes, the sperm and ovum before fertilization? There are two (interrelated) differences here, and they seem to me to hold crucial implications. First, when there is a fertilized cell, or a foetus, or a neonate, then we have a referent: something to which the expression 'this entity' is tied. There is a single and unproblematic candidate for identification and reidentification; we can talk about the person that *this very thing* will become. This is not so, on the other hand, when we revert to the pre-conception stage, to the plurality of sperm and ovum—there is no referent, no individual (individual anything) which we are talking about. Second, there is a clear sense in which the potential of sperm and ovum is 'two-staged' in a way in which that of the zygote is not—they have to combine, and only *then* have they nothing to do but enter on the (one) stage of development.

Both these features are significant; let us start with the first, the presence or absence of a specific referent. The distinction here is reasonably familiar in philosophy, and can be illustrated by simple examples. Suppose a bank manager observes one day that his branch has exactly 9,999 account-holders; suppose further that he wants to gain publicity by giving a prize to the ten thousandth customer. He tells his staff, 'The first person to open an account tomorrow will be given £1,000.' Assuming (*a*) that he is an honest man, then there is no individual *now* to whom he is referring. However, he might (*b*) be dishonest and nepotistic; he might have telephoned his nephew and told him to be sure to be first in the queue tomorrow and to open an account. In that case he is referring (secretly) to his nephew. In this latter example, (*b*), we have a parallel to the fertilized cell—there is a specific referent, someone he is thinking about. In the former case, (*a*), we have a parallel to the separate gametes: it is likely that someone will open an account tomorrow, but we as yet do not know who. In the same way, although it may be likely that one of several million spermata will fertilize this ovum, we do not know which one will, and hence do not know what zygote will result.

When our topic is personal identity, we surely must have a referent. We need some specific entity to talk about: *its* interests, prospects, characteristics, future, our relationship and obligations to *it*. So it would seem helpful, and if we are careful not unduly misleading, to draw a distinction here between sperm and egg on the one hand, the zygote on the other, and restrict our attention to the latter.

Turning to the distinction between 'one-staged' and 'two-staged' potentials, there is of course nothing *wrong*, nor even odd or aberrant, in talking of the potential that the sperm and ovum have of becoming a person. Indeed, there are many examples of perfectly legitimate two-staged potentialities to be found: for instance, the three-year-old English child is 'potentially a Russian speaker'. There is a clear sense in which this is a two-staged potentiality—first stage, he can learn the language, second stage, he can then speak it whenever the circumstances are appropriate and he feels like doing so. But this example helps us to see that there are significantly different implications to be drawn from each of the two kinds of potential here, from each stage. For note that before the student learns the language we do not call him a 'Russian speaker'; we can only say that he could become one. Analogously, before they combine the gametes cannot be said to be *a* 'potential person'; they could combine to become one, that is, to become *one*. Furthermore, there is another implication that distinguishes the two stages: there are other ascriptions which only become unconditionally applicable when the second stage is reached. It is only after stage one, after the student has learned the language, that we can ascribe to him such attributes as 'fluency', 'a Georgian accent', etc.; similarly, only after the gametes have combined into a zygote, have reached stage two, can we ascribe to it interests, prospects, needs.

In short, then, although it is not in the least incorrect to talk about the two-staged potentiality (before conception) that the sperm and ovum have of becoming a person, the sense in which they have that potentiality does not yet give us a subject to which to refer, and hence gives us nothing yet to which we can ascribe properties characteristic of actual and 'one-staged potential' persons.

The moral of all this is that we need to scrutinize carefully the precise nature of the potentiality at issue. Indeed, later in this chapter it will be necessary to do so again, for we will shortly meet potentialities—both one-staged and two-staged—of rather different kinds. Sometimes the distinctions between the various senses of 'potentiality' will not contribute to any theoretically interesting conclusion; but at other times, as is I think true of pre- and post-conception potentialities, they will.

Before moving on to discuss interests, let us pause to consider what can be said about such 'potential persons' as zygotes, foetuses, or neonates in terms of the six conditions outlined in the previous chapter. It is clear that they *now* fail to meet most of them, as can be seen if we run briefly through them. Intentional properties: it is true, of course, that some relatively unsophisticated Intentional predicates are true of a new-born child: it cries for its mother, wants food, sees the rattle. But these are indeed unsophisticated predicates, and many animals would have a stock that is considerably richer. Rationality: we would surely not be tempted to call it rational. Language use: it has no command of language until it is a year or so old—as Bentham remarked,[1] the new-born infant is less 'conversable' than a full-grown horse or dog. (Self)-consciousness: there is little reason to suppose that it has a richer consciousness or self-consciousness than many non-human animals. Finally, whatever its status as a moral *object* (which will preoccupy us for most of this chapter) it cannot do much by way of reciprocating the attitudes taken towards it; it is therefore certainly not a moral *agent*. Five of the six conditions at least, then, are not met; the only one about which we are so far uncertain is the question of the proper attitude to take towards it—its standing as an object of our practical and moral concern.

The fact, however, that the normal foetus or infant has the (single-staged) potentiality of becoming an indubitably fully-fledged person bears most centrally upon precisely this problem, the problem of the attitude we adopt towards it (condition (3) of the list in Chapter 1). In other words, it is just because it has the other five features *potentially* that it has now the remaining one, that it is an object of our practical and moral concern, *actually*. Or so I shall argue; to support this claim we need to examine the nature of a creature's interests: interests that may be present or future, short term or long term, known about or not. Discussion of interests, then, will occupy the remainder of this section.

Interests

We are familiar with the idea that the needs, wants, and interests of any creature may need respecting and fostering even if they are not consciously held; or even if they are wants, needs, or interests that may not be held currently, but which we can foresee the creature having in

---

[1] Bentham, *A Fragment on Government and an Introduction to the Principles of Morals and Legislation*, ch. XVII, s. 1, footnote to para. 4; [1948], p. 412.

the future. Thus, for example, the human needs calcium, whether this need is known to him or not. Similarly, the pig farmer should, other things being equal, ensure that there is a competent veterinary surgeon nearby even though his pigs are not only unaware of their interest in health, but are all now in the very pink of condition. Much of the time, then, it seems that desires and needs may claim our support even when the creature in question is either ignorant of them, or does not yet experience them, or both. Moreover, again if other things are equal, desires and needs should be respected—a point which asserts no more than that we need a justification for flouting them but no justification for respecting them. Someone who steps deliberately on a bee should be able to say why he did so, whereas the one who moves to avoid it has no challenge to which he needs to respond.

We can add to this the reflection that whether the wants, needs, desires, or aims are long term or short term seems to be of little intrinsic importance. Put another way, the fact that some interest will only *matter* in the fairly distant future seems not to hold much significance of itself. There are, certainly, arguments that are often perfectly respectable for preferring present interests: for taking no thought for the morrow, considering the lilies of the field, and gathering roses while we may; and it simply seems true that an immediate good may at times be more desirable than a more distant, even if a greater, good. But the general tendency is to approve the prudential attitude that, say, leads people to take out pension plans or to try to cut out smoking even when they are now both young and healthy; or, more mundanely, to get regular check-ups at the dentist; or, more grandly, to become concerned about environmental pollution. The fact that we are usually more actively concerned with interests we have now may only reflect the truth that we can typically *do* more about them.

This last point is important. It is best and most clearly defended if we exploit an analogy with spatial distance. There is, after all, the brute fact that we are usually more efficient when we try to assist people who live in our immediate neighbourhood than we are if we try to assist those living on the other side of the world. We can do more, and do it more effectively, for them. This is patently obvious; however, this patent truth in no way entails that the Englishman living in Surbiton must think that other Englishmen living in Surbiton are intrinsically more *valuable* than are Australians living in Canberra, even though he has little interaction with natives of Canberra. It is of course true that we can sometimes do something concrete on behalf of those far away: we can, for example, send money to Oxfam to help alleviate the effects of a famine caused by drought in Ethiopia. Analogously, we can do something concrete to foster our long-term interests; by taking out pension plans, we provide in some measure for our old age. But for the general run of activity and concern, immediate interests claim more of our time and our thought than do far future ones, and our neighbours and friends claim more of our time and our thought than do complete or distant strangers. The central point is that this is not unreasonable, nor immoral, nor short-sighted. For we are typically—although not always—more *effective* with respect to current interests and to local people. There is less that can go wrong when we are dealing with the immediate present, or with the person next door—we usually know more of the relevant details. Money sent to Ethiopia, on the other hand, might be embezzled, lost, wasted, or misused, just as our sensible pension plan would be frustrated if we died at the age of fifty. But none of this serves to justify any inference that distant people and future interests are intrinsically less important; when we can take effective action about remote individuals and future needs, we are considered wise and rational to do so.

What, then, are these interests for which we try to provide? Our immediate concerns, of course, can be about anything at all, and are usually highly specific: getting to this performance of the *Meistersinger*, trying to find smoked eel, trying to find any food at all, finishing the marking of a doctoral thesis, getting these shoes repaired. Longer-term interests are rarely so specific and particular, and the further away in time they are, the less specific they tend to be. This too finds a parallel in spatial distance. Those who send money to assist famine relief in Ethiopia generally send it unconditionally, knowing that it will help in *some* way—perhaps it may buy grain that directly benefits some specific family, perhaps it contributes towards buying a truck, perhaps it contributes towards the running costs of the relief team, perhaps it will be set aside for use in future irrigation projects. The object of concern is 'the Ethiopian famine', and is usually not more determinate than that. So is it, analogously, with temporal distance. We may know, for example, little more than that we shall want reasonable material comfort and financial security in old age, as healthy a physical state as possible, the opportunity to continue the pursuit of activities to which we are or will be attached, and so forth. These are interests that, in broad outline, we can predict that we will have, and we can predict this because of what we know of human biology and psychology and of the society in which we live: humans have a number of familiar and unavoidable intellectual and physical needs. By relying, tacitly, upon the laws and generalizations that hold true of the species *homo sapiens*, we can sketch—albeit in increasingly rough outline, just as with spatial distance—the wants and needs, both physical and intellectual, that we shall have in ten, twenty, or forty years' time. In other words, then, whereas we should perhaps ensure that there is a competent veterinary surgeon nearby if we are responsible for the welfare of a herd of cows, we are not obliged to ensure for them intellectual challenge or excitement—that means nothing to cows. By contrast intellectual stimulation, along with adequate medical provision, would normally be required of us if we are to any extent responsible for the welfare of other human beings. This is simply due to the different capacities of humans of cows. Such considerations are brute facts: facts about brutes.

Combining 'potentiality' and 'interests'

We can now perhaps see how the claim of an infant or foetus to be regarded right from the start as an object of moral and social concern, precisely on a par with any fully-fledged person, rests upon its potentiality—the fact that all the remaining conditions of personhood will hold of it some day; and that this claim is not dependent upon which of the other conditions actually hold of it at the moment. For the validity of its claim to be an object of practical concern is explained by the fact that the interests of the foetus are, even if predominantly long term and general, no more so than are many of the interests of adults that we are prepared to take seriously; as seriously, indeed, as immediate, specific, and short-term interests. The youth who takes out a pension plan is doing something that is rational and justifiable, but which is no more so than is the action of the parents, expecting a baby, to ensure that the future child will have the chance of a good primary and secondary school. Both concerns are equally predictable, and either might be frustrated by premature death. On the other hand, just as it would normally be folly for the youth to take precautions now against contracting mumps in old age—since there is no particular reason to suppose that he will then suffer from the disease—so it would be folly for the expectant parents to move house to a neighbourhood with a brilliant teacher of the sousaphone, since there is, usually, no particular reason to suppose that their unborn child will want to learn the instrument. Long-term interests are rarely so specific as that. Ignoring such specific

concerns as these, though, there remain a host of interests that are
predictable enough in the long term, and for which it is rational to
provide now, interests that stem from the six conditions as well as from
other implications of the potentialities of our biological nature.

3. INFANTS AS FUZZY PERSONS

So the infant or foetus is a genuine object of our practical and moral
concern. But is it *now* a person?

This problem is not a genuine one, and, for reasons that will soon
emerge, the answer does not matter. 'Person' is a term of the
vernacular, and practically all such terms have highly blurry edges—a
fact which also does not matter. We can say more or less what we like
here; and our decision will largely depend on what significance we
choose to place upon the kind of potentiality in question (where 'potentiality', of course, is also a fuzzy-edged vernacular term). Potentiality is
crucial, because the infant or foetus, viewed solely as such and not in
terms of what it will become, has probably fewer of the qualifications of
personhood than have a great many animals—it is less rational, less self-
conscious, less conversable, etc. Yet since we *can*, if we choose, regard
either foetus or neonate as persons (and the plain fact is that many
people do), we are evidently relying heavily upon this potential. There
is no fact of the matter, no true answer to the question 'person or not?'.
After all, there are hosts of examples working both for and against the
idea that something which has a one-staged potentiality to become an *F*
is also an actual *F*. Consider, on the one hand, the sleeping man who
can speak Serbo-Croatian if he is woken (i.e. potentially), who is regarded
as a Serbo-Croatian speaker; or the puppy which is potentially a sheep-
dog, but which is conventionally called one already. But equally, on the
other hand, we find that the acorn seems not to be thought of as an oak
tree, and the adolescent is clearly not middle aged. None of these
examples, of course, is a particularly close analogy to the use of the term
'person', but that too is predictable; the classificatory terms of ordinary
language are not conspicuously systematic (which is one feature that
distinguishes them from scientific ones),[2] and so the principles—usually
implicitly or tacitly held—that govern our use of them will vary from
case to case. Thus our decision will probably be arbitrary or idiosyncratic until the child is morally and intellectually mature; and, if we

---

[2] See my [1981] for a fuller defence of this point.

choose *not* to call either foetus or neonate a person, then there is no single point at which it suddenly becomes one: being a person may well prove to be a matter of degree.

It may sound strange to say that it does not *matter* whether we decide to call the foetus or infant a person or not. We probably endorse, after all, Locke's comment (*Essay* [1690], Book ii, ch. xxvii, para. 26; [1959], p. 467) that 'person' is a forensic notion, a notion of considerable moral, practical, and social significance. But note that this has already been taken into account. For a great and substantial part of this moral, practical, and social significance that we ascribe to the infant or foetus is already assured by the fact that—as argued in the preceding section—it has precisely the same general claim upon our behaviour with respect to it as do the paradigm persons, normal adults. In other words, *one* of the six conditions (the third, concerning the attitude which we adopt towards persons: they are moral objects) holds in unqualified and present form; even though the rationale for that is a function of the infant's potential to meet the other five conditions, as well as its possession (now) of interests as unambiguous and as stringent as are those of adult humans. Persons are, of course, also morally and socially significant *qua* agents, as well as *qua* objects; but here too in the case of an infant or foetus it cannot matter that they might not be called persons, since they are not (yet) rational agents and so are not (yet) morally or socially significant agents. The social, practical, and moral implications that attach to the title of personhood, then, either attach anyway to infants, or do not need to apply.[3]

4. FAILED POTENTIALS: THE 'ARISTOTELIAN PRINCIPLE'

The problem that has been looming in the background so far is, of course, what we should say about infants or foetuses which are not just

---

[3] Thus this point is irrelevant to the abortion debate. For if it is wrong, or alternatively sometimes permissible, intentionally to take the life of an innocent person, it is correspondingly wrong, or alternatively sometimes permissible, to do the same to an organism who has the same claims upon our conduct as does a person.

Somewhat to my surprise, though, the present chapter does tend to suggest that abortion and murder are about on a par. I do not myself believe this, and would remind the reader that I have discussed only one of the many strands to the debate. For instance, the woman refused an abortion has to carry a child for 9 months—and this is not something easily paralleled by an argument against murder proper; I have again and again stressed the *ceteris paribus* condition when describing conflicting interests. I must admit, though, that I am violently opposed to capital punishment; and so the extent to which the arguments here could be deployed against abortion worry me not a little.

immature, but are also savagely impaired. There are unfortunately such maimed members of the species; those for whom we can have no expectation that they will grow up to be rational, conscious and self-conscious, beings capable of reciprocating attitudes taken to them, language-users, and entities of which highly sophisticated Intentional predicates hold true. The problem arises because we have rested the argument above upon the infant's *potential* to meet all six conditions, and have claimed that this explained the fact that it already meets fully one of them, in that it requires from us the full-blown stance or attitude that we accord to fully-fledged persons. If some human creature lacks this potential, what are we to say?

We shall consider in the next chapter the status of radically impaired adult human beings (the insane or demented, psychopaths, and so forth). So the answer to the question just posed will remain incomplete until then. None the less, there are some points that we can make now.

The sole reason for regarding the undeveloped human being as something towards which we should adopt fully the attitude we take to ordinary persons (in other words, respecting its needs and desires, present or future, as much as we respect those of unchallenged persons) were argued to rest upon its potential of becoming one. As Aristotle says: 'What each thing is when fully developed we call its nature, whether we are discussing a man, a horse, or a family' (*Politics*, i. 2. 1252^{b}32 f.). This potential, in turn, was explained by the fact that it belongs to the species *homo sapiens*, and the laws of development governing the species told us what sort of creature it would become, and what sort of interests, in broad outline, it would have. Now the radically maimed foetus or infant is still a member of the species *homo sapiens*; its potential, however, is blocked off—it will never be 'fully developed' as a human, it is an abnormal member of that species.

It may be only rarely that we know that the potential is indeed blocked off. The extent of recovery that can be achieved by surgical, chemical, and psychotherapeutic means broadens each day—very recently the London Underground was full of posters showing someone in a wheelchair in academic dress, with a caption that ran roughly: 'They said it would be a waste of time sending Alys to school.' Although this advertisement referred particularly to spastics and their physical impairment and abnormality, it is easy to imagine some similar advertisement making an analogous sort of point about mental deficiency. Moreover, we cannot now predict how the medical and paramedical services will improve, although we have no reason to suppose that they will not continue to increase their scope and powers as rapidly as they have done in past decades and centuries.

So we should confront two problems that may seem at first sight to be distinct. First, what should we do and say about infants we think to be completely incurable—infants such that no measures we can take will improve their mental capacity? Anencephalic children would be a certain example: these are born with no brain at all, or scarcely any, and are incapable of awareness, reaction, activity. Those with massive brain damage (caused perhaps by intracranial haemorrhage) may have irreparable deficiencies. Many spina bifida children develop hydro-cephalus (water on the brain), which causes swelling in the brain that often damages it irretrievably. Second, what, if anything, requires us to expend money and effort (often, perhaps, substantial sums of money and inordinate effort) to improve the mental and intellectual level of infants who can perhaps be helped to some extent, but who, without these heroic efforts, would remain 'happy morons', human vegetables? Some Down's syndrome children might fall into this category, as would infants who need a series of expensive and painful operations to prevent what would otherwise be inevitable brain damage. For instance, some spina bifida children are given an operation to implant a tube and valve to prevent spinal fluid oozing into the brain and causing hydrocephalus and consequent brain damage. The two questions may seem only peripherally related to our main topic of per-sonal identity; but in so far as they concern borderline cases of persons and our obligations, whatever they may be, to ensure that individuals are enabled to *become* persons, we shall find that they are directly relevant.

I shall take first the problem of the infant who might, *if* heroic measures are taken, be pulled up out of what would otherwise be an existence at a clearly sub-personal level. For we shall see that the answer to this problem helps to answer the other.

Hope for improvement

An infant has, *qua* human, a potential to become a fully-fledged person. However, suppose it has been born with savage abnormalities, such as spina bifida. Given these abnormalities, the laws of human develop-ment, operating against these initial conditions, dictate that this potential has been cut off—in a normal environment (i.e. without heroic measures) its actual potential has been severely pruned back. Indeed, without heroic measures it is likely that many such children would die after a short and unpleasant life. But there is now yet another sort of potentiality to recognize: the potential that it has, *if certain medical steps are taken*, to overcome some of the limitations imposed by these abnormalities, limitations that have restricted its natural potential. What are the reasons, if any, for taking these medical steps?

I have already mentioned that, *ceteris paribus*, the interests of any creature should be respected. It is time to explain and defend this claim more fully. The 'should' of the proposition suggests that it is a normative—a value-laden—claim. And indeed it is; but here we can see how facts (about what it is rational to require) can engender normative conclusions. First, then, rationality presupposes that any voluntary action, or indeed omission to act, is vulnerable to the question 'why did you do (not do) that?'. Such a question may often, of course, be plain stupid—in other words, the answer is obvious and the question otiose—but an answer of a kind should always be available, even if it is only something like 'because I felt like it'. Second, empirical observation reveals that sentient creatures have certain interests, aims, goals. Thus, when asked why one acted in such a way as to frustrate those interests, the fact of those interests must be acknowledged, even if only implicitly, in any adequate answer. For example, in reply to the question 'why did you kill that wasp?', the answer 'I just felt like it' ignores, or implicitly overrides, the fact that wasps have and manifest—whether they know it or not—an interest in survival; whereas 'because it would otherwise have stung me' tacitly acknowledges (or at least does not deny) that interest, but puts the human interest in not being stung ahead of the wasp's interest in survival. Respecting interests, in other words, requires no more than that their existence needs to be acknowledged when explaining one's behaviour towards the interest-bearing creatures. It is important to recognize that there is nothing specifically moral here; the requirement stems from demands of rational explanation. If interests are facts, then rational explanation can not rationally ignore them when they are relevant.

Justification is a special case of explanation. An explanation typically tries to constitute a justification in circumstances where the question 'why did you do that?' suggests that the action might be questionable or immoral. And actions or omissions become questionable or immoral precisely when and where interests are flouted or overridden. Thus in general actions and omissions that foster or promote the interests of sentient creatures rarely require *justification*. (Like all actions and omissions, they are always subject to a demand for *explanation*.) It would certainly be odd if someone regularly maintained a generous supply of appropriate food near a wasps' nest, but the oddity is not due to the mere fact that this promotes the interests of the wasps; it is rather due to the belief that wasps' interests, in general, are largely in conflict with human interests. (I speak as someone who, aged about ten, walked into a wasps' nest; this made it apparent to me that our interests are *obviously* conflicting.) If so, promoting wasps' interests hinders human ones. If wasps were deemed totally harmless, and were thought to be pretty (like butterflies) than the act of feeding wasps would not be subjected to a demand for justification: promoting the interests of insects, *per se*, may be regarded as odd, but is not a matter for justification. Some people dote even on hornets.

In sum, then, the interests of sentient creatures are brute facts that must be acknowledged in the explanation of any action that involves them. Promoting them may require explanation, but does not require justification (*ceteris paribus*); for promotion entails that the interests are recognized. Overriding them does require justification, simply because it appears at first sight as though the agent may have failed to acknowledge the brute fact of their existence. 'Is' gives rise to 'ought'; the alleged naturalistic fallacy is here, as so often, proved to be itself fallacious.

This is a very anodyne point, though; and it does not alone get us very far. It suggests only that we should not neglect or frustrate the needs and desires, present or future, of the impaired infant; or rather, that if we were to do so we would need some justification. It by no means compels us to take action to enable an infant—for example, an infant with Down's syndrome or spina bifida—to *acquire* interests, needs, and desires that its natural development (impaired as we are now supposing it to be) would not allow it. After all, we might discover that after a few trials, chimpanzees developed an interest in watching cartoon films. This does not seem to me to suggest that we have any obligation to provide videos for chimpanzees whose welfare is in our hands. Put another way, the impaired infant has a 'two-staged potentiality' to become roughly normal: we have to take certain medical steps, and then it might develop more successfully. It does not seem that we have any obligation to get our earlier example of a two-staged potential (sperm and ovum) from the first stage of potentiality to the second stage (the zygote). Obligations arose only when we had an embryo or infant with a one-stage potential for normal development. What, if anything, is the ground for obligation towards the impaired neonate?

Evidently the argument needs to be supplemented. At the root of the matter, I suspect, is an allegiance to something that I shall call 'the Aristotelian principle', and which seems to me to be something that underpins our intuitions in these matters but which has never been spelled out. The 'Aristotelian principle', broadly, claims that every creature strives after its own perfection, and thus that any member of kind K which is not a perfect instance of kind K is in some respect something to be pitied or deplored. The stunted oak is a failure as an oak—it is not all that it might be. The puppy born with a twisted paw is deplored by the tough-minded and pitied by the tender-minded, even though it may be just as content, and in other respects as healthy, as its unimpaired siblings. There seems to me to be no compelling or convincing justification or explanation of this attitude. It is not specifically 'moral'. I think that perhaps there is something of the aesthetic about it, in so far as 'we needs must love the highest when we see it'; and perhaps there is also a feeling of waste, of lost opportunities—the puppy will never be able to run and jump, herd sheep, chase cats, and so forth. The puppy will not, it seems, mind or miss these lost abilities (as a healthy dog would, we perhaps think, if it were suddenly deprived of its former active life and then kept chained up); and perhaps for this reason we do not regard its twisted paw as a matter for *moral* attitudinizing. But the intuition of some loss, to that very puppy, remains. The puppy can never do what it should, *naturally*, be able to do. In the case of human beings, the loss strikes us as a much greater one—in part because the activities which are denied to the radically impaired seem more valuable (they are, after all, *our* activities and we correspondingly treasure them), and in part because there are so many of them: one of the things we value is the diversity and choice presented to the normal adult.

It is unclear how much the *knowledge* of the missed, or lost, opportunities is taken to matter; this is a vexed and interesting question in moral philosophy generally. On the one hand, the realization that one can never attain some standard or goal can be a source of pain which we would not experience if we knew nothing of our disabilities—if we did not realize that we might have had a chance at it. Those aware that their minds are failing them are thus in this respect more tragic than those whose senility is of such a kind that they do not notice their progressive deficiencies. Correspondingly, some spina bifida babies may grow up with roughly normal intelligence; but may well be paraplegic, prone to infections and fits, doubly incontinent, with a deformed and swollen spine. Their intelligence makes them more likely to worry about their future care, to realize what they are missing, to experience frustration and loneliness; whereas the 'happy moron' who lies all day, smiling perhaps, with part of his brain extruding through his skull, has no such mental anxiety. On the other hand, though, the wrongness of betrayal (say) seems scarcely diminished when the one betrayed proceeds in happy ignorance of the deception; and he is pitied because of the way he has (unknowingly) been treated—indeed, he may be pitied even more precisely *because* he was unaware of it. 'What you don't know can't hurt you' is only true in so far as we are talking about just one kind of hurt: there seem to be others. It is difficult to spell out just what the harm is, when the one harmed is ignorant of his loss. It is made more difficult by the assumption that the only values that really count are moral, prudential, or aesthetic values—and the loss in the cases I have been discussing is not *clearly* any of these. But it seems to me that the wrongness arises because of the *contrast* between what has happened and what might have been—with what, in the normal course of events, would have been—and that this holds whether we know of it or not. If we look, then, at the radically impaired infant, what is pitiable or tragic is not necessarily the actual present state (some impaired infants might be wholly content, and likely to live out their lives in a comfortable and secure environment), but rather his being bound to this state *rather than* living the life natural and normal to his conspecifics. We deplore the state not because it is intrinsically unsatisfactory, but because of what it is not; because of the contrast, not just because of the actuality.

The red herring to avoid here is what I shall call 'Mill's move'. Mill, notoriously, made appeal to competent judges, familiar with both sides of a debate, who are asked to say which of two kinds of life, or two kinds of satisfaction, they would prefer. This is an error, because it is simply wrong to suppose, when asking whether we would rather be Socrates dissatisfied or a fool satisfied,[4] that we, or Socrates, know from the inside both sides of the case. The pleasures of, say, playing with building-blocks or watching children's television are not (or are only rarely) pleasures for Socrates or a grown adult, but they are viable and genuine pleasures for the child or for the mentally retarded. Socrates of course would not choose such a life; correspondingly, none of us would agree to a lobotomy that deprived us of the cutting edge of most of our mental faculties—even though we had been told, and had reason to believe, that we would never be aware of our loss and would have from then on a life with all our desires satisfied. The puzzle arises because we do not know how to compare the *intrinsic* merits of the life of the

---

[4] See Mill, *Utilitarianism* [1861/1957], ch. 2, p. 14.

unhappy intellectual with those of the contented fool:

> Instruction sore long time I bore,
> And cramming was in vain,
> Till Heaven did please my woes to ease,
> With water on the brain.
>
> (Charles Kingsley)

From the inside, one cannot take or make the desired judgement:

> See the happy moron,
> He doesn't give a damn.
> I wish I were a moron:
> My God! Perhaps I am!
>
> (Anon., *Eugenics Review*, 1929)

It is crucial to realize that Socrates cannot be asked to judge from the inside, to put himself into the position of the fool. That is not possible; were he genuinely to adopt the viewpoint of the fool, he would lose the ability to assess the Socratic life. There is, however, a different kind of comparative judgement which Socrates can make, but which the fool cannot—simply because of the two only Socrates, here representing the man of normal intellectual powers, has the capacity to understand, *from the outside*, the scope and possibilities of each kind of life. The comparative judgement he can indeed make is this: he can be asked to assess the two forms of life against the standards of what sorts of life are possible, characteristic, natural, or normal for human beings (diverse and varied as those will of course be). That provides the criterion against which the fool's life fails—*whatever* the fool thinks of the matter.[5] This criterion or standard is emphatically not a specifically moral criterion. To call it aesthetic is almost as misleading, given the dubious, or at least debated, objectivity of aesthetic judgements; there is none the less something of the aesthetic about it. However, the value judgement made (and it is a *value* judgement) is as objective as are the principles governing normal human development and flourishing, precisely because it is a product of those principles; best, perhaps,

---

[5] We may not want to go quite as far as the author of Ecclesiasticus 22: 11: 'Weep for the dead, for he lacks the light; and weep for the fool, for he lacks intelligence; weep less bitterly for the dead, for he has attained rest; but the life of the fool is worse than death.' This is too strong. But it shows how seriously many take what I call in this and succeeding chapters the 'Aristotelian loss' of mental deficiency.

simply to call it 'Aristotelian'. To repeat: perhaps it is high time to acknowledge that there are values to which we all subscribe which are not specifically 'moral', nor specifically 'aesthetic', nor even specifically 'prudential'.

The impaired infant, then, has suffered a loss, an Aristotelian loss. This is a brute fact that must be taken into account, whatever judgement we may try to make about the intrinsic quality of its life. For although it is, of course, important to try to evaluate the extent to which its actual wants and interests are being met, we can now see that these are not the only considerations to bear in mind.

Given all this, we can perhaps reach some conclusion about our first problem, of the extent of our obligations towards the impaired infant whose capacity could be to some degree improved by medical methods. We have so far: (*a*) the notion that the infant, *qua* human, has the potentiality to develop as a person; plus the information that this potentiality has been blocked; plus the knowledge that something can be done (albeit with some difficulty and at some expense, and maybe with considerable pain to the infant) to remove those obstacles. (*b*) we have an 'Aristotelian reason' for saying that the impaired infant is worse off than the mentally healthy one; even though (*c*) his life may prove to hold a greater quantity of intrinsic pleasure and satisfaction than that of many normal infants, and we can do various things to meet and foster his actual present and future interests. This means that (*d*) we have reason (*ceteris paribus*) to aim for the removal of the blocks to his natural development, along with the standing reason to foster the needs and to meet the wants that he actually has. Since the greater the deficiency on the 'Aristotelian' scale, the worse the loss, then the more that we *could* achieve—the further we could get the child up the scale—the stronger would be our reasons for taking compensatory action. Put another way, we can ascribe to the impaired infant not only his actual present interests, but also the full extent of all the interests that it could come to have. And here the 'could' is determined by the two potentialities: the original potentiality *qua* human, which has been obstructed by disease or some other abnormality, and the potentiality that would be recovered if all practicable measures were taken.

Now the utmost efforts may still secure for the drastically impaired child only, let us suppose, something comparable to the capacity of the chimpanzee. In such a case we shall not have the obligations to it that we have to persons, or to normal infants (who should receive, as noted above, the *full* content of the 'stance' or 'attitude' condition (condition

(3)) that we take to fully-fledged persons). There are characteristically human interests it can now never have. However, we shall not thereby commit ourselves to adopting with respect to it the attitude that we take to chimpanzees of an equivalent cognitive level—which, for example, we experiment on in laboratories, and which we confine in zoos. It may be wrong to experiment on, or to confine, anything as intelligent as a chimpanzee; that is an issue I am leaving on one side. The point here is rather that an infant with (say) Down's syndrome, despite the fact that it may, even developed as far as it can, only score level with chimpanzees on IQ tests and the like, is yet—unlike the chimpanzee—something that has suffered an Aristotelian loss; and the existence of major losses is reason enough for attempts to compensate for them. These reasons may, or may not, be called moral ones. That depends upon one's particular moral position, and I do not find the question whether they should be called 'moral' or not particularly significant. They remain reasons, under whatever description, and need to be taken into account along with the ordinary moral reasons for fostering or not impeding the actual interests of any sentient creature.

Note though that the present and real interests that the maimed infant actually has now (in comfort, warmth, freedom from pain) may come into conflict with our attempts to mitigate his impairment. Not all operations are successful; and some deficiencies may need a whole series of painful operations. There are horror stories here. One spina bifida infant was very severely affected; he was given routine care only for the first few months of life. Aged ten months, his back was repaired and a drainage tube inserted to lessen the extent of hydrocephalus. He was later discovered to have cortical blindness. Over the next few years he had multiple orthopaedic operations, to replace dislocated hips, to lengthen his Achilles' tendon, to repair fractures, etc. Aged six, he was found to have hydronephrosis (water on the kidneys), so he needed an operation to divert the urinary passage so that urine was collected in a bag outside his body. He studies at a school for the blind, and has an IQ of 80. He finds sitting hard because of his spinal deformity, and that makes it difficult for him to keep the urine-collecting bag in place. His hips keep dislocating. Further, there are dozens of examples that can be collected of infants whose life was a continuous series of operations, but who none the less died quite early despite them; this is a life one would wish on nobody. The conclusion reached above has therefore to be qualified by a hefty 'other things equal' condition, and no answers are going to come easily here.

No-hopers

The second problem of this section was what we should do with the infant whose capacities for improvement are regarded as non-existent, and who will remain throughout its life with drastically subnormal cognitive powers. The anencephalic is a clear example; its intellectual level is below that of a chicken. Microcephalic, or irreversibly brain-damaged, children may never get above a 'severely retarded' stage, with an IQ of, say, 35.

This question has to some extent been answered already. The interests (present and future) that we can ascribe are, like the interests of any sentient creature, interests that demand respect and support—*ceteris*, as always, *paribus*. In this respect they demand the respect and support that the interests of a non-human animal at the same sort of level demand. However, again there is more to it than that; there is also the same decisive difference that we found earlier between the impaired infant and the chimpanzee, even when both were at approximately the same mental level: the infant, but not the chimpanzee, has suffered an Aristotelian catastrophe. This, as argued above, constitutes a loss to the infant; and a loss of such dimensions alone gives us reason to attempt to compensate, and would again prevent us from using the child in medical experiments or from confining it in a zoo. (I repeat that I am not suggesting that it is justifiable to experiment on chimpanzees or to shut them up in zoos; that is an issue I willingly leave aside. I am merely insisting that there are Aristotelian reasons for refusing to treat impaired infants as being precisely on a par with non-human animals of roughly equivalent intellectual standing.) The fact that some Down's syndrome infants are not able to comprehend the loss, and never will be so able, seems to make no difference to our judgement of the size of the disaster that *these very infants* have suffered.

The puzzling dilemma we then confront is the brute fact that the greater the catastrophe the feebler must be any measure of compensation. Just as the impaired infant's capacities are drastically reduced, so correspondingly are restricted its sources of satisfaction and happiness: food, warmth, security, cleanliness, and so forth may be all that we can supply. We might even be left with the thought that the only *adequate* recognition of the loss lies in the regret and helpless pity that it induces in the bystander. The massive Aristotelian catastrophe may even persuade us that death would be preferable to such an existence, particularly if the infant is visibly in pain, as some spina bifida children, with a gaping wound in the back, certainly are; or if they can only be kept alive with a drip (some Down's syndrome infants lack a proper passage from mouth to stomach, the oesophagus). If they will never acquire a reasonably rich range of satisfactions and interests, but they manifestly have a pressing, actual, interest in freedom from pain, then all one can do is to try to alleviate the pain—even if death is the most likely outcome. Those concerned with the question of nursing care (or, in the case of the foetus, of whether or not to abort) meet then the familiar and intractable problem of how to put a value upon non-existence—how to say, only how to say without paradox, that this entity would be better off if it were dead. The catastrophe itself is, as we have seen, a complex and rather abstract one, on the one hand being Aristotelian, and on the other being a disaster of which the sufferer is, and will remain, wholly unaware. If that were not intricate enough, it then has to be juxtaposed with, and set against, the 'good', or the 'bad', of non-existence. The product of such a comparison is what moves people to advocate, or to argue against, abortion; or what moves doctors to decide to give, or not to give, just 'selective treatment' in the form of 'nursing care only' to radically impaired infants—a form of treatment which may well mean, and is known to be likely to mean, the infant's early death from an infection since the antibiotics that might clear it up are withheld. (As a matter of fact, is is vastly unclear what counts as 'nursing care only'. For example, does it entail drip-feeding an infant who lacks an oesophagus? If not, the infant simply starves to death.)

It is hardly surprising that there is little if any consensus about what is the right thing to do in circumstances such as these. For the issue is, as we have seen, not exclusively a moral one, being fundamentally coloured by considerations of the kind I have called Aristotelian. Some of course may wish to call these too 'moral reasons'. If we do so, however, we shall find ourselves reverting to something closer to the Aristotelian account of ethical reasoning. This is a move which, as I have argued elsewhere [1978a], has its own substantial attractions; but to adopt it would require a considerable change in contemporary moral theory. As things stand now, Aristotelian reasons are quasi-moral, quasi-prudential, quasi-aesthetic, and quasi-something else; and, leaving out the 'something else', aesthetic arguments are certainly no more objective than are moral or prudential ones—indeed, I suppose they are generally regarded as being less so. 'Aristotelian reasons' can certainly borrow the objectivity of the scientific (psychological, sociological, anthropological, physiological) theories describing human development and human possibilities; even if some forms of life are thereby excluded as being manifestly undesirable for anybody, that still leaves room wide open for whole ranges of views about the sorts of life that might best promote human flourishing. Moreover, as we have seen, the problem examined embroils us in the notorious paradoxes of non-existence.

5. IVF EMBRYOS

The next and last instance of immaturity to consider is whether any special problems arise as a result of *in vitro* fertilization (IVF). Evidently many pressing moral and social difficulties do arise and have arisen; but our question now is of the status of the embryo with respect to its personhood and the six conditions.

In practically all cases there is presumably no difference at all between the ordinary embryo and the IVF embryo as far as everything we have said above is concerned. The interests and the claims of the IVF embryo are as much entitled to respect as are those of the foetus with more familiar origins; *whatever* the mechanics of fertilization may happen to be, its natural development (which is natural enough after it has been implanted) will, other things being equal, lead to its development as a fully-fledged human being and as a person. If medical technology advanced to such a point that embryos could develop and reach the stage of viability exclusively in incubators, then again the status of such an embryo seems no different from that of the foetus that develops in the womb; we would need, however, to enlarge our notions of what counts as 'natural' development.

It is now possible, however, to take an IVF embryo, freeze it, and store it indefinitely, to implant, or not, at some later date. Does such an entity have any claims on us at all? Is there, for example, reason to think that it has a right to be implanted and to be given the normal chances of embryonic growth and development? Or, conversely, are there objections to using it in medical experimentation and research? Put another way, we are asking what stance is the justifiable one to adopt when confronted with a frozen 'test-tube' embryo.

Such an embryo, not yet implanted, has no natural development at all, although it has a potential for one. We have, I am afraid, yet another variety of potentiality to examine. It seems that the potentiality of a frozen embryo is, so to speak, half-way between two kinds of potentiality discussed earlier in this chapter: half-way between the potentiality of the two separate gametes on the one hand, and that of the natural embryo on the other. For, like the gametes, and unlike the natural embryo, it has only a two-staged potentiality of becoming a person: just as the gametes need to combine before they attain the one-staged potentiality, so the frozen embryo needs to be implanted before *it* does. Unlike the gametes, though, and like the natural embryo, we can talk about the individual that *this very thing* might become—there is no problem of reference.

It seems to me that in trying to understand the kind of potentiality that is relevant here, the parallel with the gametes—the fact that it is a two-staged potentiality—must be the more significant for our concerns. Given what it is to be a frozen zygote, its two-staged potentiality means that we cannot ascribe interests to it at all, except conditionally: the interests it would have unconditionally if it were implanted (or, in some possible future, put in an incubator to develop). Right now it has no interests at all. Remember the earlier example of the three-year-old English child with the two-staged potentiality to speak Russian; at stage one, before learning the language, it just is not 'a Russian speaker'. A two-staged potentiality to F does not allow one to say that the object is actually, unconditionally F. Nor are there any independent reasons (*ceteris paribus*) to move it from stage one to stage two, to the state at which it will, unconditionally, have rights and interests.

To see this more clearly, compare and contrast the impaired infant whose condition might be to some extent curable, if certain steps are taken. Like the frozen IVF embryo, its potential for development into a full person is in a sense two staged: we have (first stage) to remove or minimize the obstacles that hinder it from enjoying normal human development. Only when the obstacles are removed can it achieve the second stage. But there is more to the story. Unlike the IVF embryo, the maimed infant now, *unconditionally*, has some psychological predicates true of it: in particular, it is suffering from an (Aristotelian) loss. Such a loss, I argued, gave us an independent reason for attempting to compensate, to minimize the loss; and the appropriate way to compensate could only be to try to remove the obstacles. But removing the obstacles just is to try to move the infant from stage one to stage two. The reason for trying to shift it from stage one to stage two rests upon the fact that it *already* has some stage one psychological properties: loss, suffering, harm. Put crudely, the Aristotelian reason for acting trumps the lack of reason that derives from the potential being two staged. The IVF embryo, though, has no unconditional psychological properties whatsoever, and hence (*ceteris paribus*) supplies us with no 'trumping' reason for giving it any.

There is one more point of interest here. Since we cannot ascribe any unconditional rights to the frozen embryo, we cannot ascribe to it the right to life—a right which is fundamental. It is fundamental because life is the *sine qua non* of its having any other (actual and potential) interests. One reason we cannot give it this fundamental right is the simple point, just discussed, that we can grant no rights to it at all. But even without that, there is another reason why a right to life can not be ascribed. The attempt to do so again throws us back into the centre of the paradox discussed earlier, this time from the positive rather than the negative point of view: just as we could not easily put a value upon non-existence, so we cannot readily assess the 'benefit' of an active life. Therefore, whereas we can contrast (but only from the outside) two actual lives—the life of the fool with that of Socrates, and judge that the fool (the mentally impaired) was someone who had suffered a major loss—we cannot compare and contrast the state of perpetual deep-freeze with the state of normal development. There is no content to the former, it is not an actual life. So we are unable to say that the frozen zygote would undergo a catastrophe if not supplied with the possibility of development. Analogously, it is difficult (although tempting) to say coherently that one is glad that one was (conceived and) born; again one is seeking a contrast where none can exist.

If there is no room for a contrastive judgement, then there is no obligation of any sort to implant an IVF embryo—any more than there is any obligation on a couple to conceive a child, and for similar reasons.[6] Lacking any such obligation as this, there are evidently no further obligations on us with respect to it; no interests that are coherently ascribable, no needs or concerns. There is no 'stance' that it requires us to take to it. A quite independent point, of course, is that IVF embryos have as yet no brain and no capacity for pain, and it seems that such a capacity is essential for anything towards which we take a moral stance; this would be yet a further reason for denying it that

---

[6] Some try to impose *political* obligations on couples to bear children. See for instance current Iraqi policy, as described in *The Times* of 5 May 1986, p. 5: 'Each Iraqi family must have five children so that Iraq can defend its territory, President Saddam Hussein is quoted as having said. He told a delegation of women: "The family that has fewer than five children deserves to be reprimanded harshly".' Conversely, of course, the policy of the People's Republic of China makes it a quasi-moral offence to have more than one child.

status. (Opinions vary about when the foetus is able to experience pain; conjectures range widely between nine and thirty-two weeks.) There seems, then, no reason for banning the use of early embryonic material in medical experimentation and research.

Solely from the point of view of the issues—moral and conceptual—that impinge upon personal identity, then, IVF techniques seem to set no special problems. The implanted embryo, or the embryo developing in some future incubator, requires the full application of the stance that we take to persons, ascribing to it interests as demanding as those of any fully-fledged persons. The embryo that is not in a position to develop, but which could be so placed, has no claim on us at all; there is no stance or attitude that it is proper to take to it. It goes without saying, of course, that IVF techniques pose intricate and intractable problems, moral, social, and legal. (However, it now seems possible to freeze both ova and spermata separately—rather than freezing a fertilized egg. Presumably the former strategy will attract less moral obloquy than the latter.) But these are (fortunately) not our concern here.

6. SUMMARY

The conclusions that we seem to have reached in this chapter have filled out to some extent the 'stance' condition (condition (3)). The argument has gone roughly as follows. It is hard to deny that, other things being equal, any interest of any living creature should be respected. The reason is that all that this involves is the thoroughly bland, and by no means essentially moral, claim that to frustrate the interests of anything whatsoever needs explanation or justification—which of course can very often be provided—whereas to foster them or leave them unimpeded needs no justification. The second move was to comment that future interests, interests of which the organism is unaware, long-term interests, and interests that are all of these, are as such no less important than are present, immediate, and conscious interests of the same general type; and that in those cases where our actions can impinge upon any of these interests, we may have reason to foster them but none (other things being equal) to impede them. This led us to the view that the immature human (infant or foetus) has the apparently paradoxical status of meeting in full one, but only one, of the six conditions; the paradox, however, was mitigated by the thought that the reason for this is that it *will* one day fully meet all the other five.

Such an argument led inevitably to the problem of the impaired foetus or infant, precisely because we could not ascribe to it the potential to meet the six conditions. For that reason alone, such an entity was not seen as the recipient of the full-blooded 'stance' appropriate to persons; but this did not put it on a par with such non-human animals to which it might be thought to be roughly analogous in intellectual respects, since it, unlike they, could be sensibly regarded as having suffered a major loss—a loss which may be lessened, but which was not removed, by the fact that the sufferer may be unaware of this loss. The existence of such a loss provides reasons (which may or may not be called 'moral' reasons: 'Aristotelian' seemed a more appropriate label) to attempt to eliminate, or if not eliminate at least compensate for, as much of the loss as possible. This conclusion had to be restricted by a serious 'other things being equal' condition, particularly when the compensatory operations seemed uncertain, highly painful, or both. But the various 'other things' which might or might not be 'equal' were not discussed, as the issue would have taken us beyond our immediate concerns.

The normal and healthy infant or foetus could be described as a person; only uninteresting arguments of a trivially linguistic kind would weigh for or against the propriety of so describing it. Moreover, it seemed not to matter whether it was or was not so entitled, since in either case we would have the same obligations with respect to it. The grounds for so describing it, however (supposing that we wanted to), would rest upon the potential it has of becoming a person; and so the radically impaired infant, whom we believe to have no chance of developing into a fully fledged person, has a status now that we cannot decide until we have considered (in the next chapter) what it is appropriate to say about the drastically retarded adult—for the infant with incurable mental deficiency will, if it survives at all, develop into such an adult, and so that is its potentiality.

Finally, IVF techniques seemed to add no new puzzles with respect to personal identity, except in so far as they introduced the problem of what we should say about, and what obligations or reasons for action we might have towards, the frozen zygote. We saw that the fact it has only a two-staged potential, and the incoherence of comparing active life with its absence, ensured that there were no respectable reasons for ascribing interests to such an object, nor of talking of any loss it would suffer if it were not given the opportunity to develop. As noted already, though, this conclusion in no way suggested that there were not pressing moral, social, and legal problems that are certain to arise over the whole issue of IVF.

3

Mental Deficiency, Breakdown, and Insanity

The human race consists of the dangerously insane and such as are not.

(Mark Twain, *Notebooks*)

A neurotic is the man who builds a castle in the air. A psychotic is the man who lives in it. And a psychiatrist is the man who collects the rent.

(Anon.)

1. INTRODUCTION

In this chapter we shall find ourselves turning to explore the scope of the first of our six conditions, namely that persons are rational beings. We shall not be primarily concerned with labels or titles—the question whether those suffering from radical impairment of their rational faculties are to be labelled persons or not; for whether something *is* a person may often, as we saw in the last chapter, be a matter of both decree and degree. Rather, we shall be exploring various forms of breakdown of rationality in an attempt to discover the sort of thing that human rationality, and thereby the kind of rationality that we might expect to require from any non-human candidate for personhood, involves. There will also, predictably enough, be implications for the plausible view that the notion of personhood is, to some extent at least, anthropologically, socially, and culturally determined.

2. THE SANITY OF IRRATIONALITY

The rationality of other animals is on an unbroken continuum with that of humans. This is something Hume saw clearly, and expressed with characteristic clarity and decisiveness—although, paradoxically enough, he would have wanted to deny that there was true 'reason' on *any* part of the continuum:[1]

[1] When Hume considers 'reasoning about matters of fact' (broadly, contingent matters) he has a broad and a narrow sense of the expression. The broad sense allows as

Animals, as well as men, learn many things from experience, and infer, that the same events will always follow from the same causes . . . The ignorance and inexperience of the young are here plainly distinguishable from the cunning and sagacity of the old, who have learned, by long observation, to avoid what hurt them, and to pursue what gave ease or pleasure. A horse, that has been accustomed to the field, becomes acquainted with the proper height which he can leap, and will never attempt what exceeds his force and ability. An old greyhound will trust the more fatiguing part of the chace to the younger, and will place himself so as to meet the hare in her doubles (*An Enquiry Concerning Human Understanding* [1748], s. ix, para. 83; [1963], p. 105).

Nor, of course, is animal rationality a mere matter of survival strategies and the search for food. Many animals play, too, and become bored; for example, when a dog has had enough of a stick-retrieving game it often runs off with the stick and drops it where the owner can no longer reach it. The rationality of non-human animals can be seen in many of their activities. It would be easy, but would also be unnecessary, to rehearse a long list of animal behaviour that is, by any standards, rational. Hume's sensible observation is quite as pertinent as would be any modern description of intelligent performance by, say, dolphins or chimpanzees.

But non-human animals, rational within their capacities, cannot behave rationally when the circumstances make demands that are too difficult for their cognitive abilities to absorb. As Hume notes, 'one mind may be much larger than another' *An Enquiry Concerning Human Understanding* [1748], (s. ix, para. 84; [1963], p. 107, nn. 1, 2). Couched in these straightforward terms, human minds just are 'much larger' than those of most animals—although we should acknowledge that we have few adequate ways of assessing the capacities of some large marine mammals such as whales and dolphins. Our present concern is in what this extra 'largeness' may consist, and what we take to be the nature of the rationality that persons, here again see via their standard exemplar, the human being, characteristically must be expected to have.

One striking difference is that non-human animals are incapable of, or perhaps not vulnerable to, many forms of *ir*rationality. Admittedly we do at times find some forms of madness or mental breakdown in animals; no less than humans, they too can become senile and lose the

'reasoning' any movement of the mind from an impression or from an idea, to another associated idea via the principles of association. This is common to human animals and to many non-human animals. The narrower sense is reasoning for which adequate justification can be given. Since, according to Hume, there is ultimately no adequate justification for any empirical belief, no animal—human or non-human—can possess this form of reason.

ability to detect danger or recognize friends. The rabid dog may quite literally be called mad, and, more dubiously, a nervy or inbred animal may seem neurotic, or to be suffering from phobias, hallucinations, or obsessions. But on the other hand it is difficult to think of a serious ascription to a pet of schizophrenia, an Oedipus complex, or a psychosis.

Now it may seem paradoxical to find part of the extra 'largeness' of the human mind in its potential for mental breakdown or disorder. Interestingly enough, the very same paradox is found in the familiar claim that what distinguishes our intelligence from that of *computers* is that we, but not they, can act illogically on occasion: it seems peculiar to attribute even part of our superiority over animals and computers to the fact that we can be more thoroughly irrational than they. The apparent oddity will disappear, however, if we look harder at human insanity and mental illness, and see why it is that our vulnerability to these is yet a tribute to our intelligence. (Cf. Pascal: 'Men are so necessarily fools that not to be so would amount to another mode of folly', *Pensées* [1960], para. 127, p. 40.)

The primary point, which I shall develop in some detail, is that there are forms of human irrationality which presuppose and also implicate a very complex set of rational processes. Now, that rationality is *presupposed* by certain kinds of irrationality is presumably a trivial point. For unless some creature is capable of acting prudently and thoughtfully in circumstances C—in other words, rationally—there is no point in describing it as being irrational when it fails to do so. The more interesting and substantial claim is that rationality is implicated, essentially involved, in many classical types of irrational behaviour; and its converse, that many forms of 'characteristically human' behaviour seem essentially to require strands that are dubiously rational, but which are common to 'the lunatic, the lover, and the poet'.

That needs explanation. It will most easily be made intelligible if we look at some of the claims made by Freudian theory, and at the nature of some of the explanations that abound throughout Freud's writings. The choice of Freud is not due to any conviction that his hypotheses and conjectures are necessarily superior to those of other psychoanalytic schools, but rather to the fact that his work tends to be better known than is that of others. Furthermore, as someone trained in the 'hard' sciences of medicine and physiology he knew what was required of a genuine science, and tried more deliberately than most of the other founding fathers of psychoanalysis to put his theory forward as a serious scientific one (whether he succeeded or not is, of course, quite another matter, with which we are not here concerned). This means that he is more interested than Jung, say, or Adler, in explaining the theoretical underpinning of his diagnostic methods. And as a final excuse for exploiting him: even if arguments based on Freudian theory seem suspect to some, they emerge very clearly; and all the points to be drawn from his theory will be independently supported later in the chapter.

Freud changed his mind about the relative importance he placed on many of his theoretical constructs throughout his life, but for present purposes we can ignore the fact. We are not trying to describe and assess 'the theory' in its most developed or finished form. What all would agree about, in any case, is the heavy use he makes of anthropomorphic metaphor (at all stages of his writings) to describe the workings of some of his postulated entities, such as the System Ucs., the ego, the id, and the superego. There were and are of course solid reasons for such anthropomorphization, primarily heuristic ones: few would have understood what he was saying without these helpful metaphors, and it is therefore unsurprising that they are found in greatest abundance in his more popularizing works (when writing for professional colleagues, there was less need for the crutch of metaphorical terminology). The result, though, of the ascription of this tripartite structure to the human mind was to liken the ego in particular to a rational agent struggling to cope with the demands and problems it faced from the id and superego and the outside world; and id and superego are also given intelligible rational reasons for their activities.

It is very easy to illustrate this contention:

The analytic physician and the patient's weakened ego, basing themselves on the real external world, have to band themselves together into a party against the enemies, the instinctual demands of the id and the conscientious demands of the super-ego (Freud [1963], vol. xxiii, p. 173).

Even more explicitly:

The poor ego . . . serves three severe masters and does what it can to bring their claims and demands into harmony with one another. These claims are always divergent and often seem incompatible. No wonder that the ego so often fails in its task. Its three tyrannical masters are the external world, the super-ego and the id. When we follow the ego's efforts to satisfy them simultaneously—or rather, to obey them simultaneously—*we cannot feel any regret at having personified this ego and having set it up as a separate organism.* . . . [I]t strives too to be a loyal servant of the id, to remain on good terms with it, to recommend itself to it as an object and to attract its libido to itself . . . (Freud [1964], pp. 77 f.; italics mine).

The superego emerges with a positive, and often rather sadistic, character:

during a melancholic attack his superego becomes over-severe, abuses the poor ego, humiliates it and ill-treats it, threatens it with the direst punishments, reproaches it for actions in the remotest past which had been taken lightly at the time—as though it had spent the whole interval in collecting accusations and had only been waiting for its present access of strength in order to bring them up and make a condemnatory judgement on their basis. The superego applies the strictest moral standards to the helpless ego which is at its mercy . . . (Freud [1964], p. 61).

We are introduced, via anthropomorphic metaphor, to the idea that the unconscious mind is organized and structured, consists of an inter-related web of ideas—where the term 'idea' includes propositions, thoughts and beliefs, desires, concepts, images—and which endeavours to cope sensibly and rationally in circumstances that are difficult or intolerable for it.

We should of course note that by no means all Freud's theoretical postulates involve the personification of systems and forces and the consequent ascription to them of some measure of rationality. Indeed, infantile sexuality, one cornerstone of his theory, is seen as a biological brute fact. Moreover, the instincts and drives are typically described by non-rational, mechanical metaphors such as that of a hydraulic system, of pushes and pulls, resistance and repression, of chemical reactions, electromagnetic forces, and the like. Such non-rational, causal-mechanical, phenomena are supposed to give the *genesis* of the non-conscious ideas. But after that, there is throughout his writing the central claim that symbolic action, or proto-action, or displacement activity, or of course dreams, have *intelligible purposes* to serve: for instance, by such means the beleaguered ego can escape some of the pressure from the id, or satisfy the demands of the supergo. However unfamiliar the 'mechanisms of defence' may seem to us to be, they have a job to do and a role to play: we could not manage without them. It is against this background that the patient's activities are seen to be rational, and only against such a background. Again this is easy to illustrate. Here, for example, is Freud talking of the ego and the dream work:

With the help of the unconscious, every dream that is in process of formation makes a demand upon the ego—for the satisfaction of an instinct, if the dream originates from the id; for the solution of a conflict, the removal of a doubt or the forming of an intention, if the dream originates from a residue of preconscious activity in waking life. The sleeping ego, however, is focused on the wish to maintain sleep; it feels this demand as a disturbance and seeks to get rid of the disturbance. The ego succeeds in doing this by what appears to be an act of compliance: it meets the demand with what is in the circumstances a harmless *fulfilment of a wish* and so gets rid of it. This replacement of the demand by the fulfilment of a wish remains the essential function of the dream-work (Freud [1969], pp. 26 f.).

Conscious, planned, and rational behaviour, then, and irrational, neurotic, or obsessive behaviour, are explained by the same model—the familiar, everyday model of rational explanation which starts from ideas, thoughts, motivations, moods, fears, and then uses them to help make intelligible the resulting behaviour: shows us what its purpose is. Thus there is a continuum between normal and aberrant behaviour, a continuum Freud never ceases to emphasize. We call behaviour rational when the starting-point (the ideas, fears, beliefs, etc.) is itself for the most part rationally intelligible—when the fears are appropriate to the situation, when the beliefs are consistent and well-supported, and so on. We call it irrational when the starting-point consists of elements that cannot themselves for the most part be so justified—when, for instance, the fear results from repression, or displacement, and when the non-rational and quasi-mechanical 'forces' of the libido are invoked to explain it. But after that both rational and irrational behaviour are explained in just the same way: *if* someone believes this, wants that, fears the other, then *of course* he will telephone his son ('rational behaviour'), or wash his hands thousands of times a day ('obsessive behaviour'). Voltaire, interestingly, under the heading 'Madness' in the *Philosophical Dictionary* [1764], says that madness is 'to have erroneous perceptions and to reason correctly from them'.

It goes without saying—and, again, is something on which Freud insists —that virtually all behaviour is at best more or less rational or irrational: the boundary between the two is never sharp or simple. Generally, that is, the starting-point will be a mixture of ideas (using 'ideas' in a very broad way to cover all the phenomena cited as *explanantia*); some of them are best understood by appeal to evidence, consistency, appropriateness, but others will need appeal to repression, resistance, libidinal 'forces'. Equally there is no hard-and-fast distinction between 'conscious' and 'unconscious', for there are fusions, and shades in between: the preconscious, for instance, and unconscious ideas that are not necessarily part of the System Ucs. but are merely 'not conscious'. All these can shift their status, as what was conscious may become repressed and unconscious, what was pre-conscious can emerge into consciousness, and, with some effort, even the unconscious can be acknowledged. (Later I shall dispute the merits of such division into 'conscious', 'unconscious', and so forth. Just now, however, we are accepting Freud's terminology.)

So there is a sense in which some irrational behaviour can be shown to be rational: once the starting-point is given, all behaviour receives 'rational explanation'. Conversely, unconscious factors permeate and colour our most rational and conscious activities. Dispositions, inclinations, patterns and habits of behaviour, are all said to be due in part to early projection, introjection, displacement, idealization, transference, to the inhibition or repression of infantile desires, to sublimation of unacceptable drives on to acceptable objects, to unconscious memories of primitive satisfactions and frustrations, and so forth. The conscious mind is formed *from* all this, and cannot be fully understood independently of it.

The result, according to Freud, is for the first time a *unitary* science of psychology:

Whereas the psychology of consciousness never went beyond the broken sequences which were obviously dependent on something else, the other view, which held that the psychical is unconscious in itself, enabled psychology to take its place as a natural science like any other ([1969], p. 15).

Now Freud is surely right to insist that explanations of human behaviour which stick to the level of conscious mental phenomena will be inadequate even on their own terrain. The sequences of conscious thoughts are indeed 'broken', and we cannot explain their succession. In fact, to reinforce this argument we need only look at the heroic efforts of all post-Humean associationists up until the start of this century, who tried but failed to find principles for the association of conscious ideas that were adequate, or which were at least more adequate than was Hume's triad of resemblance, contiguity, and cause and effect, to explain this succession. It cannot be done.

Whatever the merits of the theory, we are currently stuck with it:

For good or for bad, a diluted influence of Freud has now permeated our age's conception of mind, of motive, action, and morality, as no psychological theory ever before has. It influences our attitudes to ourselves and others in ways that can be separated from our believing any particular theoretical assertions about causes of behaviour or psychological structure. It shapes the styles of explanation and attribution that we are prepared to understand (Morton [1982], p. 60).

Freud modelled his explanations of abnormal or non-rational behaviour on the style of explanation familiar to all, the enterprise of showing how it could be understood as being *rational in the circumstances*; and he defended ably this sort of assimilation. Morton is here suggesting that the influence is also reversed: that we now see much of everyday vernacular explanation through the glass of a diluted version of Freud. The picture of the human mind is thus transformed. The mind consists no longer exclusively of the Cartesian self-illuminating consciousness, but becomes a rich and many-layered dynamically structured system which leaves consciousness as no more than the bare tip of an enormous and largely unknown iceberg. Furthermore, as we have seen the tip is conditioned, indeed in large part determined, by what lies beneath. Our ordinary beliefs, attitudes, emotions, dispositions, traits, moods, and styles of acting and deliberating can be explained in full only by essential appeal to a huge variety of unconscious or non-conscious thoughts which are always in the background. These in turn refer essentially to, and need to be explained in terms of, a range of instinctual needs (we need not necessarily agree with Freud about the primacy of Eros or Thanatos, but instinctual needs of some sort we must suppose), and the techniques of repression and defence that the child employs to cope with these instincts.

This suggests that the purely rational man is not only non-existent *de facto*, but also that we would find it difficult to count him as a person at all. He would have no art or literature or, more generally, imagination, no character or personality, none of the dispositions that, if Freud is right, stem from the infantile satisfaction, or frustration, of instinctual needs and desires which are then modified and conditioned by the continuing work of the mechanisms of defence—he would be unrecognizable. We cannot make sense of the idea of a person with no character at all; we cannot make sense of the idea of a person necessarily incapable of reciprocating attitudes taken to him, necessarily incapable because he could not understand likes, dislikes, prejudices, hobbies, moods, emotions, traits, and so forth.[2]

We should now turn to ask how much of all this presupposes Freudian theory essentially. The answer must be that little or none of it does. For first, a relatively minor point: even those who want to reject the *theory* put forward by Freud over the years often accept many of his less theoret-

---

[2] Hampshire [1962] argues at greater length for the indispensability of unconscious and non-conscious factors in the formation of 'conscious' or 'normal' traits, dispositions, and character generally.

ical remarks; indeed, many of those resolutely opposed to all forms of psychoanalysis would willingly agree with much of what is said in, for instance, *The Psychopathology of Everyday Life*. Second, and much more important: the conclusions that we have drawn can be developed without reference to Freud at all. Consider his alleged 'discovery of the unconscious'. It is just plainly and simply false to credit him with this (although perhaps he did indeed invent the System Ucs.). He did not discover the unconscious mind; it was, rather, Descartes who *un*discovered it, imposing upon philosophy the myth that only *consciousness* mattered. We shall explore the reasons for this later, in Chapter 6; for the moment I want only to emphasize that both before and after Descartes the importance of both conscious and non-conscious factors was generally just taken for granted. Whyte [1962], in an admirable source-book (from which all the quotations below, with the exception of the first, are borrowed) puts this beyond all doubt. Think of Heraclitus, famously noting:

You will not find out the limits of the *psyche* by going, even if you travel over every way—so deep is its nature (Diels and Kranz [1968], vol i, fragment 45, p. 161).

The interplay of conscious and non-conscious factors was well known to such as Shakespeare:

PRINCE: I never thought to hear you speak again.
KING: Thy wish was father, Harry, to that thought.
   (*2 Henry IV*, IV. v. 92; cited by Whyte [1962] p. 85)

and:

> In sooth, I know not why I an so sad:
> It wearies me; you say it wearies you;
> But how I caught it, found it, or came by it,
> What stuff 'tis made of, whereof it is born,
> I am to learn;
> And such a want-wit sadness makes of me,
> That I have much ado to know myself.
>
>   (*The Merchant of Venice*, I. i. 1; cited by
>   Whyte [1962], p. 86)

Von Wolff is among those who would agree with Freud that understanding the mind is impossible and 'broken' if we stick solely to the level of consciousness:

Let no one imagine that I would join the Cartesians in asserting that nothing can be in the mind of which it is not aware . . . That is a prejudice, *which impedes the understanding of the mind*, as we can see in the case of the Cartesians (cited by Whyte [1962], p. 102; italics mine).

Tucker in the early eighteenth century was one of many who appreciated the positive role that could be played by unconscious factors in facilitating conscious rational activity:

our [mental] organs do not stand idle the moment we cease to employ them, but continue the motions we put into them after they have gone out of our sight, thereby working themselves to a glibness and smoothness and falling into a more regular and orderly posture than we could have placed them with all our skill and industry (cited by Whyte [1962], p. 112).

Goethe was quite decided about the significance of the unconscious mind to creativity:

Take for instance a talented musician, composing an important score: consciousness and unconsciousness will be like warp and weft, a simile I am fond of using. Through practice, teaching, reflection, success, failure, furtherance and resistance, and again and again reflection, man's organs unconsciously and in a free activity link what he has acquired with his innate gifts, so that a unity arises which leaves the world amazed . . . (Letter to W. v. Humboldt, 1832; cited by Whyte [1962], p. 129).

Finally, Lichtenberg (in passages too numerous to cite) was one of several to insist that we could learn to know ourselves by studying our dreams. In short, all the elements we have taken from Freud, earlier in this section, could be illustrated from remarks made by his predecessors —whether those predecessors are poets, philosophers, scientists, or novelists. Anyone tending to doubt that should leaf through the excellent collection provided by Whyte.

In sum, then, and with or without Freud, human rationality and intelligence is unthinkable in isolation from the unconscious mind. The explanation of rational and aberrant behaviour spans an unbroken continuum. The sources of madness are also the sources of sanity.

3. WHAT IS MENTAL ILLNESS?

The preceding section may seem to have taken us some distance from the central topic of this chapter, but its relevance will quickly become clear. Let us now turn to look directly at various forms of mental breakdown and insanity, and consider what they tell us about the rationality that distinguishes human persons. But first there is the difficult project of trying to understand what sort of state is called a state of mental illness or abnormality.

Glib talk about various 'forms' of mental disturbance or illness of course conceals the notorious problem that taxonomy here is in a fluid and uncertain state. The disagreement begins with the most general level of description, with the attempt to specify mental health and mental illness. At one extreme are those like Szasz [1962] who think that the whole notion of mental illness is a myth; while at the other extreme are those who find the idea no more problematic than is that of physical illness—indeed, some of these even assume that all mental disorders will one day prove to *be* forms of physical disorders. Perhaps few subscribe to either of these extreme views in an unqualified form. But:

Over the years it has been shown that the [diagnostic] process can have a poor or questionable reliability; may be subject to inconsistency and change; often suffers from bias; tends to rely on subjective criteria; and tends to result in diagnoses of health rather than illness (Reich [1981], p. 63).[3]

We can highlight three reasons why there is so much confusion and disagreement here. One of the sources of the difficulty is the role of society. Everyone is, or should be, worried by the dangers of characterizing mental health in terms of social conformity and ill-health in terms of social deviance. Both the USSR and the USA build reference to social adjustment into their definitions of mental health; this tends to lead, as all know, to alarming consequences.[4] But it is not just these countries. For example, whenever, in whatever country, offenders found guilty of a crime are offered a choice between imprisonment and submitting to psychiatric treatment—as happens sporadically and inconsistently, perhaps, but increasingly—the same dubious, although in a sense idealistic and Utopian, presupposition must be in play: those who act against society must be ill.

---

[3] Reich backs up these claims by citing a mass of research; his references can be found on p. 85 of the article cited.

[4] Hence it is an oversimplification to regard Soviet psychiatrists as invariably willing tools of an oppressive regime. It is necessary to remember that in the USSR there has been a single dominant school (whereas in the USA and elsewhere there are dozens of competing theories), which, for its own theoretical reasons, extends the category of schizophrenia to include much that would not be so classified against the background of alternative theories. Thus many Soviet psychiatrists may genuinely believe that (for example) their 'sluggish schizophrenic' (*sic*) patients are mentally ill.

On the other hand, one cannot just *exclude* from consideration the ability of an individual to adjust to his physical and social environment. We have already noted Aristotle's insistence that man is by nature—essentially—a social animal, and that surely means that unless we can argue, in any given case, that the physical and social environment is the abnormal partner, the individual's failure to cope with it would count as abnormal, and as a deficiency in him. The critical difficulty then emerges, however: who is to determine what counts as a normal or tolerable environment, and what does not? It seems all too likely that someone who is regarded as entirely normal in one culture or society may be thought deviant or mentally incompetent in another. This sort of worry has been eloquently expressed by Laing, but several would concur with his unease. Writing particularly of schizophrenia, Laing claims:

'Schizophrenia' is a diagnosis, a label applied by some people to others. This does not prove that the labelled person is subject to an essentially pathological process, of unknown nature and origin, going on *in* his or her body. It does not mean that the process is, primarily or secondarily, a *psycho*-pathological one, going on *in* the *psyche* of the person. But it does establish as a social fact that the person labelled is one of Them. It is easy to forget that the process is a hypothesis, to assume that it is a fact, then to pass the judgment that it is biologically maladaptive and, as such, pathological. But social adaptation to a dysfunctional society may be very dangerous. The perfectly adjusted bomber pilot may be a greater threat to species survival than the hospitalized schizophrenic deluded that the Bomb is inside him. Our society may itself have become biologically dysfunctional, and some forms of schizophrenic alienation from the alienation of society may have a sociobiological function that we have not recognised (Laing [1967], p. 99; italics in original).

Laing himself has to some extent moderated his position from that expressed in *The Divided Self* [1960] and *The Politics of Experience and the Bird of Paradise* [1967], but few would quibble with the proposition that the standards of normality will and do differ from place to place and from time to time. This means that anyone who hopes to characterize sanity and madness by reference, at least in part, to the individual's ability to adapt to his society must take on the unenviable task of, so to speak, diagnosing the society itself and its norms and values.

Not only do different societies have divergent views about what counts as normality. A second source of disagreement in psychiatric classification, by no means unrelated to the first, is that all existing psychoanalytic theories are *de facto* grossly underdetermined by the data: rival theories abound and compete.[5] That means that there are many different diagnostic systems associated with these theories. Since theories in part determine observations, there will be hefty differences in what the psychiatrist looks for, what strikes him as significant or insignificant, what counts as evidence—what the patient is said to suffer from. For instance, during the 1950s about 80 per cent of psychiatric admissions in New York were diagnosed as 'schizophrenic', as against 20 per cent in London (Kleinig [1985], p. 28). This second complicating factor of course links closely with the first, in that some societies tolerate and expect pluralism and theoretic rivalry, whereas in others a particular school becomes dominant or standard, and a single theory rules the field. Presumably all would agree that psychoanalysis is so underdeveloped— and so difficult—that a humble tolerance of pluralism is the only viable option. But the more theories we have, the more variability there will be in the diagnostic taxonomies.

We can add to these two sources of confusion a third, important, claim: anyone confined in a mental institution is confined in a special society, a society-within-a-society, with conventions and standards—in other words, 'norms'—of its own. This emerges clearly from the work of sociologists like Goffman, who point out that the average mental hospital is a 'total institution', to be regarded as comparable in many respects to boarding schools, monasteries, prisons, and the like. All these differ from the uninstitutionalized life in two crucial ways. First, behaviour that seems bizarre and maladaptive to the outsider may be perfectly well fitted to blend with the demands imposed on the inmates by the nature of the institution: 'A community is a community. Just as it is bizarre to those not in it, so it is natural, even if unwanted, to those who live from within' (Goffman [1961], p. 303). Second, the greater the control exercised by the institution over its inmates, the fewer become the available opportunities for expressing misery and discomfort, and so rebellion is forced sometimes to take very unusual or peculiar forms if it is to be recognized as such:

Acts of hostility against the institution have to rely on limited, ill-designed devices, such as banging a chair against the floor or striking a sheet of news-paper sharply so as to make an annoying explosive sound. And the more inadequate this equipment is to convey rejection of the hospital, the more the act appears as a psychotic symptom (Goffman [1961], p. 306).

---

[5] This general point is ably illustrated by Farrell [1981].

In support of this claim one might note how long it took Larry Gostin, who deliberately entered a mental hospital in the USA as a patient to see for himself the conditions under which the inmates lived, to get himself discharged as sane; he had tried rational persuasion and what we would want to call 'normal' behaviour. Such behaviour might look thoroughly abnormal in a 'total institution'. Small wonder that we frequently hear about people who have been wrongly diagnosed as in some way insane and who have remained helplessly inside an institution— helplessly, because they were unable to convince anyone of their sanity. Given the circumstances in which they find themselves placed, the behaviour of the allegedly mentally ill may be as 'rational' or 'sensible' as are the hypothesized activities of the beleaguered ego in the Freudian picture, and for analogous reasons. Abnormal situations, or institutions, require appropriately abnormal behaviour.

Yet despite these three complicating factors (and there may be others), most would want to insist that, however difficult it may be to identify, mental illness is a fact. Glover ([1970], pp. 118-25) has suggested that we should try to characterize it by looking at the *harm* that is caused to the patient. In other words, a condition qualifies as a mental illness only if it harms the patient. He expands upon the idea in two ways. First, he insists that the harm must arise directly from the mental state itself, 'without the reactions of other people to my state being a necessary condition of the harm' (p. 124). Thus (Glover's examples) a habit of eating garlic, or a tendency to express unpopular political opinions, would not qualify as mental illness, even though they might harm the subject if these habits and tendencies alienated his friends or provoked the authorities. A second qualification is that any harmful condition that is to qualify as a mental illness should be of some severity and duration.

The general idea seems altogether on the right track, even though, as Glover emphasizes, it may be vastly unclear what is to qualify as 'harm', and there is no doubt but that this is a matter on which people disagree and will continue to disagree. Certainly one is likely to find a substantial measure of agreement, across all societies and all psycho-analytic theories, when the abnormal behaviour (for instance, compulsive hand-washing, severe depression, or a disabling phobic reaction such as agoraphobia) is acutely distressing to the subject himself. However, we should not leave it at that; as we saw in the last chapter, there are also reasons for saying that someone may be harmed in an Aristotelian sense even when he is himself contented and happy. This suggests that by contrasting the state that the individual is actually in with the state to which he might aspire if treated, we could have grounds for talking of another kind of harmful mental condition, one that the individual does not realize he is in. The obvious problem with this line of thought, though, is that such diagnoses will almost invariably be hard both to make and to justify; and, more worryingly, they could evidently pave the way for the abuse of psychiatry for coercive ends.

Sometimes, though, Aristotelian harm will be relatively easy to detect. Anyone would agree that an individual in a state of catatonic schizophrenia is so harmed, for he cannot function as a social animal in *any* society. This must count as harm, since if man is indeed a *social* animal, he needs to be able to survive in some society. But there are, inevitably, substantial variations in the pictures different people have of what it is to flourish in an Aristotelian way (and so there should be), and hence there will be substantial variations in diagnoses of Aristotelian harm. This complicating factor will combine with the problem we have already mentioned of assessing the sanity of the society itself, which will always leave the door open for paternalistic or authoritarian misuse of the categories of mental illness. No conclusive or compelling character-ization of what constitutes mental illness can be forthcoming, then, unless and until we reach a greater degree of consensus about what social structure or range of social structures allows for the fullest flourishing and development of the various capacities of the individual. That, though, is an issue for political theory, supplemented by psychological, biological, and sociological considerations, with which we cannot here deal.

4. CONTRASTS WITH THE PSYCHOPATH

From what we have said so far, the existence of mental illness (for the moment taken to exclude sheer intellectual degeneration) does not suggest that the patient is less of a rational creature than the mentally sane. Quite the contrary: to be neurotic or schizophrenic in fact pre-supposes and implicates the fullest and most intricate activity of conscious and rational, as well as of unconscious or non-rational, capacity. The vulnerability to such difficulties is built in to the human organism. Compare physical disease: pigs but not humans can catch swine fever, humans but not pigs can catch German measles. New diseases crop up, but even then it can in principle be seen how, and why, the human organism is, or is not, going to be threatened by them. So is it with psychosis, neurotic conditions, schizophrenia, and the like. Vulnerability to these is part and parcel of having the kind of complex mental structure that we normally enjoy, and this vulnerability is inescapable.

I am suggesting that, unless we are talking about mental decay or degeneration, the existence of mental abnormality militates not at all against the strict application of the 'rationality' condition. It is irrelevant that for practical reasons one cannot always behave towards those counted insane as one behaves towards someone counted normal. That is of course perfectly true, but reflects only their and our restricted capacity to see things from each other's perspective—it is difficult if not impossible to see the world through the mind of the schizophrenic, in terms of which the way he behaves seems, and might be shown to be, quite rational; and he for his part has temporarily, or perhaps even permanently, lost the ability to view the world as we do.

Evidently, however, the rationality condition is not the only condition we need to examine when we have cases of mental abnormality. The mentally sick may also be unable to meet fully the 'reciprocation' condition—and here we have to consider especially the sociopath or psychopath:[6] his status as moral agent and moral object.

It seems to be a characteristic of the sociopath or psychopath that his attitudes towards others are his chief abnormality; the sociopath personality, for example, is described by Julier as follows:

an individual who is repeatedly at variance with society. He is unable to make deep and stable relationships, is lacking in concern for others and incapable of guilt and remorse; he is self-centred, irritable and impatient, being liable to emotional and aggressive outbursts in the face of frustrations and delays in the gratification of his wishes' (Julier, 'Sociopathic Personality', in Harré and Lamb [1983], p. 600).

As with all general categories of mental illness, there is little agreement about any definition of the malaise, but we can hold on to one or two firmer strands. First, the psychopath typically has a history of parental deprivation and childhood disturbance; second, his EEG (electroencephalogram) is often characteristically abnormal; and third, the prognosis is usually poor. The condition quite often improves slightly with age, and in a carefully controlled environment the psychopath may be able to function adequately enough; but there seems little else that can be done with and for him. According to the British Psychological Society,

---

[6] 'Sociopath' and 'psychopath' seem to be used interchangeably in the literature.

there is no solid evidence of the effectiveness of treatment for psychopaths in this country.

It would presumably be agreed that, whether such a patient is aware of it or not, he has suffered an Aristotelian loss. All we need in order to establish this claim is the presupposition that the capacity to make 'deep and stable relationships' is one of the features that make for human well-being and flourishing, which is hardly a contentious thing to say. Moreover, it looks as though this is typically a product of the failures of parents and guardians towards the patient as a child, if indeed we can here safely make the *post hoc ergo propter hoc* move, as it seems in such a case as this we safely can. (He typically has a history of childhood deprivation or disturbance.) Thus to some extent at least his deficiency is a product of the culpable actions or omissions of others. We saw in the last chapter that the mere existence of an Aristotelian loss gave us prima facie reason to try to do something to compensate. Here we seem to have the added reason that neglect or misconduct on the part of parents or guardians when he was a child may be in large part responsible for his present, and perhaps incurable, state—a state which the abnormal EEG record indicates to be associated with some specific physical abnormality or failure of development. There can be little question, then, of what our attitude or stance to him should be. He has suffered at the hands of others, and deserves compensation for that; and here again, as with impaired infants and foetuses, we have a sentient being with interests, needs, and concerns who is also someone whom we need to compensate for an Aristotelian loss. We should, however, note that our stance to the psychopath is conditioned, inevitably, by our knowledge that he cannot reciprocate it—that he may be incapable of full recognition of the attitudes that we may adopt towards him. Most of the time we react to people as to individuals capable of acknowledging and responding to our overtures, and this we cannot do with the extreme psychopath. However, the point we need here is only that our attitude to him *should* be one that grants to the interests and needs that he does have as much weight as is granted to those of a more normal individual. Difficult as it may be to adopt such an attitude (it is often hard, for example, to *like* psychopaths) his right to such an attitude is at least as considerable as is that of sane and normal individuals.

On the other hand he does not, and cannot, reciprocate—or can reciprocate only certain kinds of attitudes and behaviours. He is thus less than a full person, failing to meet fully this particular condition; and, as far as we now know, he has little potential for improvement.

Notoriously, the certified psychopath is excused responsibility in courts of law. It may be necessary to confine him for the same general reasons as it is necessary, in crowded countries, to confine tigers. None the less, if we are clear about the severity of his condition, he is no more held responsible for his dangerous activities than are tigers on the loose in Bognor Regis. (Neither of them experiences guilt or remorse.) The label of 'criminal insanity' thus seems to be a doubly misleading misnomer: in so far as it is psychopathic insanity, it is hardly criminal, and if it were criminal, he would be attributed the free responsibility of which we consider him to have been in part deprived.

The psychopath, then, would be *unlike* the schizophrenic, the neurotic, or the obsessive in that he seems to be less than a full person. He—at least if he is one of those rare individuals who are full-blown psychopaths—seems incapable of certain forms of reciprocation, whereas with other forms of mental disturbance the ability to reciprocate is still there, even though it may manifest itself in strange, even antisocial, forms. The difference in the case of the psychopath is not because his condition is thought to be wellnigh incurable. These other conditions may be thought so too in some instances. It is rather that if we could penetrate the intricate web of conscious and unconscious thought in those with non-psychopathic mental illness, then, strange and abnormal as we may find it to be, we would—or so the theory goes—discover that the peculiar kinds of behaviour we find are indeed expressions of a reciprocal attitude to the stance taken to these patients by those around them. This is held not to be true of the psychopath.

As I have put it, of course, the position has been vastly over-simplified. Just as with the concept of mental illness itself, so also the subordinate categories of types of mental ailment are vaguely and roughly defined, and there is much disagreement about all such definitions or descriptions. The psychopath or sociopath, for instance, is sometimes classified as suffering from a 'personality disorder', and *that* is an umbrella term that is taken to include paranoid, affective, schizoid, obsessional, hysterical, asthenic, and explosive, as well as sociopathic or psychopathic, disorders (see Mayou, 'Personality Disorders', in Harré and Lamb [1983], pp. 461-3). Further, nobody would expect to find clear-cut distinctions between any of *these* categories, which are themselves roughly and crudely delineated. We can at best talk of paradigm instances of the psychopathic personality and set them against, say, something else that is relatively clear-cut, such as, perhaps, the patient suffering from catatonic schizophrenia or obsessional neurosis; and in terms of that argue that the psychopath is less of a person than the schizophrenic. As we have already noted, being a fully paid-up person will often be at least in part a matter of degree and of decision.

5. THE SUBNORMAL AND THE SENILE

The remaining problems to consider in this chapter come from the mentally subnormal and the senile: those with reduced, rather than disordered, capacity. Many relevant considerations apply to both, but there are some significant differences too.

The mentally subnormal individual we have met already, in the previous chapter, as an infant. I argued there that the impaired infant was someone who had suffered an Aristotelian loss, whether or not he could become aware of this. That discussion allowed us not only to explain why there were reasons for fostering any interests he may in fact have, both present and future, but also to show why we felt that there were extra reasons for attempting to compensate for the loss. If we consider, then, the question of the stance we need to take to him now he is an adult, it would seem that there are no significant differences between him and the normal individual—although there will of course be implications for the *forms* of behaviour that are considered appropriate to express this stance. In this respect he, both now and in his immature state, resembles the normal infant: each alike demands the full force of the 'stance' condition. Where he, both as a baby and as an adult, differs from the healthy infant is that the reason the healthy child demands the full application of the 'stance' condition rests with its potential to meet the other five conditions. The mentally subnormal, though, requires us rather to take into account the extent of the Aristotelian loss, and for that reason to adopt the full onus of the stance appropriate to fully-fledged persons.

There is little enough to add to the conclusions of the last chapter. The mentally retarded (at least the man who is very substantially subnormal) is less than a person in that he may not meet the other five conditions any more fully than does the chimpanzee; but, unlike the chimpanzee, he makes hefty demands on our consideration because of his Aristotelian loss. It is a matter of no great importance whether we allow or withhold the label 'person'; for, as we have seen already, the only reason such a label matters is because it colours our attitude to the subject labelled and to his responsibility for his actions—his capacity to reciprocate and to act in a free and responsible manner. Whether or not we call the mentally subnormal a person, it will be independently clear (so long as we are fully informed about his state) what our practical, social and moral responsibilities are to him, and it will also be clear what is the extent of his ability to reciprocate our attitudes, and to act freely and responsibly. There are one or two further points to bring to bear upon the mentally retarded, but they will be seen more clearly after we have considered the problem of the formerly healthy and normal adult who falls into senile, or pre-senile, dementia.

This character cuts across the categories we have been considering so far. He is like the mentally ill in that his intellectual capacities, some of which are breaking down, may comprise the full range of normal human ability; yet he approximates to the mentally subnormal in that he regresses, at least in certain ways, to the status of the child or the idiot. (The description of such a man as entering a 'second childhood' is not without its point.) Yet he cannot comfortably be assimilated to either category. I have suggested that someone suffering from, say, acute obsessional neurosis may be enjoying the full range of intellectual competence, disordered and abnormal though it may seem in its operations; but this is not true of the senile. On the other hand, though, because he once was such a man, and because his intellectual capacities do not fail or diminish together or consistently, he cannot simply be classified as subnormal, or in all respects like a child. It is not unusual to find a senile patient, who is, let us suppose, incontinent, unable to feed himself, and subject to childlike tantrums and tempers, who is none the less able to polish off *The Times* crossword with the same speed that he had in his intellectual prime. Those charged with the care of the senile often find one of the more tragic and distressing concomitants to be the fact that the patient shows flashes of being fully aware of the tragedy that has struck him, of being fully normal, fully anguished; and even if he lacks any awareness of his newly impoverished state, his behaviour may, on occasion, reveal the man he had once been.

One conspicuous difference between the senile and the retarded is that the senile individual needs to be recognized as someone who has had plans, projects, interests, and concerns that outrun those open to those of subnormal intellectual power. He may be supposed to have interests (e.g. in gardening, walking, philosophizing, attending CND meetings) which are cut off by the fact of his senility. It is of course true that physical deficiency too may prevent him from engaging in such activities; but physical problems would at least leave open the pos-siblity that he could pursue his interests indirectly—the physically handicapped can, for example, tell his friends and children, or write books, about how to care for begonias, what are the best routes up mountains, which philosophy books he would reread if only he were not blind, what he would say and do to support unilateralism or multilat-eralism if only he had the physical capacity. Such indirect pursuit of his former interests is barred, however, to the sufferer from senility. Now, interests, as we have seen in the last chapter, may often be long-term interests, and the fact that their fulfilment may have to wait until a future date in no way suggests, I argued, that they were less valuable than short-term interests that could be gratified immediately. The frustration of interests, then, is no less regrettable (*ceteris paribus*) if they are long-term ones than if they are immediate ones.

It is always a kind of harm to have active interests frustrated, to lose the goods of life. This again is a point that holds true whether or not the individual concerned is aware that his interests are being adversely affected; awareness seems to play a relatively insignificant role. The senile, seen in this light, suffers a loss: he cannot engage in activities with which he would have hoped to engage, cannot take to completion projects in which he has been interested. Whether or not he realizes it, his concerns have been frustrated, possibilities closed off:

it is arbitrary to restrict the goods and evils that can befall a man to nonrelational properties ascribable to him at particular times. As it stands, that restriction excludes not only such cases of gross degeneration, but also a good deal of what is important about success and failure, and other features of a life that have the character of processes. I believe we can go further, however. There are goods and evils which are irreducibly relational; they are features of the relations between a person, with spatial and temporal boundaries of the usual sort, and circumstances which may not coincide with him either in space or in time. A man's life includes much that does not take place within the boundaries of his body and his mind, and what happens to him can include much that does not take place within the boundaries of his life . . . The case of mental degeneration shows us an evil that depends on a contrast between the reality and the possible alternatives. A man is the subject of good and evil as much because he has hopes which may or may not be fulfilled, or possibilities which may or may not be realised, as because of his capacity to suffer and enjoy (Nagel [1970]; [1979*b*], p. 6).

The subnormal man, as we saw, had suffered an Aristotelian loss because of the contrast between the life he could have led and the life he actually leads. The senile not only suffers a loss of this kind—between what might have been and what is—but also another contrast: between what he *was* and what he is. This is an extra loss, inasmuch as the life he had led had been one in which he had long-term interests and activities, plans and projects, none of which he can now bring to fruition; which are now frustrated. We are not simply talking about interests he might have had (although there is that element too), but, more concretely, about interests he does have. Not merely interests he cannot ever enjoy, but interests that are cut off. He has lost something that he used to have.

Unlike the subnormal, too, the senile may be able, at least at times, to realize what is happening to him; or, when his mind starts to go, may have a good idea of what is in store. Nobody, himself included, can compare the life of the sane and the senile 'from the inside' and adjudicate on their respective merits (as was argued in the last chapter); but he in advance, and we, can say from the outside what the loss involves and how real a loss it is.

There can be little doubt, then, about the attitude that we need to take to such a man: the full measure of the stance it is appropriate to take to normal persons. This might involve not only meeting the interests that do remain to him (warmth, food, security) but, perhaps, trying to carry out wishes that he can no longer express. This might, in some cases, legitimate a decision not to take heroic measures to keep him alive if, for example, we knew that he had in the past dreaded the helpless state of dementia. In such a case there would, of course, be a delicate balance to tread between the fact that we know that such *had* been his expressed desire, and, perhaps, the fact that he now seems as content as such a man could be. We might, in other words, prefer to carry out wishes he had expressed when in full health and sanity to whatever we suppose him now, in his demented state, to wish.

It is tempting to say of the irreversibly senile that he is no longer a person. As I have been emphasizing for some time, though, there is no fact of the matter here; it is as before a matter of degree and of decision. But note that there might in such a case as the one envisaged be an added motive for saying that he is no longer a person: namely, that if one decided to withhold heroic measures for keeping him alive, one could describe this as preferring the wishes of a genuine person to those of a human being who is no longer such. The tragedy, that is, would be seen as the tragedy that has affected a person who has become something less, a tragedy which the person that he was would have wanted us to cut short.

6. SPECIESISM

I have just suggested that the decision whether or not something is a person is to a substantial extent a matter of our attitudes, as well as what is objectively the case about the individual in question. Indeed, we should not any longer disregard the role that is played by what has been called 'speciesism'. (The term is chosen, of course, to stress an analogy with racism and sexism.) Speciesism—preferring our conspecifics to non-human animals—is not unreasonable; as noted already, there just are no persons around who are *not* human beings, and so on solid inductive grounds we are usually justified in assuming that all humans are persons, and vice versa. That is, membership of the species *homo sapiens* is taken to be, and usually is, all we need to validate the ascription of personhood, and hence there is an a priori reason for adopting the 'person stance' to them alone. (This may be wrong: I say only that it is indeed *a* reason. There might be quite other reasons for adopting the same kind of attitude to non-human animals.)

There are more than merely inductive grounds, however. The title of 'person' is in some respects a parasitic one—parasitic, that is, upon the individual's ability to meet the six conditions sketched in the first chapter. This means, ultimately, that a person is something to which we could ascribe an enormous subject of the physical and mental predicates we freely assign to ourselves and others, and which justify the attribution of the six conditions. But we bestow the terms of the vernacular mental vocabulary in a highly anthropomorphic manner. (In this, I suggest, the conceptual apparatus of a *science* of psychology is, or should be, different).[7] To see this, consider how we distribute our ascriptions of mental predicates to non-human animals. Appearance is important: the pig, a highly intelligent animal, is allowed fewer of them than is the comparatively stupid koala—the koala's face is a little bit like ours, whereas the pig does not look much like us, and its squeal is less like the human's cry of pain than is, say, the yelp of the dog (which is again less intelligent than the pig). So looking or sounding like us helps; and there is a second reason too: familiarity. Those animals that spend much of their time with us, like cats and dogs, receive a greater allocation of mental predicates than do those that are comparatively strange. We have more of their behaviour to observe; and they share our lives, often enjoy the same foods, seem to take pleasure in some of the

[7] See my [1981].

same things (warm fires, walking, chasing balls). Above all, we have to hand none but the 'characteristically human' mental predicates by which to describe and explain it. (Crude behaviourism just does not work, for mice or for men.) Note that it was as we steadily grew better able to explain the behaviour of stars, trees, streams, and the weather in *physical* terms that we correspondingly cut back steadily on the anthropomorphization of our natural environment. Before we achieved this improved understanding of the physical world, intentional explanation was all that we had available; better some explanation than none. Ascription of mental terms to explain the behaviour of plants, computers, animals, and indeed other people, is sometimes explicitly instrumentalistic (*faut de parler*, or 'as if' ascription), sometimes less so. That does not matter; what justifies such ascriptions is that they should work, and work better (more conveniently, with better predictive power, with more accuracy) than any alternatives, so that we can act *as if* these things were like us in relevant respects. So when we find animals that look or sound a little bit like humans, or which share our lives and become the subject of discussion, it is not surprising that we tend to 'spread' ordinary mentalistic predicates on to them as well.

This suggests that the human being is not merely the only actual person that we happen to have found. It suggests that we are just not going to call anything else a person unless it meets the six conditions *in the same sort of way that we do*; unless it were thought to be sufficiently like us. (Hence: 'if a lion could talk, we could not understand him', Wittgenstein [1963], p. 223ᵉ.) The human sets the standard—whether or not 'person' is a culturally relative term, *it looks to be species relative*. This would mean that 'person' is not a natural-kind term, but is rather one whose ascription depends upon what attitude we have to the individual as well as upon what is actually true of him. We shall return to this in the very last chapter.

If, or since, this comparability to ourselves matters (matters to us), then we must note that the mentally ill, the senile, and the mentally retarded are, since they belong to the same (human) species, as like us as it is possible to be. If we find it easy to ascribe mentality to koalas on the grounds of a slight facial resemblance, it will be impossible to resist the tendency to ascribe everything we can to our impaired conspecifics. Invariably we shall want to give them the benefit of the doubt, and if it is true (as I have not argued here)[8] that much of our explanatory apparatus should be construed instrumentalistically, there will in any

---

[8] I have argued this more fully in my [1983a] and [1987].

case be no right or wrong of the matter. When we add to this the thought that it is not merely the physical resemblance of the mentally handicapped to the normal that helps determine our attitudes, but also the fact that we may have further attitudes of love, pity, sympathy, and kinship, the existence of speciesism in calling other organisms 'persons' needs no more explanation. Nor does it usually matter; for, as we have seen over and over again, the actions that are appropriate to take that affect other beings are in fact typically independent of the title 'person': we can try to clarify our obligations to the mentally disabled without reference to whether or not they are indeed persons. Perhaps being a person is not such a big deal after all.

4

Fugues, Hypnosis, and Multiple Personality

Oh, when I was above myself
I was a curious pair;
My lower feet still walked the street,
My uppers trod on air.
Said folk 'You must come down a peg,
We know not where you stand';
So reaching up I pulled my leg
And took myself in hand.

(M. H. Longson)

1. THE UNITY AND CONTINUITY OF CONSCIOUSNESS

In the last chapter we found that consciousness seemed not quite as all-important as the Cartesians have traditionally persuaded us to believe. Yet on the other hand consciousness, or 'a special kind of consciousness' (the wording was left deliberately vague) was listed as the sixth condition of personhood listed in Chapter 1. Hence, presumably, it should be extremely important to our concerns. It is thus high time to look more directly at what this troublesome notion involves. This we shall do in the present chapter and the two following.

A preliminary warning—a promissory note—about the strategy of the next three chapters. Chapter 6 will in fact argue that 'consciousness' is so fluid and flexible a notion that it is not well suited to generate sound philosophical or scientific conclusions. As a term in the everyday vocabulary, there is of course nothing wrong with it: the worth of vernacular terms lies in their utility, and the test of their worth is survival; and the term 'consciousness' has survived. For our normal (i.e. not specifically philosophical or scientific) purposes, it works fine.

But not all everyday terms, however legitimate in their own (common-sense) domain, pick out a phenomenon which theoretical accounts do or should take seriously—consider 'the will' or 'sakes'. I think, and will argue in the sixth chapter, that 'consciousness' covers such a diverse heterogeneity of *disparate* phenomena that, when engaged in philosophical investigation of the mind, we should resort instead to a corresponding diversity of alternative expressions competent to capture this disparity. This chapter and the fifth, however, will treat the notion of consciousness *as though* it were unproblematic, and will bend attention rather on conscious 'unity' and 'continuity'. Treating consciousness as though it were straightforward will, I think, throw up so many difficulties and inconsistencies that the reader should be softened up for the direct attack, in the sixth chapter, on the theoretical viability of the term itself. A further ambition of these two chapters is to show that even though the notion of *consciousness* fails to meet the increasing pressure on it, there is much to be said in general about 'unity' and 'continuity' as such: these can remain as central tools in the understanding of personal identity.

To return to our topic: somehow central to the issue of personal identity is the old and powerful idea that persons have a *unity* or a *continuity* of consciousness. However hard it may be to characterize either consciousness itself, or a unity/continuity of consciousness, there seems something right about the intuition behind the belief that a person is something which, in Locke's familiar terms, is and can regard itself as:

a thinking intelligent being, that has reason and reflection, and can consider itself as itself, the same thinking thing, in different times and places; which it does only by that consciousness which is inseparable from thinking, and, as it seems to me, essential to it (*Essay Concerning Human Understanding* [1690], Book II, ch. xxvii, para. 11; [1959], vol. i, pp. 448-9).

This chapter and the next will examine Locke's claim, in the guise of a claim that something we call very vaguely a 'unity', or a 'continuity', of consciousness is a necessary condition of (and thus essential to) personal identity. Chapter 5 will pursue this examination in relation to the apparent split in consciousness caused by commissurotomy; Chapter 6 turns to consider consciousness directly.

Let us first look at conscious *unity*. What is involved in the intuition that this matters centrally? Unity as such (that is, when we do not add the qualifier 'conscious') is very commonly scrappy, or missing. We know, for example—and have been long familiar with the idea—that there is considerable disunity, incoherence, disharmony, failure of mesh, between conscious and *non*-conscious mental phenomena. As we saw in the last chapter, we do not even have to give the credit for this to Freud; the existence of a subterranean mind which may or may not jibe with our explicit self-reports was a thought taken for granted from

Heraclitus onwards—recall Shakespeare describing Prince Harry's exercise in wishful thinking ('[t]hy wish was father, Harry, to that thought'). That being so, we evidently tolerate some degree of disunity in general as a brute fact about people; why should the importance of unity be so enhanced when we restrict ourselves to the conscious level?

Suppose, though, that we do so restrict ourselves. Suppose that we bracket the domain of abnormal behaviour and of depth psychologies, and keep to everyday thought and action, to the sorts of things we can describe without recourse to explicit theory. Even then, though, we find that we are not necessarily as unified, even on the conscious level, as we might like to think. I shall cite a few examples to support this claim; but I will not go into details at this point, since we shall need to examine them all more thoroughly in the next chapter. These examples illustrate both an *absence* of unity, and positive *dis*unity. Absence of unity: consider the phenomenon of (successfully) divided attention, when an agent can do two unrelated things at the same time. Disunity or conflict: consider the weak-willed, who is torn between wants and desires that are incompatible; or note that our emotions and feelings about something or someone often clash inharmoniously; and there is also the disunity of the self-deceived, who holds beliefs that are not consistent with one another.

But someone might object to this last example that the self-deceived is not conscious of his disunity, so his difficulty is not due to a breach in the unity of *consciousness*. Such an objection points to the problem, which will be explored at length in Chapter 6, that what is and is not conscious is often very far from clear, and particularly when beliefs are in question. For instance, we are presumably not aware (in the sense of thinking about explicitly) most of the indefinitely large stock of beliefs that can be securely ascribed to us—such as your belief and mine that eating chips does not affect television reception, that no lizards are chartered accountants, that Jaruzelski's wife had parents. These are trivial consequences of other things we believe. Such beliefs, of course, can become consciously held, and citing these three will have made them fleetingly become so; but there is a colossal number that will never cross into the spotlight of conscious attention. Are they therefore nonconscious? This is obscure. But if, on the basis of the fact that they could (easily) be admitted into conscious awareness we call them 'conscious' by courtesy, so to speak, then the penalty is that we must recognize substantial 'disunity of consciousness'. For we rarely pursue far the implications of our explicitly held beliefs; were we to do so, then it is plausible to suppose that all sorts of hidden inconsistencies and contradictions would come to light. After all, it is just when we do examine the implications of our claims that we unearth contradictions.[1]

Leaving unity for a moment: how strong a *continuity* of consciousness do we require? For whatever Locke may have thought—and opinions differ on this—we want to allow that there must be some gaps in the continuity of consciousness. When asleep and not dreaming one is not conscious, or thinking, and so one is not 'the same thinking thing' as anything; and we are all familiar with the fact that there are patches of our life that we have just forgotten. So we should admit that there are discontinuities, no less than there are disunities, in the lives of normal and perfectly healthy people.

Thus even in ordinary life the 'Lockean principle', or as I shall sometimes call it, the 'Lockean condition', needs some modification and weakening; phenomena like weakness of will indicate disunity, dreamless sleep a lack of continuity. The extent to which it will need such modification, though, will most easily be seen if we look at more dramatic cases where the principle fails (even though some of these examples are 'dramatic' only because they are more uncommon than weakness of will, or sleeping, and not because the breakdown of the principle is more extensive). We shall see, I think, that with one exception the concept of a person seems to survive all the violations of unity and continuity of consciousness that we can throw at it. This should allow us to see more clearly just what kinds of unity and continuity we require a person to possess, and just where breaches of either do indeed start to threaten the notion of a person.

2. FUGUES AND EPILEPTIC AUTOMATISM

We might start by considering fugues, because these can be relatively unproblematic. Some are very short lived; others can last for months or even years. The best-known example is perhaps the one described by William James ([1890], pp. 391-3), of the Revd Ansel Bourne. Bourne, on 17 January 1887, left his life as an itinerant preacher in

---

[1] To forestall misunderstanding, I should anticipate some of the remarks in ch. 6 and say here that I am *not* arguing that there is a stock of these tacit beliefs, somehow 'there', which are, somehow, in conflict. I want to take an instrumentalist attitude to most propositional attitudes (see Wilkes [1986] and [1987]. In any case, the claim here does not presuppose realism. There is inconsistency whenever, by *whatever* mechanisms, conflicting beliefs—tacit or explicit—can be ascribed or self-ascribed.

Rhode Island and travelled a considerable distance to a country town in Pennsylvania, where, under the name of Brown, he managed a small shop which he had opened. He was quite amnesic for his past life as a clergyman; it was two months before he 'came to', and awoke one night in fright as Ansel Bourne, finding himself in a bedroom that he had never seen before. Ullmann and Krasner [1969] describe an even longer fugue state of fifteen months, during which a sober businessman, a pillar of his community, went off and worked as a manual labourer at a chemical plant. In each case we find a double amnesia: during the fugue phase, both remembered nothing of their former lives, and, after recovery, neither remembered his doings during the time 'out'. Bourne, it is true, managed to remember his life as Brown when undergoing hypnosis with James, but after the trance had worn off his amnesia for that period returned.

Here the large-scale breakdown of the unity and continuity of consciousness, which afflicted Bourne and the businessman twice, does not tempt us to deny them a continued identity over the course of their adventures. (Some might want to claim that it *should*; my point here is only to appeal to our actual practice to show that in fact it does not.) The reasons why it does not will become clearer later, but we should now note the following. To take Bourne as an example: although much of his factual memory failed him completely, a lot else that he had learned must have stayed ('united') with him; he did not have to relearn the language, for instance, and he seems to have had no difficulties with acquired skills like harnessing and driving a horse and cart, or handling money and change. What other capacities and traits remained unimpaired we do not know—the case is not described in enough detail, and maybe James did not know the answers. Memory, in short, comes in many shapes and forms; the loss of a large set of personal memories may leave unimpaired the retention of many factual propositions (that Washington is the capital of the USA, say, or that there are 100 cents to the dollar), and many rememberings-how.[2] So 'complete amnesia' is rather a misleading label for the fugue condition; even though, to be

---

[2] The well-studied amnesic patient H.M. (for a survey see Corkin *et al.* [1981]) has almost complete anterograde amnesia—i.e. he cannot learn new information. But he is able to master motor and maze tasks, and learned to solve the Tower of Hanoi puzzle—even though each time he was confronted with a task, or the puzzle, it felt to him as though he were seeing it for the first time. (H.M. had an operation for epilepsy which involved bilateral mesial temporal lobe ablations.) So H.M., among other such patients, seems to be able to 'remember how' without any ability to 'remember that'. The reader is invited to recall the scepticism about memory on the 'marbles in a bag' picture expressed in ch. 1.

sure, *some* features of his character must have changed (or so we assume). What does seem clear is that we can manage with fairly dramatic breakdowns in the unity and continuity of consciousness: we regard this as one and the same man. (A question to keep in mind: of the competences and the knowledge that certainly stayed 'united' with Bourne—the abilities that he must have retained—how many do we want to describe as *conscious?*)

Exactly the same holds also, for evident reasons, for shorter-term fugue states such as those seen in epileptic automatism or transient global amnesia. In both such conditions the patient has a brief fugue; after recovering he can remember nothing of the 'lost' period. Those overtaken by epileptic automatism, a condition which might last for a few seconds or a few hours, typically show either purposeless behaviour patterns (such as buttoning and then immediately unbuttoning a jacket), or else fairly stereotypical ones, involving well-learned routines (such as putting out cat food, brewing hot chocolate). But some such overlearned behaviour may be highly sophisticated: there was one instance of a doctor, caught up unexpectedly by an attack of epileptic automatism while interviewing a patient, who yet managed to conduct a reasonably efficient medical examination—as he discovered from his notes when he recovered and saw that he had successfully examined his patient (although he had no recollection of doing so). Whatever he was or was not amnesic for, he clearly retained his (sophisticated) medical skills and his habit of taking full notes of his checks and tests. Transient global amnesia, which probably results from a short-lived ischaemia,[3] shows patients to all outward appearances behaving quite normally; but after they recover (and the attacks rarely last for more than about five hours) they remember nothing of their activities during this period.

So it seems that short- and long-term fugue states do not pose a problem for the issue of reidentification. That is, it seems clear that each of the individuals cited is one and only one person throughout. Thus it is already evident that we cannot be too demanding in our requirements for a unity or continuity, since our judgements of 'sameness of person' allow for disunities and discontinuities on a large scale. This should not be thought surprising. For—surely—epileptic automatism or transient global amnesia are in fact no more puzzling than

[3] Ischaemia is a brief blocking of the blood supply to regions of the brain. Transient global amnesia probably results from a temporary failure in the blood supply to temporal lobe structures. However, some conjecture that transient global amnesia can result from focal epileptic discharges, in which case it would merely be another term for epileptic automatism.

sleep, which equally interrupts the power of conscious recall. They strike us as odder, certainly, but that is because we are so well used to the breakdowns of conscious unity and continuity during sleep (familiarity breeds neglect), whereas these short-lived amnesias are rare, peculiar, and hence striking. Longer-lasting fugues interrupt the unity and continuity of consciousness more dramatically and drastically; but, if they do not seem to disrupt our intuition that we have, unproblematically, one and the same person here, that must be because the unity or continuity of consciousness, or perhaps even consciousness itself, are not quite as important as one might at first think.

3. HYPNOSIS

The dissociations that hypnosis can induce make this point clearer yet. Undeniably we take it for granted that the hypnotized subject is one and the same person as the individual who agreed to be hypnotized, whatever may happen to him under hypnosis. I admit that there is considerable scepticism—often well founded—about the validity of some of the effects described as occurring with hypnotized patients. Certainly many of these effects may indeed be due to deceit, extreme suggestibility, or role-playing. On the other hand, it is usually possible for the critical and well-informed observer to detect the dissembler; and people like Hilgard (see e.g. his [1977]) provide such careful documentation and so many double-checks that the chance that his subjects are deceiving him is well nigh minimal. Genuine hypnotic states can give us not only the sorts of amnesias that we find in fugue states, but, as we shall see, they reveal an extra twist as well.

To take the amnesia first: it is possible, and fairly typical, for the hypnotized subject to act in a way that is quite dramatically out of character, and to have afterwards no recollection of what he said or did under hypnosis. This gives him the same sort of qualitative and quantitative gap in conscious continuity that we found with cases of fugue. However, there is not only a diachronic gap, a failure of continuity; there seems also to be at times a synchronic split, a failure of unity. An example or two would make the point clearer.

One way of distinguishing the genuinely hypnotized subject from the one who is merely pretending is by instructing the subjects not to see a chair (a negative hallucination) and then asking them to walk in a straight line which would put the chair right in their path. The unhypnotized subject who has been asked to pretend that he is hypnotized walks straight along and crashes into the chair (unless, of course, he knows a bit about the behaviour of patients under hypnosis). The genuinely hypnotized subject, however, goes around it. We can thus tell the two apart; and the split that I mentioned comes in with the fact that the hypnotized subject seems both to see and not to see the chair—he sees it, for he avoids it successfully, but he does not see it, for when asked to describe the room he always leaves the chair out, when asked to sit will not use it, and so forth. He does not comment on his detour around the chair, though, and when shown that he did not walk in a straight line he is typically either puzzled or (sincerely) tries to rationalize his action: 'I just thought I'd like some variety', or 'your picture caught my eye and I thought I'd go over there to have a closer look'. (Incidentally, such *ex post facto* rationalizations should not be damned as deliberate dishonesty. They are peculiar, certainly, and difficult to comprehend; but the very widespread prevalence of such attempts at rationalization in virtually all subjects—in hypnosis, mental illness and confusion, hemispheric neglect,[4] commissurotomy patients, and elsewhere—is so widespread that we should accept it as a phenomenon and admit that the patient genuinely believes what he is saying.) Anyway, it looks prima facie as though we can say he is both aware and not aware of the chair.

A second example introduces the so-called 'hidden observer', often seen in action during hypnosis. Hilgard [1977] gives many examples of this; we might consider one of them, the phenomenon of hypnotic anaesthesia. This is particularly interesting, and shows us a split in consciousness of a very marked form. One experiment, conducted by Hilgard, is to get the subject hypnotized, and then tell him that he is going to feel no pain. Then one hand and arm are put into a stream of circulating iced water. This is very rapidly felt as painful by the unhypnotized, who cannot under these circumstances keep up the pretence for very long. The successfully hypnotized subject, though, can sit there with his hand and arm in the water for long periods,

---

[4] Hemispheric neglect is a condition in which patients with a lesion to one half of the brain virtually ignore the side of their body contralateral to the lesioned hemisphere, and fail to report, or respond to, stimuli presented to the contralateral side. This is evidently bizarre: how can anyone ignore half of the world, and half of themselves? It would seem that such a condition should be very upsetting to the patient. However, 'neglect' patients are rarely worried. They may rationalize the dilemma by denying that an arm or a leg belongs to them at all, by denying that their visual or sensory field is impaired, or by admitting that there is some impairment, but making light of it and regarding it as insignificant.

untroubled and saying that he is untroubled. However, if in his other hand he has a pencil and paper (usually so placed that he cannot see it), and if he is encouraged to write or indicate what he is feeling, then the 'hidden observer' may complain bitterly about the intensity and unpleasantness of the pain he is experiencing. (And in fact the hidden observer may observe much more than we realize. Ordinary anaesthesia may not anaesthetize him. Many patients who have been hypnotized after a routine operation involving routine anaesthesia have proved to be able to recall in detail conversations held while the operation was in progress between the surgeon and the anaesthetist: see Cheek and LeCron [1968].)

The objection might perhaps be made to the example of hypnotic anaesthesia that neither state of the hypnotized subject—the state in which he denies pain, and the state in which he complains about it—is strictly a conscious state, so that there may be no violation of the unity of *consciousness* here. But that would be a hard line to defend, for it requires an account of what a 'strictly conscious' state may be; we met the same objection, and noted the same difficulty, when discussing self-deception in Section 2 above. Surely one of our clearest tests of consciousness, at least for human subjects, is verbal or linguistic output (bating for the moment certain possible exceptions like sleep-talking; we shall return to discuss the 'language test' of consciousness in Chapter 6). Yet the subject undergoing hypnotic anaesthesia can talk sensibly to the hypnotist about the absence of pain, and simultaneously can write sensibly about its intensity. So to say that he is not *really* conscious merely requires one to say more clearly what one is understanding by '(strictly) a conscious state'. So for the moment I shall ignore that objection, content to point out that it creates as many difficulties for the objector as for his target, precisely because of the obscurity of 'consciousness' in such cases.

Prima facie, then, it looks as though we lose any unity of consciousness here. In fact we might even say that we have two consciousnesses, each perhaps internally united, working simultaneously but separately—somewhat like what we apparently find under experimental conditions with split-brain patients (to be discussed in the next chapter). If we add to this the amnesia that often attends states of hypnosis (in other words, an amnesia that can often be made to follow states of hypnosis), we get a double dimension of split in conscious unity and continuity, and Locke's principle seems to be in yet further trouble.

None the less, we have no doubt about the singleness of the person before us here. There is one and only one individual, and *he* is being hypnotized. This, at least, is how our practice runs: we seem not to consider hypnotic subjects as challenging the concept of personal identity. We apparently tolerate breakdowns such as these in the unity and continuity of consciousness. (As already noted, if we hardly ever dreamt we would find dreams just as bizarre as we now find hypnotism and fugues; but as things are we regard the disunity and discontinuity seen with dreams to be perfectly normal.) The substantial point is that the dissociated states we have discussed so far show how weakly the prejudice in favour of the unity and continuity of consciousness often needs to be taken; whatever else is true, the unalloyed assertion of what I am calling 'the Lockean principle', or 'the Lockean condition', needs to be modified in order to tolerate our clear intuition that the subject before, during, and after hypnosis is one and the same person.

4. MULTIPLE PERSONALITY: CHRISTINE BEAUCHAMP

So far, I expect that few would disagree. Since 'the Lockean condition' stumbles over such everyday phenomena as sleep and self-deception, it is scarcely surprising that it is hard to fit on to fugues or hypnosis. The plot thickens, though, when we get to multiple personality; even though (as we shall see) this is, in a sense, just more of the same. First, though, we should consider what kind of condition it is.

Previously classified as one subclass of 'hysterical neuroses, dissociative type' it has now been to some extent distinguished from the hysterical neuroses and is rather classed along with other dissociative states like fugues, psychogenic amnesias, and so forth. Certainly it can no longer be thought of as an exclusively hysterical disorder (see Confer and Ables [1983]). We saw in the last chapter how fluid and fraught is the taxonomic classification of abnormal conditions, and so this sort of revision and reclassification should not be thought surprising.

It is necessary again to argue, even if only briefly, that we indeed have here a genuine phenomenon—that there is such a condition as multiple personality. For it may look as though with this, as with certain other medical complaints, nature follows art. In the late nineteenth century, when multiple personality was taken as a genuine diagnostic category and philosophers and scientists were fascinated by it, there was a wave of reported cases. But then the increasing scepticism of the mid-twentieth century seemed virtually to abolish the condition. (Of sixty-three patients admitted to Bellevue hospital in 1933–4, all said to be suffering from 'loss of identity', not one was declared to be a case of multiple personality; schizophrenia, manic depression, psychosis, aphasia, amnesia, cerebral arteriosclerosis, pre-senile dementia, cerebral trauma, epilepsy, and carbon monoxide poisoning sufficed as diagnostic labels; see Sutcliffe and Jones [1962].) Moreover, there are *very* sound methodological reasons for dropping or at least suspending belief in multiple personality as a discrete and identifiable phenomenon. After all, the condition is an unusual and an intriguing one, so doctors naturally treat potential cases with keen interest and attention—thereby providing strong positive reinforcement to the patient to develop distinct and distinguishable alternate personalities. It is highly likely that role-playing, whether conscious or unconscious, whether in childhood or in the surgery, is an essential element in the aetiology of the condition.[5] Finally, contemporary psychiatry has largely abandoned the almost automatic resort to hypnosis as a method of therapy. This is significant, for after reading case histories it is hard to avoid the impression that repeated hypnotism often had the effect of defining and solidifying alternate personalities which, if not thus encouraged, might have dissolved away again.[6]

On the other hand, though, what remains important is this: with or without the encouragement of doctors; with or without the prior existence of strenuous role-playing; whether we call it multiple personality or just an acute form of *grande hystérie* suffered by some psychoneurotic patients; allowing all that, we do get, and have had, patients with symptoms that cannot be adequately described in any terms other than those provided by the 'multiple personality' category and classification. Furthermore, there has been much independent evidence from the relatives and friends of the patients that testifies to the existence of puzzlingly split states well before, and independently of, any medical intervention. Nor does the condition seem to be exceptionally rare; Howland [1975] has noted that over 200 cases have been reported in the literature, and it is impossible to guess at the number of cases that have gone unreported. Whatever the *genesis* of the trouble, many of these patients have become genuinely split and cannot then get out of the problem by making a New Year's resolution to stop playing games. Furthermore, we now have techniques more reliable

---

[5] See Taylor and Martin [1944], or Congdon, Hain, and Stevenson [1961].
[6] See Harriman [1943], Gruenewald [1971], or Greaves [1980].

and more objective than the (theoretically guided and motivated) opinions of doctors. These opinions were admittedly often a product of their own prejudices—either that there was no such thing as multiple personality, or that there was indeed such a thing and what fun it would be if the patient proved to have it! The tests I have in mind are psychological, physiological, and psychophysiological, and one or two illustrations of their use may be helpful.

Ludwig *et al.* [1972] examined Jonah, a twenty-seven-year-old man whose alternate personalities called themselves Sammy ('the Mediator'), Usoffa Abdullah, Son of Omega ('the Warrior'), and King Young ('the Lover'). (Jonah—'the Square'—was also called 'Jusky'—a democratic decision reached on the basis of taking the initial letters from the names of *J*onah, *U*soffa, *S*ammy, and *K*ing *Y*oung.) All four personalities showed, quite consistently over time, significantly different reactions *in propria persona*, and with each alternate, in repeated EEG (electroencephalogram) tests that looked for alpha and theta wave frequency and amplitude, or for the conditions of alpha-blocking (eye-opening, for instance, often blocks alpha wave activity). The four also showed systematic differences on GSR (galvanic skin response) tests to emotionally laden words. King Young, for example, responded strongly to words denoting sex, Usoffa Abdullah, to terms of fight, violence, and bloodshed. Their VERs (visually evoked responses) to light flashes differed systematically too. Tests of paired-word learning showed some transfer of learning from Jonah to the other three, but no transfer between the other three and none from any of them to Jonah. These are not the sorts of results that can be produced intentionally by a single subject bent on tricking a gullible doctor.

Some different cases: Confer and Ables [1983] put their patient Rene several times through the MMPI test (the 'Minnesota Multiphasic Personality Inventory'), which threw up great differences of character, traits, preferences, and dispositions between the primary personality and each of the major alternates—differences which no layman could have predicted or prepared for, and so hard to explain on the supposition that the patient was deliberately fooling the doctor. Similarly, Eve Black and Eve White proved to have some differences in microstrabismus (a transient loss of oculomotor parallelism; see Condon *et al.* [1969]). One physical variation between these two showed up even without elaborate tests or equipment: Eve Black was allergic to nylon, Eve White was not (Thigpen and Cleckley [1957]).

Thus we have some *hard* data to add to the mass of evidence that Morton Prince described ([1905]; reprinted in his [1968], from which page references are taken) in his early, but very thorough, analysis of Miss Christine Beauchamp.[7] Prince did not, of course, have available the various tests, just described, which were developed later in the century. But since his description is so clear and full, I shall discuss the problem by reference primarily to his treatment and not to later works, on the reasonable assumption that if he *had* been able to use these tests, they would have fully endorsed his judgement that he was dealing with a thoroughly split individual. His discussion is particularly instructive because, in a work written for fellow scientists rather than for the popular market, he tries to explain his theories, justify his conjectures, and make explicit his assumptions. (The better-known book-length treatments written more recently were intended as popular paperbacks and we miss in them Prince's theoretical and critical stance.)[8] Moreover, he wrote before Freudian theory had swept the USA, and so his book is not shadowed by that potent figure. I shall therefore describe as briefly as possible the salient features of Miss Beauchamp's predicament, and then, with reference to this and one or two other cases, particularly that of Jonah/Jusky, consider the implications for our overall problem.

Following Prince, I shall call the patient as she lived until 1893 'Christine Beauchamp'. She was then eighteen. She had been a nervous, ailing, impressionable child, prone to headaches, somnambulism, daydreams, and trances; she had been neglected by a mother she adored and maltreated by her father.[9] In 1893 she was working as a hospital nurse, and on one stormy night had a succession of three shocks, each alone sufficiently alarming to one of a nervous constitution.[10]

The patient whom Prince saw for the first time five years later I shall call, as he does, '*B1*'. (Of course, she was not labelled '*B1*' until much later, after she began to have competitors for the name 'Christine Beauchamp'.) *B1* was otherwise known as 'the saint'. She was a woman morbidly reticent, morbidly conscientious, a bibliophile, deeply

[7] This was not, of course her real name.

[8] e.g. Schreiber [1975], and Thigpen and Cleckley [1957].

[9] A repressed, puritanical childhood, often including neglect and physical or sexual abuse, seems a pattern common to many cases of multiple personality.

[10] First, she saw illuminated in a lightning flash a patient in a white nightgown, who grabbed hold of her; then she saw her boyfriend's face outside a second-floor window (he had climbed a ladder to suprise her); and finally—although Prince is somewhat coy about this—it seems that the same boyfriend found Miss Beauchamp and attempted what to her seemed near-rape, illuminated only by flashes of lightning.

religious, patient, and long-suffering, with 'a refinement of character out of the ordinary' and 'great delicacy of sentiment'. She had been advised to consult Prince because of her insomnia, fatigue, headaches, nervousness, and depression. Prince at once hypnotized her (such patients are typically very easy to hypnotize, although it is counter-productive with multiple personality patients who have any degree of psychosis). *B1*'s hypnotic state came to be called '*B1a*', but *B1a* was never considered to be a distinct personality—she *was B1*, but was a *B1* who had less reserve and restraint when in a hypnotic trance, and hence who was better able to talk fully and freely about her condition. *B1a* knew of, and claimed as her own, all *B1*'s thoughts and actions; *B1*, as is common for hypnotized subjects, was amnesic for all she said and did as *B1a*. I shall represent this asymmetrical knowledge by an arrow: one arrowhead to represent knowledge of actions, another to represent knowledge of thoughts (Fig. 2).

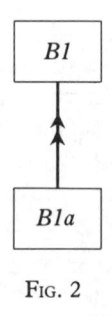

F<small>IG</small>. 2

One day under hypnosis the patient referred to *B1* not, as before, as 'I' but as 'she'. When asked why she did not think of herself as *B1* (who then, having no rivals, was of course simply called 'Christine Beauchamp') she replied, 'because she is stupid; she goes around mooning, half asleep, with her head buried in a book; she does not know half the time what she is about' (Prince [1968], p. 28). This personality proved to know all of *B1*'s and *B1a*'s thoughts and actions—often, indeed, she was able to describe *B1*'s dreams in greater detail than could *B1* or *B1a*. But she denied that they were *her* thoughts, dreams, and actions. She claimed rather to have existed as an intraconscious[11] personality right from Christine Beauchamp's early

---

[11] The technical term for a subordinate consciousness that is aware of the primary personalities' actions but not thoughts is 'co-conscious'; one aware of both actions and thoughts is 'intraconscious'. Thus Sally was intraconscious to *B1* (and, as we shall see,

childhood. *B1* and *B1a*, on the other hand, knew nothing of this personality. Prince at first called her by Miss Beauchamp's own name, but she disliked and despised *B1* so much that she chose eventually to be called 'Sally' instead. So in Fig. 3 we need to supplement Fig. 2.

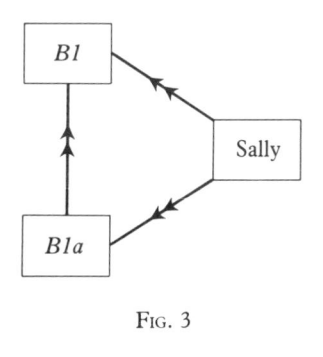

FIG. 3

Prince was fascinated by Sally. He used to get her repeatedly by hypnotizing *B1*, who then either turned into Sally directly, or turned into *B1a*, from which state Sally could easily come when summoned. She remained as a hypnotic state of the individual until one day she contrived to get her eyes open, and there she was: an unhypnotized, merry, and carefree individual, in full control of the body and with every intention of keeping it that way. After she had once managed to get her eyes open she was able to 'come' more and more often, with or without the prior hypnotism of *B1*. Much of this was Prince's responsibility, for he did little at first to discourage her—she amused him by her vivacity, irresponsibility, flirtatiousness, and verve: 'there was a delightful attractiveness in [her] absolute disregard of responsibility; she was a child of nature' ([1968], p. 53).

The rise of Sally did the unfortunate *B1* no good at all. *B1* knew nothing of her (it was some time before Prince informed her of the new development), and as far as she was concerned the times when Sally was 'out' were times she lost completely. For example, she lost an entire Christmas Day. More painfully, she lost the whole of a ten-day period in hospital to which she (*B1*) had explicitly asked to be committed; Sally amused herself by pretending to be *B1*, and the hospital staff, impressed by '*B1*'s' absence of depression and fatigue, discharged her. Thus *B1*

co-conscious to *B4* and intraconscious to *B2*). Co-consciousness is represented in the figures by a single arrow, and intraconsciousness by a double arrow.

gained not at all from her difficult and courageous decision to undergo hospital treatment.

Sally in fact hated *B1*, and spared no pains to make her life a misery. Prince believed that the implacable hatred was fuelled by jealousy of *B1*'s superior attainments and the love and respect she received from her friends. For Sally, although she claimed to have been present as a coexisting consciousness throughout Miss Beauchamp's life, was far less well educated—she was easily bored, so had not paid attention to school lessons or difficult books. She could not, for example, speak French, whereas *B1* was fluent (a fact Prince often exploited to forestall Sally's interference in his plans for *B1*); and her command of grammar, spelling, and syntax, and the range of her vocabulary, were much inferior to that of *B1*. Jealous or not, it is clear how much Sally disliked *B1*. She would tear up her letters, conceal money and stamps, destroy sewing and knitting, or perhaps sew up the sleeves of *B1*'s clothes. She sent through the post to *B1* parcels containing spiders, spent money lavishly on unsuitable clothes, and for a period kept *B1* on an 'allowance' of 5 or 10 cents a day. Her friends were not *B1*'s friends and her tastes differed from *B1*'s; so *B1* often found herself coming-to in a circle of alien faces, with a drink or a cigarette in her hand—though she rarely drank and hated the taste of cigarettes. Sally broke *B1*'s appointments and walked out of the jobs *B1* had worked so hard to keep. At one time she even thought of killing her, and needed to be reminded of the consequences to herself of such an action. Sally of course had all the advantages, knowing, as she did, everything about *B1*; whereas *B1* could know nothing directly of what Sally was doing and planning. Yet—perhaps unwisely—*B1* continued to visit Prince, as her anguish steadily deepened.[12] Disturbed by Sally's effect on *B1*, Prince eventually tried to suppress her, but failed in this completely.

Prince was in a way fond of Sally, otherwise known as 'the devil'. But he was less taken by the next personality, an alternate who just arrived one day, unheralded and unexpected. This individual, labelled '*B4*' by Prince, remembered nothing that had happened since the night of trauma in 1893, six years earlier. Indeed, on her first appearance (in Prince's surgery) she thought that it was still that same night. She failed to recognize Prince; struggling to come to terms with a situation almost

---

[12] In fairness to Prince one ought to say that his suggestions to *B1a* often proved effective in removing for several days *B1*'s headaches, insomnia, depression, and exhaustion. On the other hand, a summer spent in Europe (and thus away from Prince) found *B1* almost entirely untroubled by Sally—the longest such period since Sally first came on the scene.

impossible for her, she retreated into aloof reticence, determined to conceal by any means available her embarrassing ignorance of the last six years.

Sally was highly excited by the advent of *B4*. She found that she was aware of *B4*'s actions but not of her thoughts (thus was 'co-conscious' rather than 'intraconscious' with her—one arrow in the figures, not a double one), so it was some time before she discovered that *B4*'s pretence to knowledge was no more than that, a pretence. When Sally discovered this she was highly indignant at such a deception, and contemptuously dubbed *B4* 'the idiot'—the first of her many rash underestimations of *B4*. *B4* had a hypnotic state which stood to *B4* just as *B1a* stood to *B1*, and was termed *B4a*; so we now have Fig. 4.

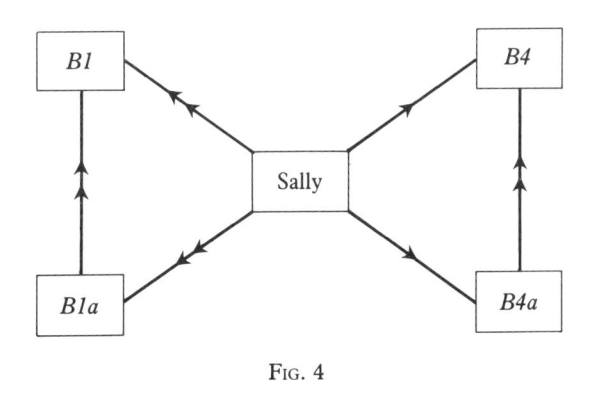

Fɪɢ. 4

B4 knew nothing directly of either *B1* or Sally. Prince thought of her as 'the woman' of the trio—possibly a judgement revealing some degree of male chauvinism, since he describes her as prickly, hot-tempered, impatient, fiercely independent, and aggressive. Certainly she was someone who ardently resented the position in which she found herself. Quickly despising and discounting what she heard of the wretched *B1*, *B4* set out on battles royal with Sally. Sally in these forays had the obvious advantages of knowing all *B4*'s actions (though *B4* could often mislead her by speaking to herself in French, or by pretending to have a headache when she did not—something Sally discovered with indignation only when *B1* 'came out'). Sally could exhaust *B4* physically, frustrate her arrangements, deny her sleep, hide her belongings, and so tended to win the first rounds; but she in turn could eventually be brought to heel by *B4*'s sincere ultimatum: one more outrage, and *B4* would commit the lot of them to an asylum. *B1* had to pick up whatever she could from indirect evidence—from the remarks of friends, from finding letters written by Sally and *B4* to each other, from the jobs and places in which she found herself—and from her point of view, things were degenerating rapidly.

Sally and *B4* were forced into an uneasy working alliance by a development alarming to both of them. Prince discovered that *B1* deeply hypnotized and *B4* deeply hypnotized—getting 'below' *B1a* and *B4a*—became one and the same, called *B2*. This hypnotic state claimed to *be* both *B1* and *B4*, accepting all their thoughts and actions as her own. She seemed, moreover, to combine the virtues of both with the excesses of neither. However, she knew nothing at all of Sally, even though Sally knew (as she did with *B1*) all her thoughts and actions. So

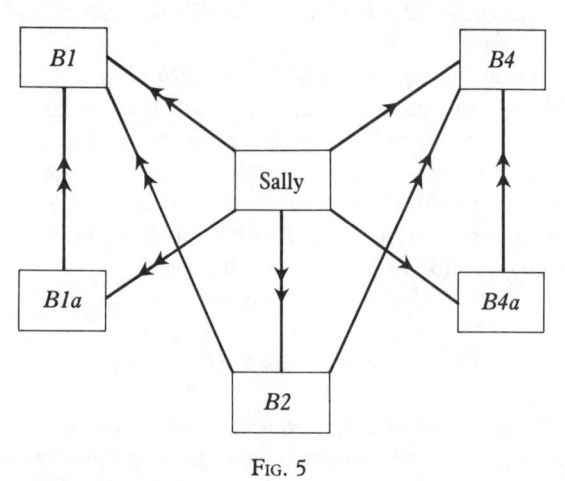

Fig. 5

now we get Fig. 5. *B2*'s memory went right back (with lacunae only for the periods when Sally was 'out') to early childhood. She seemed, moreover, a sober, responsible, and well-balanced individual. *B2*, Prince thought, was 'the real' Miss Beauchamp, identical with the pre-1893 Christine Beauchamp. However, whenever he tried to wake *B2* out of the hypnotic trance, she never woke up *as B2* but would split, via *B1a* or *B4a*, into *B1* or *B4*.

To *B1* and *B4*, life as *B2* was equivalent to death. From their point of view they ceased to exist when *B2* was present, despite the fact that *B2* claimed to be both of them. *B1*, characteristically, was ready to meet meekly her own extinction. *B4*, though, was determined to fight. She made a partner of Sally who, although not 'killed' by the rise of *B2*, would have been 'squeezed' (her own term) back to her passive status as a coexisting consciousness by a healthy *B2*, and Sally much preferred a lively and active existence. Thus, for example, *B4* planned a flight to Europe, which was frustrated only just in time; *B4* and Sally broke appointments with Prince; and determined autosuggestion by *B4* made it difficult for Prince to hypnotize her to get *B4a* and thereby *B2*. Eventually, though (in 1904), they were defeated. Sally admitted that she had recognized in *B2* the pre-1893 Christine Beauchamp, and that it had been her subterranean influence which had 'split' *B2* back into *B1a* or *B4a* whenever Prince tried to wake up *B2* as *B2*. She withdrew her interference, and, after completing her autobiography and a Last Will and Testament, voluntarily committed herself to what she regarded as extinction. And thus *B2* at last woke up as—Prince contends—Christine Beauchamp.

Then it was all over bar the shouting, and bar Sally. *B2* proved to be quite stable, splitting back into *B1*, *B4*, or Sally only when under severe strain. When *B1* or *B4* did emerge, it was for them as though they had woken up after a coma of several months; as for Sally, she returned to the position that she said she had occupied until 1898, that of an intraconsciousness existing alongside Christine Beauchamp. So we can now round out the full diagram as Fig. 6 (opposite).[13]

5. HOW MANY MISS BEAUCHAMPS?

Now for the primary question (a question difficult to frame in a way that is not grammatically suspect): how many people was Christine Beauchamp between 1893 and 1904? It should be clear that it matters not at all for this problem whether the condition of multiple personality is or is not something that psychiatry ought to recognize as such, or whether it is or is not an avoidable phenomenon initiated by role-playing and unwisely encouraged by an undue use of hypnotism. However it is produced, whatever its aetiology, so long as we accept the

---

[13] Fig. 6, like the account offered above, is much simplified. It leaves out, for example, Sally's hypnotic state (which played no very active part in the story); it omits several further but relatively fleeting personalities; it simplifies the coding (*B1a* was first called '*B2*', Sally was first *B3*, then 'Chris', and eventually elected to be called 'Sally'). The reader is urged to consult Prince's book in case some of the simplifications prove positively misleading.

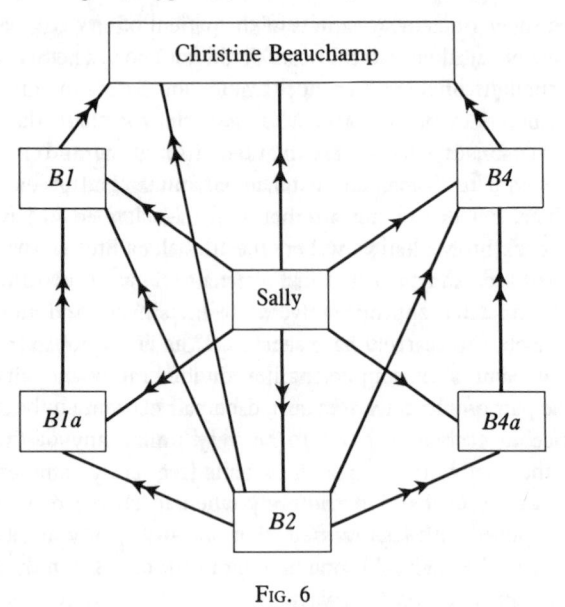

Fig. 6

general truth of the data provided by Prince and supported by the more recent analyses mentioned above, the questions of personal identity, of the role of a unity or continuity of consciousness, and of the role of unity and continuity generally, arise urgently. It is difficult to describe the case except in terms appropriate to four persons (and I have not tried to avoid this question-begging mode of description: the debts from the begged question will be repaid); but nature need to be no party to our phraseology. As we shall see, the various criteria purporting to tell us what it is to be a person are not decisive.

Bodily considerations

Strongly in favour of saying that there was *one* person throughout is the fact that only one body is involved: one genetic constitution, one pair of hands, one mouth, and so on. Biologically speaking there is just one *homo sapiens* here, one human being. And that is strong evidence, simply because we all do in fact take it much for granted, as we have noted already, that persons and bodies come related one : one.

There is, however, one incidentally puzzling fact here. Let it be agreed that there *is* only one body, of a specific physical description. All the same, the various personalities of the patient often disagree strongly about their physical characteristics. We do not know whether Sally, *B1*, and *B4* thought of their own appearances in their own idiosyncratic ways—Prince does not tell us. What is certain is that other cases of multiple personality show very marked disagreements on what 'the body' looked like. Rene, for instance, definitely had green eyes and auburn hair, but one of her alternates, Jeane, claimed to have brown eyes and dark brown hair; another, the flirtatious Stella, was a blonde and dressed accordingly. Her third alternate, Sissy, claimed to be four years old, and acted appropriately; while the sinister and violent male alternate, Bob, can scarcely have seen what Stella saw when 'he' looked in a mirror. Sybil's sixteen personalities divided into eight pairs of near-twins (one pair of which were males), each pair claiming to be similar in appearance to each other, but to be very unlike any of the others. Further, the doctors treating such patients frequently comment on the different ways each handles the body when in charge of it: this personality slouches with legs crossed, that one sits primly, back straight, on the edge of the chair; this one has an oncoming glint in the eye, that one looks depressed and far away.

That is interesting;[14] but cannot of course defeat the *brute* fact that, like it or not, the various personalities do indeed have to make do with but one body. And this is a prima facie argument for saying that there is only one person there. But we cannot regard this alone as conclusive, precisely because the one : one relationship is something that we *might* need to call into question.

The six conditions

Let us look next at the six conditions and see if they can help us out. Most militate in favour of affirming plurality: each of the three dominant personalities meets four of them handsomely. Consider how (complex) Intentional predicates are true of each of the Beauchamp family separately. All can use language—two of them can use two. Each claims consciousness and self-consciousness. All are as capable of rational thought as are most ordinary people. So four conditions are clearly satisfied. It is the remaining two conditions, to do with 'attitude' and 'stance', that need examination: what attitude to Sally, *B1*, and *B4*

---

[14] Curiously enough, multiple personality patients seem not always bothered by this anomaly, sometimes, indeed, insisting that their bodies are quite different from the body of another alternate. The obvious inconsistencies that this provokes are ignored or shrugged off.

(or, what attitude to 'Christine Beauchamp') was, or should have been, taken by Prince; and how did they (or she) reciprocate such attitudes. Let us consider first the attitude taken *to* them (her), for here we will find considerations pulling both ways.

On the one hand, this condition can be used as evidence for the claim that we have one person here, deriving from what we are accustomed to do, what we are accustomed to say. It is just a plain fact that the doctors in charge treat these patients as single individuals to be cured. Prince had no doubt but that his job was to 'find' and to 'cure' *the* real Miss Beauchamp. There were, I think we should agree, good reasons for him to do so; *B2*, or 'the real Miss Beauchamp', functioned much better than had any of the others, once she was established in virtually sole charge of the body.

It is worth mentioning, though, that it is not invariably the case that singularity is better for 'the patient' than plurality. It seems that the 'cure' was less effective with Jonah/Jusky; for him/them, apparently, multiplicity was better suited than unity. (The full title of Ludwig *et al.*'s [1972] discussion of Jonah is 'The Objective Study of a Multiple Personality: *Or, are Four Heads Better than One?*'—italics mine.) Notwithstanding Jonah/Jusky, though, we can see why singularity is usually preferred. It is typically much more convenient, since the uniqueness of the body jibes poorly with a plurality of owners. Sally and *B4*, for instance, were most annoyed whenever they 'came to' and found themselves in church, or engaged in one of *B1*'s charitable or altruistic activities. *B1* in turn could become ill with worry when she found herself with a cigarette in her hand. It was immensely time-consuming for all three if the body had to be bathed up to six times a day (each of them wanted two baths, and if Sally had bathed first in the morning, *B1* might have another one, then *B4*; and then in the evening they might all go through the same routine again). We can guess what difficulties even Jonah/Jusky might have had, despite the fact that Jusky was in general more stable and efficient than the reunited Jonah, if, say, Sammy had wanted to be a ballet dancer and Usoffa Abdullah had thoughts of becoming a Sumo wrestler. The fact that several of Sybil's sixteen alternates wanted to take 'the' dose of a prescribed medicine meant that the body was getting much more of it than any doctor intended; nor did her bank balance prosper, when each alternate wanted her own wardrobe of clothes (see Schreiber [1975]). In general, one body per person is just much easier.[15]

---

[15] As Fagin puts it: 'Some conjurors say that number three is the magic number, and

All the same, despite the fact that we probably would agree with Prince's presupposition that it was *Miss Beauchamp* to whom he took the 'help-treat-cure' stance, there is a paradox here still. For note that in the relevant period, before *B2* appeared, *he did not have 'the real Miss Beauchamp' to take an attitude to*; the fact that he felt he must cure 'this patient' was rather an attitude towards someone he had not yet met! Even so, though, I think we have to agree that his overall stance was to a single, albeit absent, individual; he took himself to be treating one woman.

However, the 'stance' condition also works to support the thesis that we have *several* people here. We have been arguing so far that Miss Beauchamp seems to have been a *single* object of moral concern: our attitude to her is, at least most of the time, the attitude we take to a single sick person. But we cannot be consistent here, and notably Prince did not try to be. For he *also* regarded each member of the trio as an individual object of concern. He was worried about the effects on *B1* of Sally's practical jokes; he sympathized, quite genuinely, with *B4*'s agony when she told him that he was killing her; and, although he deplored Sally's childishness and occasional spitefulness, he was also amused by this 'carefree child of nature'. So as well as treating the (elusive) 'real Miss Beauchamp' as a single person, he treated each of the three personalities as one too. The 'stance condition' is thus a two-edged weapon for use in deciding on the number of people here.

What then of the 'reciprocation' condition? This cannot pull in favour of saying that only one person ('Miss Beauchamp') was present during the crucial period. For until the advent of *B2*, she was not there at all. It rather pulls in favour of saying that there were indeed three responsible, reciprocating agents here. Prince certainly regarded all three as such. He firmly (for example) ticked Sally off for her tricks and follies, and would lecture her sternly; he criticized or approved of *B4*'s plans for finding a job, or for taking a holiday; and he commended *B1*'s sweet and self-sacrificing nature. All the alternate personalities were thus treated as moral and prudential agents, with respect to other people, with respect to each other, and with respect to their own selves. Prince is by no means alone in taking such an attitude to the diverse personalities of a patient—it is practically impossible to avoid. Sybil's alternates often showed their own attitudes and concerns to problems *common* to them all: for instance, the two male alternates often did

some say number seven. It's neither, my friend, neither. It's number one' (Dickens, *Oliver Twist*).

useful jobs around the house, Vanessa took a job in a launderette, while Marcia submitted a pop song to an agent—all to assist with the financial situation.

Thus five of the six conditions suggest that there are several members of the family Beauchamp; and the sixth is ambiguous.

Further considerations

Leaving aside the six conditions, we can find further arguments in favour of affirming plurality, and the rest of this section will list these. None of these is conclusive; each has some weight.

The first consideration derives from the very marked differences in their characters and personalities. It is true that differences of character are not enough, alone, to justify claims that we have more than one person—we all know how much our own moods and styles of behaviour can swing, and how the 'roles people play' vary from context to context. So consistency of character cannot as such be a 'condition of personhood'. All the same, and despite role-playing and mood swings, we can and do identify the distinct personalities and character traits of our friends. And, as we read Prince, it emerges that each of the Beauchamp trio not only had swings of mood, and adopted different attitudes in various circumstances; they also had, each her own, *overall* character. They had entirely distinct, though each internally consistent and coherent (within natural limits), preferences, prejudices, outlooks, moods, ambitions, skills, tastes, and habits. Some of these differences have already been mentioned; Prince ([1968], pp. 288-94) lists some of the specific dissimilarities between *B1* and *B4*. For example, *B1*'s appetite was poor, *B4*'s healthy; *B1* liked her coffee unsweetened and black, whereas *B4* took hers with sugar and cream; *B1* never, *B4* regularly, used vinegar and oil in cooking; *B1* liked soups, milk, broths, brown bread, vegetables, and ice cream, all of which *B4* avoided. *B4* was 'extravagantly fond' of smoking and drinking, but *B1* rarely drank and never smoked. *B1* preferred sober, loose clothes, with low-heeled boots and no rings or brooches; *B4* bought tight, brightly coloured clothes, high-heeled boots, and jewellery. *B1* read devotional books, but *B4* the newspapers. *B1* visited the sick, attended church, sewed, and knitted, all of which bored *B4* to distraction. Perhaps surprisingly, it was *B4* rather than *B1* who was terrified of the dark. Then again, one's 'self-image' is often said to be an important constituent of personality; if so, it is relevant to remember that multiple personalities often regard their physical appearance very differently, and maybe *B1* and *B4* did too—certainly they dressed in violently opposed styles. Whatever the validity of this last point, though, I believe that the accumulation of such differences as these allows us to say that we had very different character types here. A further point in conclusion: a 'character' is a certain kind of unity and continuity of character *traits*, without which we would be unable to describe it; but note that there is no implication in this anodyne remark that the unity/continuity must be 'conscious'.

A second indication (no more than an indication) of plurality is that each of the Beauchamp family could have managed for long periods in sole charge of the body. Indeed *B1*, before she came to see Prince, had had the body to herself for several years. *B4* could have survived well in any circumstances, probably better than *B1* alone: she was a tough lassie. Sally had various remarkable abnormalities; for example, she never experienced ill-health, pain, tiredness, hunger, or thirst, and claimed never to sleep. (Usoffah Abdullah, Son of Omega—one of Jason/Jusky's alternates—was a bit like this too.) Nevertheless, she showed that when she was in a relatively responsible mood she could take adequate care of herself, remembering the necessity to eat, drink, lie down, and so forth. Of course, all would have liked to have had the body solely to herself; had Prince confirmed any one of them in undisputed charge of it, anyone would have agreed that here was 'the' Miss Beauchamp. Each came across as a relatively normal individual, however dissimilar they were from each other in character and temperament. This degree of autonomy does not hold true of all the cases of multiple personality to be found in the literature, where we find personalities most of which are less well rounded than at least the three main figures of the family Beauchamp. For instance, as already noted, the personalities of Jonah/ Jusky were specialized to deal with specific sorts of incident. Here again, though, it seems that each could have managed alone, even if not always very adequately. Of the sixteen personalities of Sybil, on the other hand, it seems highly improbable that either of the two male alternates could have managed well with a woman's body; and Rene's four-year-old alternate Sissy would have been helpless by herself for long. However, if we stick to Miss Beauchamp, there then seems no doubt about the adequacy of *at least B1* and *B4*.

A third, equally non-conclusive, argument for regarding the family Beauchamp as a plurality is that it is by no means obvious, as one reads the book, that *B2* is indeed going to come out at the top of the heap. There is even room for some scepticism about whether Prince was correct in picking on her as 'the' real Miss Beauchamp; it is evident that his views on which contender had the best title changed from time to time, and were to some extent determined by what he thought a young lady at the turn of the century *ought* to be like. Certainly he had Sally's confirmation that *B2* was the same as the pre-trauma Christine Beauchamp, but it is paradoxical, to put it mildly, to take the word of that young lady in the circumstances. If *B4* had succeeded in her plan of escaping to Europe, who would have ended up in charge? Maybe Henri de Montherlant was right: 'It is through chance that, from among the various individuals of which each of us is composed, one emerges rather than another' ('Explicit Mysterium' [1931]).

There is a fourth indication: we should observe that Miss Beauchamp's plurality was not only diachronic—Sally, *B1*, and *B4* by turns—but also synchronic. For whenever *B1*, *B2*, or *B4* were in control, Sally coexisted as a second consciousness, aware of all their actions and of the thoughts of at least *B1* and *B2*, while keeping her own counsel. Her consciousness was substantially independent of that of the personality in charge of the body at the time. We have already seen that Sally observed, as an amused spectator, *B1*'s dreams, even being able to give a fuller account of them than could *B1*. Predictably enough, then, she could also watch and report the confused and chaotic thoughts of *B1* in delirium. Then again, if either of the other two were walking along in a trance, not noticing much around them, Sally might be attending with keen interest to details of the passing scene. Indeed, she could be alert when the personality in control of the body was completely un-conscious: chloroform, which suppressed the consciousness of *B1* and *B4*, seemed to have no effect on Sally's. (Compare the 'hidden observer' revealed by hypnosis, who sometimes seems immune to normal anaesthetics.) Conversely, though, she could switch off her attention when either of the others was engaged in something that bored her (so that she alone proved ignorant of shorthand, which *B1* and *B4* both decided to learn, and she could not understand French, which Miss Beauchamp had learned as a schoolgirl). All in all, we find with Sally the synchronic duality of consciousness that is also a feature of split-brain patients under certain experimental conditions. She would have agreed with Oscar Wilde: 'One's real life is so often the life that one does not lead' (*L'Envoi to 'Rose-leaf and Apple-leaf'* [1882]).

It is true that to get a simultaneous *manifestation* of a second con-sciousness, or at any rate a manifestation that was not fleeting and unpredictable, artificial circumstances were required just as they are usually required to induce a split in commissurotomy patients. For example, after *B4* had destroyed an autobiography that Sally had been at pains to write, *B4* became somewhat remorseful and allowed her hand to be used 'automatically' by Sally to rewrite the document. Thus Sally wrote with '*B4*'s hand', while *B4* commented caustically upon what appeared on the page before her. This situation was no less contrived, in its own way, than are the experiments on split-brain patients.[16] But on top of this Sally provided quantities of *ex post facto* evidence of her simultaneous existence, not all of which could be dismissed (although Prince was laudably sceptical about some of it) since it helped explain and make intelligible some otherwise inexplicable lacunae in *B1*'s own account of her experience. So there was evidence of synchronic duality for all, or almost all, of the time, with the sole exception of the periods in which Sally herself was 'out'. (This point, of course, only works to suggest that *Sally* was a discrete individual.)

A fifth and final argument for regarding *B1*, *B4*, and Sally as distinct persons appeals to intuition: to the consideration of what it must have been like from the inside, from the first-person perspective. The best way of putting this is in terms of Nagel's well-known question (Nagel [1974/1979*b*]), 'what is it like for an *X* to be an *X*?'. I have argued that intuition is a problematic and dangerous tool to use in consideration of problems of personality identity, and I am myself unsure just what is being asked by the 'what is it like . . . ?' question.[17] However, since Nagel's question appeals so strongly to the intuitions of so many, it would be remiss not to consider its weight in this instance.

It is an interesting and puzzling fact about the topic of personal identity and personal survival that the answer one is tempted to give in response to assorted puzzle-cases may differ depending on whether the question is framed in the first or third person. For instance, even if it seems sensible to say of another person that after (say) a thought-

---

[16] This again tends to oversimplify the position. Sally was able, by a technique she described as 'willing', to induce positive and negative hallucinations in both *B1* and *B4*; she could induce aboulia (failure of will) or apraxia (inability to act), especially if the primary personality was, as she put it, 'rattled'; she could tease *B1* by making her transpose letters in the words she was writing; and so forth. But these and similar instances cannot of themselves indicate the co-presence of a secondary consciousness as clearly as does the arranged phenomenon of her automatic writing.

[17] I am most perplexed about Nagel's question. Put simply, I do not think that I do know what it is like to be me. That is, I could write a tediously long self-analysis, which would seem to me to give any reader as much information as I have on this score; but I am sure that this is not what Nagel means. But if not, then I do not know what he does mean. I explore this problem in greater detail in ch. 7.

experimental body-swap, one of the resulting individuals would be 'more or less' him, of oneself one tends to think that either the result will be *me*, or it won't: no degrees about it.[18] So we find, I think, with the Beauchamp family. Because *B4* ceased to exist as far as she was concerned when *B2* was in charge, *B2*'s survival meant death, extinction, for *B4*; as it also did for *B1*. It was little or no consolation for either to be told that they did in fact survive as *B2*, that *B2* claimed each of them as herself. This refusal to be consoled seems reasonable enough—consider the difficulty of persuading anyone that he had continued to exist as an active agent over a lengthy period of time of which he had absolutely no recollection, simply on the grounds that an individual, of whom he knew nothing directly, claimed to *be* him. There is, in short, *nothing* that it was like to be 'Miss Beauchamp' during the time that she was split up into the three dominant personalities. There was, however, something that it was like to be Sally, something that it was like to be *B1*, something that it was like to be *B4*. Whatever the difficulties with the tool of intuition in philosophy, when it comes to the fundamental and heartfelt claim 'that's not *me*', as each of these three personalities would say about any of the others, we surely ought not to disregard it lightly.

If we press this line of reasoning, then, we seem to be pointed in the direction of affirming multiplicity. Just the same difficulty, of course, arises with the less dramatic dissociations we mentioned briefly at the beginning of this chapter; there seems nothing that it is like to be the Revd Ansel Bourne that would include both his fugue and his normal state, and nothing that it is like to be both feeling and not feeling pain when undergoing hypnosis. However, with these cases we have a great deal that points us in the direction of singularity; with multiple personality this consideration is yet another of a number of factors suggesting plurality.

Summary

The brunt of the argument suggests that we ought to conclude that during the period from the appearance of Sally and *B4* to that of *B2*,

---

[18] It may be *wrong* to say that there are 'no degrees' allowable in answer to the question 'will that be me, or not?' Ingenious thought experiments have been brought in to suggest that 'more or less me' might sometimes be the most appropriate thing to say. But such thought experiments must meet the conditions imposed on legitimate thought experiments which were suggested in ch. 1. Until one is proposed that does meet them, we should hold on to reality: this is not the way that our linguistic habits have it. At minimum, then, our actual prejudice for 'no degrees!' must be taken seriously.

Prince had three people to deal with. Arguments in favour of affirming plurality are more numerous than those suggesting singularity. What we ought to say and what we do say, however, may not always jibe.

6. UNITY; AND THE GREEKS

Few will like the suggestion that there might be three people jointly occupying one body. To the extent that we dislike it, the foregoing tends to encourage the conclusion that with Miss Beauchamp the concept of a person breaks down completely. Powerful and intuitively plausible considerations militate in favour of plurality; fewer suggest uniqueness, but the 'one body per person' presupposition is also powerfully persuasive. If one shudders from allowing that there are three people here, the only alternative seems to be to say that the concept 'person' has fractured under the strain. That is the negative result. It is important in that with it I can bear out the claim of the first chapter, not only that truth is often stranger than fiction, but that actual puzzle-cases serve better than thought-experimental ones to probe and test our concepts. Multiple personality patients present us with situations in which all the facts are in, or can in principle be collected (albeit they need careful handling, description, and interpretation). We no longer need to ask what we *would* say; we can look and see what people—the people literally and actually involved with the patients on a daily basis, in the world as it is—*do* say. And here it appears that we have no clear consensus about what to say: the concept of a person fails to cope under this particular strain. But, as I remarked in Chapter 1, we learn much about a concept by discovering where, and why, its remit ends.

More positively, though, such cases should compel one to reflect more deeply upon the degree and quality of unity and continuity—*whether conscious or not*—that we should require of an individual who is to be considered a single person. The example of Miss Beauchamp highlights the enormous importance of the normative pressure on personhood, without which we would surely have rested content with saying that she was several people; persons are, very centrally and significantly, what society thinks persons ought to be. B4's struggle against her own extinction stood no chance against Prince's insistence that proper people are single and unitary people.

If society's norms are what help determine our judgements about personal identity, it would not be surprising to find that different ages and cultures sometimes have slightly different attitudes to the significance of unity. Particularly interesting is the extent of psychological *dis*unity that Homer, especially the Homer of the *Iliad*, allowed his characters, while he simultaneously and unproblematically regarded them as single individuals.[19] We shall discuss the ancient Greek picture at greater length in Chapter 7, but it will be helpful to introduce the Iliadic picture now, since it holds particular relevance for cases of multiple personality.

The archaic Greek disunity (as we would now regard it) was not just psychological, but extended to the body. From vase paintings of the eighth century BC we can see that the human form was thought of as an articulated collection of limbs—the arms, legs, torso, and head are pictured as prominent and rounded, while the joints are unstressed and wasp-like. This corresponds well with the absence in Greek of a singular term to designate what we mean by 'body'. Apparent candidates, such as *soma* or *derma*, need to be translated as 'corpse' and 'skin' respectively. When Homer needed to talk of the living human body, he used one of two plural forms both meaning 'limbs'—*melea* and *guia*. So man was seen as a physical aggregate. More crucially for our purposes, the *Iliad* portrays him as a psychological aggregate as well, despite the fact that Homer also uses the personal pronouns and proper names in a wholly unembarrassed way. Decisions, for instance, could be made by the *thumos*, the *phren* or *phrenes*, *noos*, *kradie*, *ker*, *etor*, or by the individual; action could be initiated by any of these but also on occasion by the hands, feet, or knees. One example (there are hundreds available) will illustrate the point. In the following lines Zeus is talking of Achilles: 'Let him take thought then in his *phren* and his *thumos* lest, strong though he may be, he may not be able to endure my attack . . . his *etor* thinks nothing of declaring himself equal with me, whom even the other gods fear' (*Iliad*, xv. 163 f.). The point to note about this and other such passages is not so much the plurality of centres of thought and motivation (anatomically and psychologically distinct though they may be) but rather the coexistence of descriptions of their activity with references to 'him' or 'Achilles'; a single individual just was a plurality of that kind.

After Homer this 'one over many' fades considerably (indeed, it is already less noticeable in the *Odyssey*). Today we seem to require a very stringent unity, the modern-dress version of Locke's description of the person; a continuity and a unity of consciousness. It is surely worth

---

[19] See especially Snell [1953], Adkins [1970], and Jaynes [1976].

reflecting that even though Homer may have been too liberal for our present social, moral, legal, and political tastes, our present emphasis upon a unity of consciousness might for its part be unduly restrictive, so that some compromise position should be sought. For, first, the intuition that the unity and continuity of consciousness are centrally important runs into difficulties (as we have seen) not merely because we have but a fuzzy grasp upon what is meant by the terms, but also because of the oddities of fugue states, trance states, hypnosis, and multiple personality (and the intuition does not have an easy ride with the everyday phenomena of sleeping and dreaming, self-deception, weakness of will, and divided attention either). Second, to stress the unity or continuity of *consciousness* inevitably highlights the tip of the iceberg of mentality that is conscious mentality, thereby fostering the bias, established by Descartes, in favour of one particular kind of account of the self.

Inasmuch as the extent of unity and continuity required of a person is determined in part by social norms, it appears that we *need* no such strong and stringent conditions as those that have traditionally been taken to be involved in 'unity and continuity of consciousness'. What we require is enough consistency and stability amongst all of a man's mental states (whether conscious or not) to enable us to treat the individual as a single Intentional or rational system;[20] so that, for example, most of the time his behaviour can be shown to be intelligible against the background of his past behaviour and experience, so that most of the time we can hold him responsible for his activities, applying praise and blame appropriately, so that most of the time he can steer a roughly consistent and autonomous path, seeking reasonably effective and practical means to an ordered set of short-term and long-term goals. Unity and continuity of consciousness evidently help enormously—if by 'unity and continuity of consciousness' we mean *inter alia* his recognition and acceptance of past actions, and of intentions for the future, as his own. Nevertheless adequate functioning (and 'adequacy' will be relative to the demands of the society) may be compatible with extensive dissociation on this conscious level.

Were we to weaken our requirements on unity—in other words, were we to acknowledge that persons are or might be less well integrated than 'unity of consciousness' seems to require—there might be several advant-

---

[20] 'Intentional system' is a term usefully coined by Dennett [1971]. Briefly, an Intentional system is one whose behaviour can best, or at least most perspicuously, be described and/or explained in terms that deploy intentional (or 'intensional') terminology; i.e. by reference to states which are 'about' things.

ages. It should mean that we would have less initial suspicion of psychological theories that, like Freud's at one stage, hypothesize a tripartite structure of superego, ego, and id, or which add to our model of the mind a postulate of a dynamic and systematic unconscious. Perhaps we would—and should—be less troubled by the present trend among cognitive psychologists to ascribe 'characteristically human' predicates to systems and subsystems in the brain. At a different level it might help to clear obstacles from the path of some psychological research. To take just one example: Geschwind [1964] has suggested that weakening our requirements on unity might benefit many branches of the science, particularly developmental psychology (the association cortex, which as its name suggests 'associates' various psychological functions, is ontogenetically the most recent, and hence is the last part of the brain to lay down its connections; young children may be much less unified than we tend to suppose). Presumably the investigation of senile dementia too may be similarly handicapped by the difficulty of squaring strong constraints on unity with the manifest evidence of several kinds of disunity and incoherence. Turning to traditional philosophical issues, it is not impossible that the paradoxes of self-deception and *akrasia* might be eased a little.

That is all speculative. What seems less so is that apparently nothing can alleviate the problem posed by such as Jonah/Jusky and Miss Beauchamp. Here we see the fracturing of the concept of a person.

5

Being in Two Minds

Like Robespierre, I thought I was Joan of Arc and Bonaparte.
How little one knows oneself.

(Charles de Gaulle)

1. THE PROBLEM INTRODUCED

We continue the examination of the sixth condition, the 'special form of consciousness' condition, and its 'unity' or 'continuity', by turning to look at the peculiar data provided by split-brain patients. These patients are people who have suffered from severe and uncontrollable epileptic seizures, and the operation called commissurotomy is a drastic but often effective way of mitigating the effects of these attacks.[1] One by-product of the operation, however—as we shall see—is to raise a question about the number of centres of consciousness, or minds, that commissurotomy patients, and by extension normal people too, may have. Worse: if we assume that there is one mind per person, we start to question how many *people* there are in the commissurotomy patient's body, or, by extension, in the body of normal people. If there are indeed *two*, as some argue, this will clearly have dramatic implications for the question of the identification of persons—it would challenge most forcefully the working assumption that there is (roughly speaking) one person per body. These questions arise because commissurotomy presents us with the clearest and most drastic instance of conscious disunity that one could imagine: an individual with two coexisting streams of consciousness. All this will be described more fully below; but first we should give a rough outline sketch of what is known about duplication and specialization in the brain.

---

[1] Later this comment will be clarified and qualified. There are various forms of the operation, and varying success rates from them.

2. OUR TWO BRAINS

Much of our knowledge of hemispheric duplication and specialization has of course come from commissurotomy. However, there were well-informed speculations and guesses well before that; first, perhaps, with Marc Dax in 1836, and then in increasing abundance after Paul Broca in the 1860s discovered 'his' speech area in the left frontal lobe. Now, with the advent of new techniques (such as EEGs, evoked potential analysis, the Wada test, CAT scans, PET scans, CT scans, measuring blood flow with radioactive isotopes, NMR scans)[2] we have hard data that can be elicited without commissurotomy, and from normal as well as from lesioned brains. These data are doubly 'hard', in that the results are decisive, but it is not quite clear what they are decisive *for*: their interpretation is a very vexed issue. Anyway, since the data are to some extent independent of commissurotomy patients, I shall sketch very briefly and in rough outline how the hemispheres are thought to divide or double their functions, before going on to sketch the split-brain operation and its effects.

In general each hemisphere (left and right) controls, and receives input from, its contralateral side. For example, the left half of the visual field of each eye feeds information into the right hemisphere, and vice versa (although input from *peripheral* vision is not segregated). The left hemisphere has primary motor control over the right arm, hand, and leg, the right over the left. There are exceptions to, and modifications of, this general rule, though. Some senses are not lateralized very crisply; hearing is one example. Tastes are equally accessible to either hemisphere. Smell is *ipsilaterally* organized—that is, the right nostril

---

2 EEGs are electroencephalograms—patterns of electrical activity detected by electrodes placed on the scalp. Evoked potential analyses average the EEG waveforms that follow successive presentations of a given stimulus. The Wada test briefly anaesthetizes one hemisphere by the injection of sodium amobarbital into the carotid artery on one side of the neck. CAT scans detect activity by the enzyme choline-acetyltransferase, thereby allowing one to trace the links between cells. PET scans (positron emission tomography scans) detect the radiation emitted by positron-emitting isotopes injected intravenously. This allows one to get an image of the metabolic rate in any region of the brain. CT scans are computerized tomography scans, used to reconstruct images of a brain-slice; this helps especially to pinpoint lesions in the brain. Blood flow can be detected by injecting Xenon 133, a radioactive isotope, into the carotid arteries; this emits gamma radiation which can be measured. NMR scans are nuclear magnetic resonance scans. Hydrogen atoms 'resonate' in the water molecules of living tissue, and this resonance can be detected by radiowaves and a large electromagnet. It allows one to calculate very accurately the density of brain tissue. There are various further techniques which I do not cite.

feeds in to the right hemisphere, and the left in to the left. Moreover, to muddy the picture further, both hemispheres control, and receive kinaesthetic input from, the muscles of face and neck; each also has some (relatively crude) ipsilateral control over the limbs of the body.

Apart from dividing most sensory input and bodily control between themselves, the two hemispheres show specialization, as well as division, of labour. This seems to hold true for strands, or facets, of many competences; but two instances of specialization are distinctive and striking, and have been much discussed in the literature. One is speech production: in *most* people (probably about 95 per cent of right-handers) this is primarily controlled by the left hemisphere. The right has a certain capacity to comprehend speech (the extent of its capacity is much debated),[3] and can sometimes read, write, and utter some words; but typically it can produce rather few. There are some people in whom this lateralization of capacity is reversed, so that the right hemisphere gets the power of speech rather than the left; in particular, left-handers. Even then, though, about 70 per cent of left-handers still have speech controlled by the right hemisphere. Some people show a less marked monopoly of speech by left (or right) hemisphere than do others. For example, there is some reason to suppose that the cerebral hemispheres in women's brains are in certain respects less crisply specialized than they are in men's brains. However, for reasons of simplicity I shall proceed by using as an example the typical right-handed male subject, in whose brain the left hemisphere is articulate, the right almost dumb. The right hemisphere, though, has the second distinctive specialization: it is considerably superior to the left in constructional, manipulo-spatial, tasks.

I add here a short parenthetical paragraph. It is perhaps no mere coincidence that these two (language and manipulo-spatial ability) are the major functions that seem dominated by left and right hemispheres respectively. For it looks as though they might both compete for cerebral space in the same area of the brain, in and around the inferior parietal lobule. Language, as Washburn and Harding [1972] have conjectured, may have derived from the primitive need of manipulatory

---

[3] The right hemisphere has sophisticated cognitive abilities, some of which rely on language. For instance, it can match a word with an associated item picked out from an array (e.g. if given the word 'comb', the left hand may pick up a brush). But the precise nature of its linguistic abilities is much contested. Generally speaking it will associate pictures of things with other pictures that *look* similar; that is, if shown a picture of a cake, it will pick on a picture of a hat as the 'nearest' alternative, whereas the left hemisphere goes more by function, and will select a picture of a knife and fork.

animals to *name* and *request* the objects and tools that they *used*. Suppose that this hypothesis is correct; then it is significant that linguistic and manipulo-spatial capacities, if they are to function adequately, both require the same sort of (cross-modally convergent) neural mechanisms. Thus it would be no accident that the developing linguistic capability should begin in a region heavily implicated in tool-using; and that it should start to oust from one of the hemispheres the manipulo-spatial capability, since it needs to exploit the same mechanisms and hence the same region of the brain (see Gazzaniga and LeDoux [1978], pp. 55 ff.). This is only a conjecture at present; whatever the genesis of the specializations, though, these two capacities are agreed on all hands to divide reasonably sharply and clearly between the two hemispheres.[4]

There is a whole host of further capacities the performance of which seems to be unequally divided between the two half brains, but I shall not list them here. It is essential to remember that there are very considerable individual differences, and the data are abominably hard to interpret. Furthermore, even when there is broad agreement, it usually remains broad: for example, although most would agree that the left hemisphere is dominant for language, just *how* it is dominant, and what the right hemisphere does or does not contribute to language comprehension and production (metaphorical understanding? humour? tone of voice?), is hotly debated. Measurement of blood flow during linguistic activity shows that the regions of the right hemisphere corresponding to the language centres of the left are about as active as the latter, and so they presumably contribute a significant amount. Conjectures about different differences between the two, such as their respective roles in emotional experience, are supported; but supported by very slippery and inconclusive evidence. The issue has been further muddied by those rightly labelled 'dichotomaniacs'—people who want to find in the left hemisphere their pet prejudices like 'the Western mind', and in the right, 'the Eastern mind'; or who write articles entitled 'Ten Ways to Develop Your Right Brain', and other such nonsense. Moreover, whatever may be the variable amount of hemispheric differentiation, which is very much a matter of mystery at the moment, it is important to remember that there are numerous functions they divide almost

[4] If this conjecture holds up, then we have some further indirect evidence for the idea—adumbrated in ch. 1—that the '6 conditions' on personhood should be increased to 7: adding tool construction and use. That is, it would suggest that it is no accident that humans excel other animals both in tool-making and tool-manipulation, and in linguistic ability.

equally: the fact remains that each hemisphere can see, hear, smell, taste, and recognize objects by touch, and each can control bodily movement—there is a vast amount of *duplication* of capacity.

Now this duplication and specialization of capacity may seem at first sight to be just a scientifically interesting fact, which need not necessarily engage philosophers. It is, of course, a *very* interesting fact, encouraging research into the details of the specializations of the two hemispheres; and it requires one to explain why in almost all animals we find cerebral duplication—why has nature been so liberal? Alone, though, the interesting fact poses no conceptual puzzles. It does not do so because of the great cerebral commissures. These are the bands of nerve fibres, millions of fibres, which link parallel regions of the two hemispheres and transmit data received by one to the other. The net result is that each hemisphere gets the information that may have been received initially only by the other.

But conceptual and theoretically intractable puzzles do arise, and arise very strikingly, with commissurotomy. The nature and history of the operation should now be briefly described.

3. COMMISSUROTOMY

Commissurotomy is surgery carried out in an attempt to alleviate the worst effects of intractable epilepsy, and involves cutting through part or all of one or more of the cerebral commissures. These are the bands

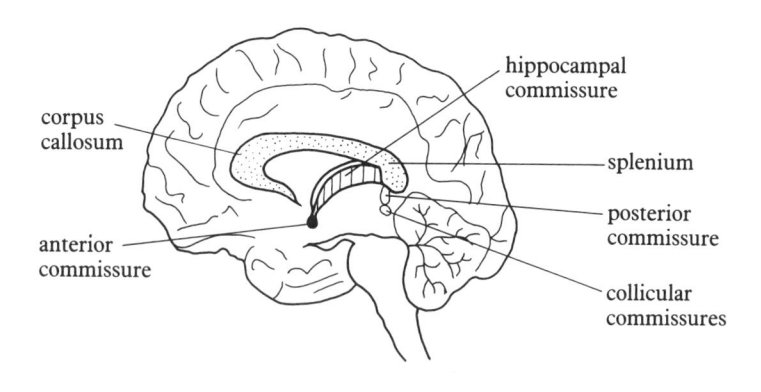

Fig. 7

of nerve fibres which link the left and right cerebral cortex (see Fig. 7). The corpus callosum is the largest of these—consisting of several million nerve fibres—and it is this, or part of it, that is usually sectioned.

Van Wagenen, in the 1940s, was the first to operate on human subjects, and he sectioned the forward (anterior) half of the corpus callosum. (With a couple of patients he also cut through a separate fibre-band called the anterior commissure.) However, the operation did not give him the results for which he had hoped. Although the patients suffered few after-effects from the surgery, and in some of them the severity of the epileptic attacks was alleviated, the improvement was irregular and unpredictable. So before long this method of treatment was discontinued. In general, what surprised all concerned was the very *absence* of symptoms after this major surgery, surgery which involved cutting through so many million nerve fibres. Akelaitis, who tested Van Wagenen's patients post-operatively, famously failed to find any behavioural change at all, apart from occasional relief from the severity of the epileptic attacks. This led Lashley to suggest that the function of the corpus callosum was to prevent the half-brains from sagging—a kind of internal scaffolding—while McCulloch sardonically conjectured that the corpus callosum was there to transmit epileptic seizures across from one cortical hemisphere to the other.

This failure to spot facts which we have now learned to take for granted should not be thought surprising. After all, in the normal run of things the saccadic jumps of the eye ensure that each object viewed is seen in both half-fields, and hence by each hemisphere; peripheral vision, in either half-field, generates input to both half-brains; and, since people can usually see what each hand is doing, each hemisphere, not only the contralateral one, will have information about what the hands are up to. Moreover, not everything is *crisply* lateralized. Each hemisphere, as we have noted, has *some* ipsilateral control over its own side of the body. The ears supply some information to their ipsilateral hemispheres, even though the auditory signal is stronger to the contralateral side. Taste, and input from the face and neck muscles, are not lateralized at all. It needs to be stressed, too, that patients with such severe epilepsy as to justify a drastic operation like this often have substantial brain damage elsewhere as a by-product of constant and major epileptic attacks, and so occasional oddities in behaviour would not in the 1940s have been found particularly remarkable.

The verdict changed in the following decade. In the 1950s Myers and Sperry (Sperry [1961]), working mainly with cats and then with chimpanzees, showed that sensory input to each half-brain could be segregated after total section of the corpus callosum. (With their experimental animals, they sometimes severed the optic chiasm as well; this meant that input to each eye went only to its ipsilateral hemisphere, since the contralateral channels had been cut. Thus it became much easier to explore the effects of segregating visual input.) This encouraged people to try commissurotomy again on human patients. The cats and chimps seemed to suffer no ill effects from the surgery; and neurosurgeons guessed that the failure of Van Wagenen's operations may have been due to the fact that the surgery was not sufficiently heroic—that he had not disconnected the two cortical hemispheres completely enough. Vogel and Bogen, then, performed complete commissurotomies on a number of epileptic patients—see for instance Bogen, Fisher, and Vogel [1965]. *This* more drastic operation did indeed dramatically reduce the severity of seizures. But not only that: ingenious and elaborate tests showed up further exciting and often bizarre consequences of the hemispheric disconnection.

The last stage to mention in the history so far is that improved techniques, such as those described in note (1), have now made it easier to locate more precisely the areas of the brain thought most likely to transmit epileptic discharges. This has allowed surgeons to return to a more limited commissurotomy, cutting only the fibres connecting the suspect area with the opposite hemisphere. Not only is the surgery less drastic, but it has of course enabled researchers to study the functions of specific parts of the commissures by examining the effects of this partial commissurotomy. I cite this recent development for completeness; none the less in what follows I shall describe the effects of the complete commissurotomy, since the greater the apparent splitting of the mind, the greater the alleged problem for personal identity.

The easiest way of describing these results (although—as I shall argue later—by no means the most perspicuous way) is by talking in terms of a divided consciousness. If the experimental set-up can be so arranged that the input is sharply lateralized (so that only one hemisphere receives it) then the unity of consciousness is lost. Dozens of examples could be given, but one or two will be enough to illustrate the phenomenon. Here is one often cited in the literature. L.B., an intelligent eleven-year-old commissurotomy patient, was given a pipe to hold in his left hand; a screen prevented him seeing what he was holding. The pipe was removed, and he was then asked to write, with his left hand, the name of the object he had just held. The left hand is of course primarily controlled by the right hemisphere, which had received the 'pipe' input from the left hand's tactual sensing of the pipe. Slowly and laboriously L.B., with his left hand, wrote 'P' and 'I'. At this point the left hemisphere took over—using its ipsilateral control over the left hand—and, changing the 'I' into an 'E', swiftly wrote 'PENCIL'. The right hemisphere took over again, crossed out the letters 'ENCIL', and *drew* a pipe.[5] More generally, whenever there is visual input to the left half-field of each eye (and the information in the left half-fields can be isolated from information in the right by using a tachistoscope, or by Zaidel's visual occluder, the Z-lens)[6] this goes only to the right hemisphere; the speaking left hemisphere does not get the information; and hence the patient cannot say what it is that the right hemisphere has seen. The right hemisphere, though, is well aware of what object it was, and can prove as much by pointing to a picture of it, picking out the object from a randomly assorted pile of objects, or by inducing a frown when it hears the left (speaking) hemisphere guessing wrong.

Of the many case-studies in the literature there is another which illustrates particularly clearly a direct inter-hemispheric conflict, and this is in the domain of constructional tasks. The right hemisphere (left hand) is typically much better at such tasks than is the left. However, Sperry asked one of his commissurotomy subjects (W.J.) to recreate, with his *right* hand (left hemisphere), patterns shown on a number of cards. He had a number of blocks to fit together into the right shapes. The film Sperry took of the experiment shows W.J. making rather a poor job of it with his right hand.[7] Slowly and steadily, though, the left hand creeps in, brushes aside the right hand, and starts building rather more efficiently. The experimenter is seen pushing away the intrusive left hand. After a little while, along comes the left hand again. This time we see W.J. grasping the wrist of the left hand with the right, and pushing it away himself. But you can't keep a good hand down; after

---

[5] I think that Levy [1969] was the first to discuss this case. Nagel, who describes it in his [1971], first informed me of it.

[6] A tachistoscope is a device that flashes stimuli for very brief periods on a screen to the left or right of a midpoint on which the subject is fixing his gaze. The exposure is so brief that there is no time for the eye to move to focus on the stimulus, and so only the contralateral hemisphere receives the input. Zaidel's Z lens consists of a contact lens that blocks off one half of the visual field of either eye. Thus, if the other eye is patched, the subject wearing the lens can be given time to look at the stimulus, and yet only one half-field (i.e. one hemisphere, in split-brain patients) will receive the information.

[7] I saw this film in Princeton, in 1971.

another pause, in creeps the irrepressible left hand once again. This time W.J. takes his left hand in his right, pushes it away—and sits on it, to stop it interfering further.

We should add that there *are* occasional instances of right–left conflict and inconsistency even outside these artificial experimental set-ups. There are not many of them, though, and the few that exist tend to be given undue weight, by being rehearsed in the literature over and over again. For example, a patient has been reported whose one hand spurned a dish of food while the other was trying to pull it closer. Another patient found each hand choosing different clothes to wear in the morning; and reported that every now and again her right hand would slap her awake when she was in danger of oversleeping. There was even one patient, with a left hand that had behaved aggressively to his wife, who made Gazzaniga remove himself rather smartly from the vicinity when he saw the 'hostile' left hand pick up an axe. Fascinating as these case histories undoubtedly are, we do not need them for our present purposes: the splits which are artificially induced alone pose difficult problems. Moreover, it is essential to re-emphasize that any epileptic patient ill enough to need such surgery very often has associated brain damage. It is too often forgotten that fewer than half the total number of commissurotomy patients are competent enough mentally for the results of their post-operative tests to be usable—there are too many effects that could easily be due to damage in other regions of the brain. Thus it is by no means clear that the sorts of conflict illustrated above are necessarily due to callosal section. Indeed, concentration upon these rare but dramatic conflicts in everyday situations is even counter-productive. It tends to divert attention from the documented *problems* (rather than conflicts) that trouble split-brain patients after the operation, even outside the experimental situation: they find it hard, for instance, to associate names to new faces (see Levy, Trevarthen, and Sperry [1972]), and those patients who were good at geometry before the operation found it much harder afterwards. There are subtle and hard-to-measure consequences of commissurotomy, by no means all of which have yet been detected.

Let us turn to the philosophers' interpretation of the data, and to the difficulties or paradoxes for understanding personal identity.

4. PHILOSOPHICAL PERPLEXITIES

It is the manifest conflict of knowledge, purpose, and behaviour, shown by the commissurotomy patients in experimental situations, that has attracted the attention of philosophers and of theoretically minded scientists. It has seemed to both Nagel [1971/1979*b*] and Puccetti [1973, 1981] that the concept of a person is fractured, or at least jeopardized, by these findings. Nagel, for example, warns:

the natural conception of a single person controlled by a mind . . . may come into conflict with the physiological facts . . . it is possible that the ordinary, simple idea of a single person will come to seem quaint one day, when the complexities of the human control system become clearer and we become less certain that there is anything very important that we are *one* of (Nagel [1979*b*], p. 164).

Puccetti, at least in his first paper, goes further, concluding that 'even in the normal, cerebrally intact human being there must be two persons, though before the era of commissurotomy experiments we had no way of knowing this' ([1973], p. 351). His later article talks rather of two *minds*, but in the 'Author's Response' to the discussion of his paper he insists that he has not abandoned 'the two-person view . . . on grounds that I cannot make sense of one person having two minds' ([1981], p. 119).

Nagel and Puccetti reach these interesting conclusions by arguing that the unity or singleness of conscious control—which is, as I understand them, taken to be the same as a mind—is lost, or perhaps duplicated, in such patients; and that this observation licenses the inference that we are dealing with two people (Puccetti), or at least not clearly or simply one (Nagel). Puccetti adds the claim that if commissurotomy patients are really two people, then we must agree that all *normal* individuals are dual persons as well.

The argument from the experimental data to the fragmentation, or bisection, of the person runs roughly as follows.

First, there is the proven fact that one of the patient's hemispheres cannot use any information that is available solely to the other. If we try to describe what this can mean in terms of the patient, rather than in terms of his half-brains, we want to say that he knows and does not know that *p*; that he acts purposefully and does not know that he is acting; that he disagrees with and disputes his own judgement; that he is both aware and unaware of an unpleasant smell; that he hears and does not hear an order—which he obeys. This certainly seems to give us a split in the unity of consciousness—*whatever* we are going to understand by that phrase. The central thrust of this is nothing less than a violation of the law of non-contradiction. We break this law as soon as we permit ourselves to say that one and the same entity both knows and does not know that p, for nothing can, at time t, be said to ϕ and not to ϕ. Therefore, since brain bisection provides us with cases in which *somehow* the patient knows (ϕs) and *somehow* does not know (ϕ), he cannot himself be the subject of such attributions—*there must logically be two different subjects.*

Second, each hemisphere by itself does have its own unity of consciousness. There is *intra*hemispheric, even if not *inter*hemispheric, integration of information and purpose, and each half-brain can sustain complex, conscious, and organized cognitive activity. Put another way, an individual with a hemispherectomy of either hemisphere has a unity of consciousness. (A hemispherectomy is the surgical removal of the cerebral cortex of one hemisphere.) Therefore the brain-bisected patient has two unities of consciousness.

Third, to have a mind is, or requires, a single such unity, so these patients have two minds; or at least they do not clearly have one mind. We may want to quibble with the idea that 'mind' is so closely tied to 'unity of consciousness'; this is something to which we will return. For the moment, let us accept it.

Fourth, minds and persons are related one:one.

So therefore, fifth, a commissurotomy patient cannot be a single person.

Finally, sixth, the only difference between normal people and commissurotomy patients lies in the commissures, which are simply channels of communication; thus we are in fact as fragmented, or bisected, as they are, even though we may not realize this. In fact, if we *are* tempted to go along with Puccetti and say that there are two minds post-operatively, it is certainly the best explanation by far of such a puzzling fact to say that there were two minds pre-operatively as well, in people without a bisected brain. Otherwise one, or both, of these minds would be new—not having existed before. It is evidently extremely difficult to say of either, or of both, that they have just sprung into existence: each has consciousness of itself as the same 'thinking intelligent being' as the patient before the operation, each has capacities which had to be learned and developed over time.

Pucetti, in his later [1981] paper, adds a slightly different argument. He notes that if a word like *teacup* is projected on to a screen tachistoscopically, *tea* to the left of the midpoint on which the subject is asked to fixate his gaze, and *cup* to the right, then the subject's left hemisphere sees, and can report on, the word *cup*, while the mute right hemisphere sees, and can indicate non-verbally, that it was *tea* that it saw. The normal subject, of course, sees *teacup*. How does he manage this? The obvious suggestion is that we have some fusing mechanism. But according to Puccetti there is no evidence that there is any such device. If we reject the hypothesis of such a fusing mechanism, then

in the callosally intact human brain the word *teacup* is seen at the same time in both cerebral hemispheres, half the word registering in area 17 and the other half (probably) in the prestriate cortex (Sperry [1970]) of each hemisphere. If this is what really happens, consciousness does not span both hemispheres; otherwise, without the fusing assumption, we normals would see *teacup teacup* instead of just *teacup*. Thus, with regard to vision, a split brain does not produce a divided mind but deprives two minds of visual input to the ipsilateral half field (Pucetti [1981], p. 95).

(We shall leave discussion of this argument until the last section (Section 11) of this chapter.) Commissurotomy does not create two minds; it simply allows us to acknowledge the two minds we all have, since post-operatively they can act independently. Before the operation there were still two tapdancers (Puccetti's simile); they simply performed in perfect unison, although one, usually the verbally articulate left, is boss—the right is a 'cerebral helot'.

5. THE LANGUAGE OF BRAINS

There can be little doubt that commissurotomy sets us a *puzzle*. The prima-facie violation of the law of non-contradiction is puzzle enough, even without the further argument that the operation shows that we are not really unified, or that we are all really dual persons.

Before we go on to deal with the puzzle, there is one concession that must be made at once to those who want to talk of two minds: that it is and must be perfectly legitimate to ascribe to either hemisphere the psychological predicates ('sees', 'hears', 'thinks', 'knows', etc.) that are required to describe the behaviour we find. I have indeed been making such ascriptions freely myself, in the preceding sections. L.B.'s right hemisphere knew perfectly well that his left hand had just held a pipe. His left hemisphere guessed, and guessed wrong—so it did not know. We cannot dodge the issue by linguistic manipulation such as 'he knows with his right hemisphere but does not know with his left one', for this just leaves the problem lurking beneath the carpet: does *he* know, or not? (If a normal person points 'with' his left hand, *he* indubitably points, even if his right hand does not.) The reason for the concession is very simple—we just have no alternative; an entirely parallel argument justifies our ascription of psychological predicates to animals and sophisticated computers. We can wrap such ascriptions, whether to half-brains, animals, or computers, in scare-quotes if we like. But this only indicates that we find the uses rather novel and are a bit 'scared' by them, that we regard them as being to a greater or lesser degree extensions of the terms, that we expect that these ascriptions will not behave in all respects like the central cases.

The crucial point is that the unavoidability of such ascriptions is justification enough for their employment. In fact, too, this concession is not as serious as it may seem. We are, or should be, increasingly familiar with the idea that entities other than single human beings can be legitimately ascribed the so-called 'characteristically human' predicates—even if we protect the ascriptions with scare-quotes; Freud, after all, did just this with ego, superego, and id, Plato did much the same 2,000 years earlier, and work in Artificial Intelligence and in neuropsychology would founder if trammelled by the arbitrary constraints of linguistic propriety. Moreover, this is no more than a special case of the wholly general point that the sciences (all sciences) adopt, and then adapt, terms from the everyday vocabulary—such as the 'spin' of electrons, 'reward' neurons, the 'charm' and 'colour' of quarks; and even terms which we now perhaps do not regard as 'borrowed', since they are so well established: 'force', 'mass', 'energy', 'field', or natural 'selection'. Psychology has the same right to extend or redefine everyday terms. We should not, of course, ascribe *more* than we have to; Lloyd Morgan's Canon instructs us always to seek the simplest and most modest explanation when interpreting the behaviour of an animal. For instance, we would prefer to say that a dog was cowering because it feared a beating, than that it was cowering because it feared the pains of hell-fire. We should adopt this maxim when talking about computers and half-brains too, ascribing the minimum that is needed to describe the behaviour. But that minimum we must have. Later, in Section 9, we shall see that ascribing *minds* to half-brains goes considerably beyond what Lloyd Morgan's Canon would permit: even if the right hemisphere knows (or, 'knows') that *p*, it does not necessarily follow that it has a mind.

We return now to examine the difficulties identified in Section 4. In the next section I shall introduce a slew of cases that offer, to a greater or a lesser extent, many of the same paradoxes; these were touched on in the preceding chapter. After that, we shall consider what would count as an explanation for them: what sorts of explanations we should be seeking.

In the last chapter our attention was primarily devoted to the breakdowns in the unity or continuity of consciousness, and in unity and continuity more generally, shown by abnormal states such as fugues, epileptic automatism, hypnosis, and multiple personality. We touched briefly upon some breakdowns seen in everyday life, but did not go into much detail. Now, though, it is worth looking harder at these familiar, everyday phenomena; for we shall see that the bizarre and *outré* results of commissurotomy have many echoes in quite 'normal' goings-on.

1. We might start with the not uncommon state of being unable to realize something fully—when the fact has, as it were, to penetrate our understanding at several levels. Proust's Narrator describes such a situation when he is attempting to come to terms with Albertine's departure:

at every moment there was one more of those innumerable and humble 'selves' that compose our personality which was still unaware of Albertine's departure and must be informed of it; I was obliged—and this was more cruel than if they had been strangers and had not borrowed my sensitivity to pain—to describe to all those 'selves' who did not yet know of it, the calamity that had just occurred, it was necessary that each of them in turn should hear for the first time the words 'Albertine has gone' (Proust, vol. xi, p. 17 of Scott Moncrieff's translation [1969]).

We should note that this state of affairs is amenable to description in other terms. We could, that is, describe it more prosaically as the development of the Narrator's realization that Albertine had gone, which would avoid the contradictory '*A* knows and does not know that *p*' without splitting the person into discrete 'selves' who become the subjects of knowledge and ignorance. Proust's way of describing the state of the Narrator, however, seems as accurate—given that the description is phenomenologically valid—as it is forceful; and remember that he has no interest in giving a description suitable for philosophical or scientific theory. Clearly, as Proust has depicted him, the Narrator does not, when thinking about Albertine, have a unified consciousness, an integrated mind. But we can describe the state in other ways, and Proust most certainly did not expect us to start wondering about ontology: about the *number* of selves involved and how they should be counted. Furthermore, a point that I shall stress consistently: in other respects, in other contexts (when not thinking of Albertine), the Narrator could be 'unified' enough. The 'disunity' held only for his thoughts about Albertine's departure—although, as Proust depicts him, the loss of Albertine was something that dominated almost all his thoughts.

2. Next, we might take the extremely common phenomenon of divided attention. This is especially relevant to split-brain patients; for they, under experimental conditions, can sometimes perform concurrently two tasks which a normal individual would need to do consecutively. (This has been shown most conclusively with monkeys, but there is some evidence that it also holds in certain circumstances for human patients.) There are activities which people can, attentively and with little or no detriment to either performance, do simultaneously. For example, they can read and listen to music, drive a car while conversing, dig a ditch while thinking of Fermat's last theorem, or, like President Ford, chew gum while walking. Occasionally two highly sophisticated things can be done simultaneously without the agent's realization; I know someone who discovered to his own amazement that he had completed a crossword while remembering only the vigorous argument in which he had been throughout engaged. There are no general criteria for telling what activities can, and what cannot, be conducted together,[8] except perhaps that one cannot use the same parts of the body in two ways at once (one cannot run while swimming, or watch the television while reading a book). Certainly the joint performance of two or more activities can be detrimental to the successful conduct of either—it is unwise to be engrossed in conversation while negotiating difficult traffic, and the greater the attention paid to a book, the less one can appreciate the music being played. Thales fell into a well, too absorbed in his thoughts to realize where he was heading. Nevertheless, much of the time two or more activities can often be performed together with a high degree of efficiency.

Now, when we thus find two activities successfully performed simultaneously, we do not ascribe a duality of minds, nor a split in the unity of consciousness; instead, we tend to applaud the talents of the agents. It is only sustained and radical impairment of efficiency—when the division of attention is irreparable, and successful action impossible—that might lead us to say that the individual's mind was somehow

---

[8] Kinsbourne and Hicks (in Kinsbourne and Hicks [1978]) have been trying to provide an explanation of successful and unsuccessful divided attention in terms of brain structure and function.

unintegrated, or that his unity of consciousness was lost. Even then we would probably attribute the milder term 'scatterbrained' before we began to count minds or wonder about the mental ontology. The mere capacity to do two disparate things successfully, or an occasional failure to divide attention without impairing performance, would never lead us to such a serious conclusion. Note again that on other occasions, engaged in different activities, there is no reason to suppose an individual is not as 'unified' as one would wish; the 'division' here is temporary and local. Divided attention is only a mark of disunity, of a split mind, where it fails, and fails in a radical and sustained way— otherwise we do not have someone with two minds but rather one person, who may be either abnormally talented or slightly scatter-brained.

We do not then *withdraw* the attribution of an integrated mind, or of a unified consciousness; but it is becoming most unclear what this notion of conscious unity and integration is doing, what role it is playing. He who reads a book while listening to music is not combining or integrating his auditory with his visual stimuli (contrast this with the man who identifies the speaker he hears with one of the people he sees, who *is* integrating his sensory inputs). There is no integration of any kind between a driver's driving and his argument with a passenger about the guilt or innocence of Richard III (contrast here the driver who gives a learner a running commentary on what he is doing). So in what sense is the man who divides his attention integrated, or unified? Perhaps, it is sometimes suggested, because he is able to say what he is doing. But if we are to use the criterion of 'being able to say' to pick out the constituent elements of the integrated mind or the unified consciousness, then we must beware that we do not beg the question against the commissurotomy patient. Most split-brain subjects (P.S., studied by LeDoux, Wilson, and Gazzaniga [1977], is a rare exception, to whom we will return in Section 7) can report linguistically only on the contents of the left hemisphere. On the other hand, the right hemisphere can understand a question and *indicate* what it is seeing or doing, so there is some justification for saying that both hemispheres are in some sense 'able to say'. Thus it is not inevitable that this criterion must beg the question against the right hemisphere of the split-brain patient. However, 'being able to say' is for independent reasons an unattractive criterion: it rules out too much. The driver who talks animatedly while he drives may be quite unable to say what he is doing with his hands, feet, and eyes. If he is an experienced driver, he is presumably not aware of every gear change, each acceleration, every turn of the wheel, even when he is driving with care and attention; and if the conversation is sufficiently interesting, he may be able to say little if anything about the road, the flow of traffic, his speed, and so forth. There is little conscious integration here, nor need for any—and yet he is not driving *unconsciously*. (This line of thought will be pursued further in the next chapter.) There seems, in fact, to be no sharp distinction between the way the commissurotomy patient knows or does not know what he is doing, and the way the talkative driver knows or does not know. The idea of conscious integration and unity have so far provided little help.

3. As common as divided attention is our next semi-parallel: the states of mind summed up in such phrases as 'being in two minds' or 'a conflict of emotions'. Now we often analyse such inconsistent states by arguing that there is, on close inspection, no flat contradiction. We may say either that, for example, the apparently contradictory states of wanting to go to London and not wanting to go to London are elliptical and misleading ways of reporting the non-contradictory wants: wanting to see a play in London, and wanting to save the cost of the journey to London. Alternatively, we might interpret the 'not wanting' as 'wanting not', and argue that there are two logically consistent, although not practically compatible, desires: wanting to go to London, and wanting not to go to London. (A very simple, but important, point: the position of the 'not' is what matters here. Compare the wants of the smoker who is addicted but who would like to give up the habit. He wants to smoke, and he *wants not* to smoke; it is not true of him that he does *not want* to smoke. If it were, he would have violated the law of non-contradiction. This is the sort of reason why we teach undergraduates elementary logic.) The same approach could work for emotional conflicts; Jack may be glad Jill has left (she was not happy there), and sorry that she has left (he will miss her company). Such accounts—and here I am not concerned with their merits or their defects—dissolve the blatant contradiction. But they can do nothing, evidently, about the incompatibility of these wants and emotions in the face of action, they cannot dissolve uncertainty or hesitation, nor secure against indecisive changes of mind. All the same, it seems that we do not want to say that such conflict states give evidence of more than a trivial sort of mental disunity. We do not suspect two minds at work, and in fact if we say that such a man is 'in two minds', we do not take ourselves literally. Moreover, and yet again, when he is not brooding on the reason for his current indecision, the agent may be fully integrated

and 'unified'; the disunity concerns one small aspect of his activity and concern. Mental disunity, as before, only arises as a serious possibility if and when the individual becomes systematically incapable of deciding on, and adhering to, a single course of action.

4. Another example of 'being in two minds' is the notorious problem of *akrasia*, or weakness of will—a puzzle which is no nearer solution than it has ever been, for reasons I shall come to in Section 9. Fortunately a detailed discussion is not relevant to my purposes. I want only to draw attention to one prevalent account (or perhaps it is just a redescription?) of the question—the account which reifies and anthropomorphizes parts of the mind, generating two or more volitional elements, each with its own reasoning and appetitive centres. Such an account conforms to our idioms that describe the weak-willed; for we may say that he is struggling with himself, that his better (or worse) self prevails, that his desires defeat his reason, and so forth. The akratic gives us the clearest prima-facie case so far of non-integration and disunity. His thoughts, desires, and actions do not jibe; his behaviour is inconsistent and may be marked by hesitation, remorse, regret—regret even in the very instant of action. His disunity and non-integration, such as they are, have much more significant and far-reaching consequences than have those of the commissurotomy patient. The comparison here is interesting because the account just adumbrated also splits the individual, by dividing the akratic into two or more subjects of the conflicting mental attitudes. However, since *akrasia* does not tempt us to draw similarly drastic conclusions about the concept of a person, and presumably does not do this because we feel that there *is* some alternative account, then we should not jump the gun when it comes to commissurotomy.

At the risk of boring the reader, I shall emphasize yet again that, as in all the other examples given, the disunity may be noticeable *only* in circumstances where the opportunity for disarray—the temptation to succumb—arises. There might be impeccable 'unity' in other contexts.

5. In important respects, then, *akrasia* parallels brain bisection. There is, however, a difference which many find crucial. The honest akratic can tell us about his mental conflict, which the commissurotomy patient usually cannot; he is restricted by the fact that the left hemisphere, in general, is the only speaking hemisphere. So it would be as well to cite another semi-parallel, that of self-deception.[9] A familiar

---

[9] Fingarette, in his book on the subject [1969] goes so far as to conjecture that this phenomenon could be attributed to the fact of brain duplication. But there seems to me to be no evidence for this conjecture.

account—the merits of which do not concern us—claims that to get a true case of self-deception we need someone who both believes *p* and believes not-*p*, and who, while affirming *p*, is prepared to deny not-*p*, which by hypothesis he also believes. (Anything less than this is said not to be full self-deception but is rather ignorance, idleness, confusion, or wishful thinking.) Since the subject is deceived he, like the commissurotomy subject, is unable to report on his disunity, of which he is either not aware or at least not fully aware. (We noted in the last chapter that it was most unclear whether self-deception counted as a breakdown in the unity of *consciousness*, or not.) The parallels here with commissurotomy are close. The 'deceiving' element is so purposive—self-deception is highly motivated—and the resultant behaviour is rationalized in such a sophisticated way, that we tend again to reify and anthropomorphize parts of the mind. Thus once again we can be led to postulate two elements in the individual, each with a purposive mind, acting against each other. This conflict state is no less difficult to understand than the state of the split-brain patient, and may have far more serious, because generally malign, repercussions upon behaviour. But we do not start wondering about *numbers* of minds here—we do not think there are literally two. One reason we do not do so, I believe, is that we are simply used to the phenomenon. Commissurotomy is unusual; and it may perhaps escape our attention that the problems it raises are, to some extent at least, familiar. (In Chapter 3 we saw that states of, say, hypnosis or epileptic automatism were no more problematic, philosophically speaking, than is dreaming; but the former are unusual and therefore striking, while the latter is an everynight matter.) A second reason by now scarcely bears repeating: the self-deceived is unified enough for the rest of the time, for the vast bulk of his activities and deliberations.

So much for the everyday phenomena. We should not forget, either, the abnormal conditions discussed in the preceding chapter: fugues, hypnotic states, epileptic automatism, multiple personality. With the exception of the last, these seemed not to shake the concept of a person. It was one and the same man who went through several months in a fugue state, or who behaved grossly out of character when hypnotized. Multiple personality, I argued, did threaten the adequacy of the concept of a person: there were considerations pushing strongly in favour of saying, and of denying, that there were several people in one body.

None of these parallels is particularly close, nor need we expect them to be. The moral to draw from them, though—if we shelve for a

moment the radical dissociation seen in some cases of multiple personality—is that they show that we do in fact freely tolerate, and do not
count against the attribution of a single mind, many common and uncommon instances of deviant, irrational, inconsistent, hesitant,
incompatible or conflicting, and inexplicable mental processes or states;
further, that the successful performance of two or more unrelated
activities is an object rather of admiration than worry. Indeed, the disunities, in general, stood out against a solid background of 'normal'
unity and integration.

It is important to note that all the examples listed above gave us *more*
instances of disunity and non-integration, and had far *greater* and more
consequential effects upon everyday purposive behaviour, than does
brain bisection. Commissurotomy does not in general bring about far-
reaching behavioural oddities. One reason is probably that the split is
(usually) only on a conscious level, and I have suggested that consciousness may be only the tip of the iceberg of mentality; maybe the bulk of
what matters for 'unity' lies below. But another reason is that the
paradoxical behaviour under experimental conditions is a product, and
a *transient* product, of those conditions. For although there are some
reliably reported cases of occasional hemispheric conflict in everyday
life, these are very much the exception rather than the rule. As we have
already noted, they may for all we know be due to further undetected
brain damage (to which epileptics are very liable). The conflicts seen in
experimental conditions are generally conflicts of knowledge and belief,
and do not usually impinge upon desires, emotions, moods, dispositions,
attitudes, character, personality—on any of the long-term characteristics
that go to make up a person. Just as we see from most of the semi-
analogies above, the split exists only against a massive background of
consistency, coherence, integration—in short, 'unity'. Proust's Narrator
perhaps has the least unity; for owing to his fascination with Albertine
he was rather thoroughly discombobulated, in almost all his thought
and action, by his loss of her. This example, of the 'everyday' instances
cited, gives us someone whose disunity is radical and far-reaching; but
even there we treat him as one person, albeit someone who finds it
harder than most to lead a 'normal' life under the circumstances.

However that may be, the mind of a person, no matter how we understand it, must be *far* more than a number of transient conscious beliefs,
and cannot possibly be individuated in terms of these alone. Indeed, the
fact that the hemispheres manifest specialization as well as duplication,
monopolizing as well as sharing the labour, makes it clear that their

contributions to competence, character, and personality are *comple-mentary*. Even the command of language, which is specifically the job of the left hemisphere, seems to need the right hemisphere for full and normal functioning; how, precisely, is not yet clear, but there is some evidence that the right brain allows (*inter alia*) for the recognition of metaphor, humour, and maybe for the detection of varying tones of voice. It seems that both hemispheres must contribute their specific talents to get balanced emotional states; each appears to control different strands of our emotional range (see Sackheim *et al.* [1982]). Further examples of this complementarity could be multiplied indefinitely.

7. P.S.: AN APPARENT EXCEPTION

I should discuss here a patient who may seem to threaten this last point. P.S. was one of the rare commissurotomy patients whose right hemisphere had a good command of language (probably because of earlier damage to the left hemisphere). This meant that although his right hemisphere could not command the speech centres, he could with his left hand (right hemisphere) spell out words in Scrabble letters in answer to questions. He showed on several occasions that his two hemispheres could take different attitudes to people, objects, activities. In particular, his right hemisphere wanted (or, if preferred, 'wanted') to be a racing driver; the left opted for a career in draftsmanship. The right hemisphere frequently liked things less than did the left, giving lower ratings on a scale of five ranging from 'like very much' to 'dislike very much', when a word was presented to one hemisphere or the other. LeDoux, Wilson, and Gazzaniga comment:

> Each hemisphere in P.S. has a sense of self and each possesses its own system for subjectively evaluating current events, planning for further events, setting response priorities, and generating personal responses. Consequently, it becomes useful now to consider the practical and theoretical implications of the fact that double consciousness mechanisms can exist (LeDoux, Wilson, and Gazzaniga [1977], p. 420).

Does this not indicate that the split between the two hemispheres can be much wider than I have suggested, and that the hemispheres may even be said to have their own personalities, traits, dispositions—may be distinct and different at more fundamental levels than the transient conscious one?

Well, we have a problem here in interpreting the results. Quite often P.S.'s two hemispheres agreed on their likes and dislikes (and then, significantly, he was in a much better mood than when they disagreed). Our problem, though, is that the data are subject to various interpretations—we do not know how far P.S. was (deliberately/consciously or not) fooling, or perhaps entertaining, his interrogators. Moreover, when a subject has considerable left hemisphere damage, as P.S. has, it is difficult to know what factors to pick on as the causes of the occasionally noted discrepancies. We shall have to wait and see—wait for more evidence. Remember that ESP (extra-sensory perception) has notched up thousand upon thousand of 'positive' instances, but the scientific community, by and large, is yet sceptical.

Till more evidence reaches us, the following considerations are relevant. First, P.S. functioned normally enough outside the testing situations (in that respect quite unlike multiple personality patients, or indeed Proust's Narrator). So here too we have overwhelming 'unity' practically all of the time. Second, surely a sceptical interpretation—one that suggests that P.S. was, consciously or unconsciously, giving the researchers what he thought they wanted—is a priori more plausible than is its denial, since for most of his life his two hemispheres had enjoyed full co-operation: it was share and share alike until he was sixteen, his age at the time of the operation. Third, the description of the results needs to be examined. There is some evidence to the effect that the hemispheres specialize when it comes to the emotional burden. To summarize, in a way that neglects the complications of the experimental findings (not all researchers agree, to put it mildly): left-hemisphere damage typically brings depression and anger, right-hemisphere damage brings indifference and euphoria. The emotional tone dominating in each of P.S.'s hemispheres could well, on occasion, explain a difference in the attitudes each took to the target words. Yet such a coloration by the emotions suggests scepticism about the genuineness of the linguistic reports offered, especially when P.S., in a more placid and happy mood, had both hemispheres agreeing with one another. It certainly does not force us to conclude that there is a *separate* 'sense of self', or *separate* systems 'for subjectively evaluating current events', etc.

If future operations, and improved experimental techniques, show that many commissurotomy patients consistently manifest the kind of character difference that P.S. seems—sometimes and *in*consistently— to manifest, then, and only then, the split-brain operation will seem to me to indicate that the integrity of the notion of a person has a problem. Even so, it is far less worrying than is any full-blown case of multiple personality. I shall wait and see.

8. CONFABULATION AND THE DRIVE TO MINIMIZE DISUNITY

To return to the data provided by the majority of commissurotomy patients, it is worth noting that even in the carefully designed experimental circumstances where the hemispheres are deliberately pitted against each other, there is a very strong drive to minimize the disunities that result. (We have already commented on this in Chapter 3.) This drive, which is almost certainly not a conscious or deliberate one, should not be underestimated. One of the obstacles to research upon commissurotomy patients is the hemispheres' skill at confabulation, their exploitation of all the non-commissural channels of information— they will seize every opportunity to give and accept clues, they guess, use frowns and smiles (for the face is common territory) to fill each other in. When the left hand is holding (say) a comb, it will often run a finger along the teeth, thus providing the left hemisphere with the sound-cue necessary to identify it. If the left hemisphere guesses wrongly about what the left hand is holding, the right hemisphere, hearing the mistaken reply, will provoke a frown, which spurs the left hemisphere to guess again; or the right hand may try to draw letters on the other hand to give it a clue (see Puccetti [1981], p. 97).

Furthermore, we should always remember that subcortical connections are untouched by commissurotomy. The anterior, posterior, and collicular commissures too are left intact, as is (and must be) the brain stem. Right back in the first chapter I quoted Dimond suggesting that the subcortical structures might be *more* important for high-level cognitive processes than is the cortex. Whether or not they are more important, the data suggest that they are at least *as* important; and it is simply not known what role the brain stem, mid-brain, or paleocortical organs play in assisting 'confabulation'.

Confabulation, then—conscious or unconscious, psychological or physiological—enables the patient to minimize much of the interhemispheric conflict. Furthermore, brain-bisected people and animals alike endeavour to avoid situations in which the hemispheres are openly opposed. One of the examples which has been cited above to illustrate the striking *conflict* between the two half-brains can also be used to show the drive to avoid it. This is the case of the eleven-year-old boy, L.B., who had held in his left hand (concealed from view) a pipe. As already described, when asked to write with his left hand what he had been holding, he started to write 'P', 'I'; but then the left hemisphere took over with its ipsilateral control and wrote 'PENCIL'. The right hemisphere, resuming control, then used the hand to cross out 'ENCIL', and went on to draw a pipe. Clearly this shows overt conflict. But equally significant is the fact that L.B., usually a cheerful and co-operative subject, actively disliked and refused to engage in experiments of this sort, and had to be persuaded to complete this one.

Monkeys also show a tendency to avoid conflict. Trevarthen [1964] severed the commissures and the optic chiasm in a group of monkeys; this meant that each eye fed into the ipsilateral hemisphere alone. The right eye/hemisphere pair saw the left half-field, and the left eye/hemisphere pair saw the right. Then, blindfolding one eye at a time, he trained the right hemisphere/left hand to select a circle rather than a square, and the left hemisphere/right hand to pick the square not the circle. When each hemisphere had learned its trick perfectly, he removed the blindfold and presented the choice to both eye/hemisphere pairs at once. The interesting result was that the monkeys showed virtually no hesitation in preferring one option over the other—some chose the circle, others the square—and then they stuck to it. [10] In other words, unless conflict cannot be avoided, there is none. (Brain-bisected monkeys may sometimes find themselves tugging at the two ends of a peanut with each hand, but this lasts only as long as the monkey is not noticing what it is doing.) All in all, the *lack* of disunity is at least as surprising as are the rare and artificially induced instances of conflict. We should remember that Akelaitis in the 1940s failed to find any significant behavioural disorders at all in the split-brain patients he studied.

The disunities shown by commissurotomy patients are then to a very great extent the product of unnatural and experimental conditions. Since that is so, it is instructive that we find confabulation, and the same strong drive to minimize disunity, in the other experiment-dependent condition we have discussed, the hypnotic state. Hypnotism, and post-hypnotic suggestion, provide examples of people behaving

[10] It seems—at least as far as we know at present—that non-human animal brains do not in general manifest hemispheric specialization. There are, however, exceptions: one conspicuous such exception is birds. Lesions to right and left hemispheres in bird brains result in markedly different deficiencies in their ability to produce their characteristic song.

irrationally and aberrantly, clinging to contradictory beliefs, claiming not to see an object whose outline they are tracing with their fingers, even when their eyes are focused upon it. They too, though, deny the manifest inconsistencies and try to rationalize their behaviour, often in highly ingenious or far-fetched ways. Just like commissurotomy patients whose left hemisphere has not received the relevant input, they protest or pretend that all is normal and rational. So we see once again the strength of the drive to assert unity—to deny that there are inconsistencies of knowledge and behaviour; this seems to be a brute fact, and it goes a long way to help explain why commissurotomy patients avoid situations where there will be manifest conflict, why they refuse to recognize them when they occur, and hence why they tend not to reveal the occasional conflicts that may indeed crop up from time to time.

The case of hypnotism has also, of course, been used to support the argument pressed above: we saw in Chapter 4 that we did not allow it, any more than we allow fugue states or self-deception, to disrupt our concept of a person. Yet the (experimentally induced) disunities of hypnotism are, yet again, typically *more* marked and bizarre than are the (experimentally induced) conflicts of brain-bisected patients. It adds one extra strand to the argument, though: one of the reasons why we are reluctant to suspect several minds at work in the hypnotic subject is precisely because we know that the peculiarities of behaviour are the product of the artificial context; outside that very special context we find normal integration and unity. The implications for our interpretation of the split-brain behaviour are evident.

To sum up this section and Section 7, then: the disunity and failure of integration shown by commissurotomy patients is no more serious than is that shown by normal people in countless familiar and unfamiliar situations. There is nothing exceptional about their disunity except the surprising novelty of the experimental results. The disunity holds against a background of 99 per cent unity. It is not far-reaching, does not consistently disrupt ordinary purposive action, tends to affect *only* the level of consciousness, and is avoided whenever possible. Of course we have a problem here—that it would be absurd to deny. For it is highly tempting to say of a split-brain patient, in the experimental situation, that at one and the same time he both ϕs and does not ϕ—that he knows and does not know, hears and does not hear—but this is a temptation that we have met often before. To split the subject into two (or more) minds, or persons, is only one recourse; and the parallels listed above have been selected to show that there are no independent grounds for such a drastic step in *this* case. The reasonable alternative is much less exciting: to point out carefully and systematically the difficulties of attributing either knowledge or ignorance to the person himself, and, where the evidence for both knowing and not knowing appears strong, to ascribe indeed knowledge to one hemisphere, ignorance to the other—while insisting that this is a far cry from ascribing a duality of *minds*.

9. HOW SHOULD WE EXPLAIN CONFLICTS?

Part of the point of Section 7 was to show how much disunity we tolerate, even in everyday life; we saw in Chapter 4 how much we tolerate in abnormal circumstances. Some of the semi-parallels cited were long-running philosophical puzzles, such as self-deception and weakness of will; but whether or not they had drawn the attention of philosophers, most were very familiar. Commissurotomy, though, is not only striking but also rare, and this is part of its attraction.

The philosophical difficulties arose because there seemed no way of describing the behaviour so as to make it rationally intelligible. But this, I shall argue, is inevitable—and provides no reason for drawing radical conclusions. We cannot make self-deception or *akrasia* rationally intelligible either: *within our common-sense framework for psychological explanation*. I will now defend this claim briefly.

There is substantial agreement in the literature that we approach other human beings with the presumption that they are, broadly speaking, rational. Put another way, we presuppose that their behaviour can be explained in terms of our framework of Intentional predicates: in terms of their wants, reasons, hopes, fears, decisions, calculations, interests, beliefs. We employ what has been called a 'principle of charity' (roughly: interpret the behaviour of others so to make them seem as rational as possible), or a 'principle of humanity' (roughly: interpret it so as to make them seem as much like other human agents as possible), when trying to understand them. We start out, that is, from the assumption that they will generally seek appropriate means to their declared ends, that their assertions will be founded on evidence, that most of the time they are telling the truth, that they have reasons for their actions, that they are like us. The common-sense mode of explanation is just this: to show how an apparently puzzling piece of behaviour is in fact a rational action for the agent to perform—making routine allowance, of course, for slips of memory, errors in reasoning, and the like. Put another way, we *begin* by assuming that they are, by and large, as 'unified' or 'integrated' as are most of us most of the time. This is what it is to make purposive behaviour intelligible.

Often, as we have just seen, behaviour cannot be understood in this way, by the rational/Intentional framework, and then we have difficulties —such as the notorious paradoxes of self-deception. These difficulties, we can now see, are insoluble within the common-sense framework: they must be, because we are, hopelessly, trying to show how irrational or non-rational behaviour is, after all, rational. That is all we can do with the common-sense framework of psychological terms, since that is what it is for.

Earlier (in Chapters 3 and 4) we looked at some candidate explanations for abnormal behaviour, these of Freud and the ancient Greeks. Both sought to *supplement* the everyday common-sense psychological framework by finding rationality somewhere else—the Greeks in the behaviour of the gods, who had reasons for interfering with the heroes' behaviour; and Freud with such postulates as the (anthropomorphized) superego, ego, and id. Thus supplemented, it becomes possible to see why Agamemnon was so stupid as to steal Achilles' slave-girl, or why someone might 'have reason' to wash his hands thousands of times a day. There is then a clear sense in which both these accounts (and of course others, such as demonic possession, malign or benign witches, etc.) kept the presupposition of rationality; they just ascribed it to a wider range of entities than did the unadorned everyday picture, the picture that serves us so well when the behaviour is normally rational.

Now some peculiar behaviour cannot be understood within the everyday framework of rational/Intentional explanation, even when that has been supplemented. Here is just one such case. Consider a man who can write quite fluently, but cannot read a word he has written; his eyesight is fine, though, and he can recognize anything you set before him—except letters or words, and colours. Sometimes he can even read numbers. He is not colour-blind, even though he cannot name seen colours; because he can match and sort colours, can tell you *that* blood is red, the sky blue, grass green, and so on. This condition, which is fairly rare, is called 'pure alexia': we met it in Chapter 1. It is, note, wholly unintelligible to common sense. For, when we (as laymen) try to explain behaviour, we just take it for granted that someone who can write, see, and read numbers, can read words too; that someone who can distinguish between red and orange colour chips by sight, and knows how to use the terms 'red' and 'orange' correctly, can tell you which chip is red and which orange. If we did not make such banal (tacit) assumptions as these, we would be lost when trying to understand normal behaviour. Why is pure alexia not then a major philosophical puzzle, as intractable as self-deception—or indeed commissurotomy?

There is an explanation for pure alexia, although it is not a 'rational' explanation. The explanation, though, makes it perfect intelligible in another way. I outlined it very rapidly in note 16 to Chapter 1, but now it will be as well to redescribe it more fully (although still non-technically). I shall oversimplify considerably (relying on Geschwind and Fusillo [1966]; the reader is urged to consult the original paper or Geschwind [1974], ch. 9). The explanation runs like this. Pure alexics have typically a complex brain lesion, involving destruction of the left visual cortex; thus only the right hemisphere receives visual input. Furthermore, the splenium (part of the corpus callosum which, you will recall, transmits information between the hemispheres) has degenerated or has been split. The rest of the corpus callosum, and the anterior commissure, is intact. It is the splenium, however, which is the part of the corpus callosum that links the visual regions to the other hemisphere. Language functions are typically in the left hemisphere; but now in our brain-lesioned patient there is no longer a *direct* link between the visual regions in the right hemisphere and the left hemisphere's language centres.

When the pure alexic sees something like a hammer, the left hemisphere receives no direct visual information itself, since its visual region is destroyed. The right hemisphere receives the information, but cannot pass it over to the left via the splenium. However, the right hemisphere has millions of nervous connections to other parts of the brain, and—to put it crudely—the 'hammer' information will evoke associations else-where. We pick up and use the hammers we see, we hear the noise they make, we feel their weight. Still speaking very crudely, then, the 'hammer' information is sent to regions of the right hemisphere other than the visual cortex (the motor cortex, or the auditory cortex, for instance); and from there can cross over the intact parts of the corpus callosum to the language areas of the left brain. So the patient can name the hammers, and suchlike objects, that he sees. But colours, letters, and written words are, by contrast, almost exclusively visual—we cannot identify them by touch, smell, taste, sound. Consequently visual input from written words, or from colours, has not encouraged the formation of associations with the auditory cortex, the motor cortex, etc. Thus the information 'red' could travel to the language centres *only* across the splenium, and that has been destroyed. Sometimes the ability to read numbers is preserved; that oddity now becomes intelligible when one recalls how counting is often learned on one's fingers. Numbers may thus have strong connections with 'touch' and 'movement' regions of the brain. Clearly, there is nothing to prevent the patient from writing, from describing the colours of the sky or grass, from matching and sorting colour chips. The complex combination of ability and disability is fully understood: so—QED.

Pure alexia is now no longer *philosophically* puzzling. Given the explanation, we can see why it is so; why, indeed, it must be so. An explanation, albeit as crude and simplified as that given above, allows one to understand it, even to the extent that we could make some predictions that are in principle testable: for instance, that if the patient had learned letters as a child by playing manually with block letters, he should now have less difficulty with reading; or that he might have trouble naming other objects that are almost exclusively visual, such as (perhaps) clouds and shadows. The availability of this explanation removes the earlier paradox; even though, note, we are no nearer than before at showing how this spotty recognitional performance is *rational*. It is not rational; but the demand to make it appear so has vanished completely. Non-rational explanation has *supplanted* the rational/ Intentional model (just as meteorological explanations of thunderstorms have replaced rational/Intentional anthropomorphic explanations via angry gods). There are a lot of such cases; see my [1980] for discussion of a long list.

This means that we now have two clear extremes to consider when we find behaviours that are prima facie unintelligible or abnormal. One of them extends and supplements the rational/Intentional model (the ancient Greeks, Freud); the other drops this model entirely, and supplants it by another. These are extremes, and the behaviour we continue to find perplexing will be somewhere in between, requiring a bit of the rational/Intentional—'extended' or not—and a bit of the neurophysiological. Where they meet, we have to cope with the problem of the relationship between psychological and neuroscientific levels of description . . . otherwise known as the mind–body problem. (A good example of this mixture is reactive depression, and poses hefty conceptual problems: how do we link, say, Seligman's account in terms of 'learned helplessness' with an account in terms of a deficiency of the catecholamine transmitter substances at synapses in the limbic system?)[11] The point, and the moral, survives this complication, though, for the moral is this: we cannot and should not expect an explanatory apparatus, developed precisely to explain what is rational and sensible about human purposive action, to cope with the non-rational, the irrational, or the not-sensible. It must be supplemented, or supplanted.

This section and its predecessors have tried to show both: that commissurotomy is only one of a large and diverse number of 'split' behaviours which we cannot render rationally intelligible; and that this failure is not only predictable but even inevitable. Familiar with our inability to show abnormal behaviour to be normal, irrationality to be rational, we have learned to tolerate the disunities.

10. COUNTING MINDS

We are now in a position to make a few more general points. So far we have seen how unhelpful are the ideas of a 'unity of consciousness' or a 'mind' when it comes to any difficult cases. There is far too much common disunity, too many instances of a mind without perfect integration, for these concepts to be theoretically useful. We have just seen that vernacular notions—which make up the rational/Intentional framework of common-sense explanation—cannot and should not be expected to cope with the disunity; in the next chapter we shall tackle the notion of consciousness head-on, for much of the difficulty lies there. But before starting off on that project, let us return to examine explicitly the vernacular concept 'mind', which we have already seen to be elusive, and reconsider its relation to the 'unity of consciousness'. For part of the problem posed by commissurotomy, I believe, is that philosophers have underestimated the vagueness, and chameleon-like flexibility, of the term 'mind'. (Many languages—ancient Greek, and Croatian, for example—have no term with more than a very rough overlap. We shall return in Chapter 7 to examine in some detail the reasons for the interest in the concept of the mind.)

There is no theoretically coherent account of what minds are, and no reason to suppose that the term 'mind' refers to anything that it is necessary to individuate, nor to anything that we can count:

If you give someone a piece of your mind it is senseless to ask for it back. If a weight is taken off someone's mind neither grammes nor grains will measure it.

[11] Clark ([1980], ch. 1) has an interesting discussion of precisely this problem.

Someone who casts his mind back does not find that his mind is some way behind him. Although someone may have something at the back or front or in the corner of his mind, we can make no legitimate deductions about its shape. Statements of mental topography cannot be taken at face value. To appeal to such statements in support of the view that people have minds with familiar properties would be like arguing that people have handles because they sometimes fly off them . . . Just as the fact that people sometimes have a change of heart says nothing about the efficacy of heart transplants, so most occurrences of the word 'mind' offer no direct support or threat to theories about the nature of minds (Squires [1971], p. 347).

Now the mere existence of inconsistent idioms is of course no argument against the theoretical integrity of the concept that features in them; if that were so, then we would have even greater problems than we do already when studying the notion of time (see Bouwsma's highly entertaining article [1942] on that subject). The point is rather the combination of the inconsistent characterizations of the mind with the fact that the notion is theoretically, descriptively, and explanatorily dispensable: anything that scientists need to say in terms of minds they can say more easily without. For, a point that can scarcely be repeated often enough, a term of the vernacular has countless roles to play *other than* those of systematic description and explanation. The term 'mind' has come into the vernacular as a relatively convenient way of picking out a heterogeneous range of psychological features that happen to interest us, us as laymen; and its survival shows that we have uses for it—but those uses may not be, and I would argue that they certainly are not, confined to systematic description and explanation. We are not, or are not usually, interested in terms only because they are scientifically central (think, for example, of 'fence' and 'ornament'). In short, that a term flourishes in the vernacular provides as such no grounds at all for the inference that it refers to anything (a property, state, event, process, whatever) which should be acknowledged by a theory bent on systematic description and explanation.

Perhaps that is going a little too far. It may be argued that the term 'mind' has a role in scientific theory: to pick out the subject-matter of all post-behaviourist psychologies (indeed, I have suggested as much in my [1983b]). It is, presumably at least, our most general term for psychological capacity and competence. As 'our most general term for psychological capacity and competence', though, it has as such nothing to do with, and does not yet presuppose, anything like a *unity of consciousness*. An implication of unity in general, in the sense of integration, is indeed carried by the vernacular term; since we find—and indeed presuppose—that our psychological capacities and competences usually work together consistently and coherently, we are used to the notion of mind as the integrated set of these features. But as we have seen, the vernacular gives us no licence to conclude that this integration demands a strong 'conscious unity' at every point, in all circumstances— a unity that would not permit even transient breakdown—and, looking around, we have seen how much disunity the term 'mind' can tolerate.

Thus, if the least misleading true statement we can make about a mind is that it is the most general term for the more or less well-integrated sum of our psychological events, states, dispositions, traits, and processes, then it is evidently going to be very much more than a unity or an integration of *conscious* mental phenomena. Hence it will take a good deal more to disrupt it. We seem to attribute a mind to an agent (and, remember, we are now talking about our everyday attributions, not of scientific theory) when there is a sufficient degree of integration amongst a sufficient subset of all his mental states and processes—conscious, pre-conscious, subconscious, non-conscious, and unconscious—to enable him to function adequately in a roughly normal range of environments. This will demand considerable overall integration; it presupposes, among other things, the capacity to subordinate ends to one another in a flexibly ordered hierarchy, to adopt efficient means to a given end, to quell overmuch vacillation and hesitation—in other words, to have what might be called a 'life plan' of a realistic sort, plus the capacity to attempt to realize it. Thus the law of non-contradiction cannot be used to determine how many minds an individual human being may have. As soon as we accept that there will always be inconsistencies and contradictions in any agent's set of psychological attitudes, one contradiction more or less does not present a *new* difficulty. Minds are not thus attributed or withheld. Rather, we say that a mind is lost when the agent is unable to order his principal aims and goals into a realistic pattern (and there is no implication here that this must be a consciously mediated order), and is unable to follow a means–end pattern of action. Then he may be said not to know what he is doing, and we may talk of 'the ruin of a fine mind'. Briefly, we use the language of 'minds' to encapsulate the facts of complex, adaptive, purposive behaviour. The systematic and consistent behaviour of the normal person indicates the degree of integration that we expect to find when we ascribe minds.

If this is so, then evidently a man with a left, or a right, hemispherectomy (the operation that removes the cerebral cortex of one hemisphere) is a person with a mind, albeit a maimed and impaired person. But it would be grossly mistaken to infer from this that someone with no hemispherectomy but with a severed corpus callosum has two minds. For 'mind', unlike some other psychological concepts, cannot be ascribed to anything less than a single organism. (It is, I repeat, a term of the vernacular, so we are tied to the meaning that we find there.) The brain, the half-brain, and a man are all readily identifiable and reidentifiable particulars. A mind is not; we identify minds via the functioning and structure of the entities which have them. A mind achieves particularity, can be identified and reidentified, parasitically, only in terms of its realization and actualization, without which it is nothing.

We cannot say, except in a somewhat Pickwickian sense, that the brain 'has' the mind. We attribute minds *to people*, on the basis of experience and action, and for that we need to find coherent, planned, and purposive activity within the world as we know it. Still less can we say that one or both hemispheres 'has' a mind. One blank reason is that we cannot separate them or their functions; I repeat yet again that the bulk of cerebral activity, even after commissurotomy, engages both (the divided cortex is a small fraction of the total brain mass, which is predominantly undivided). So we just do not have 'separate half-brains'. But we can now see too that we could not in any case conceive of a body running simultaneously under two minds, given what it means to ascribe a mind to somebody: if behaviour is (relatively speaking) controlled and rational, we say there is a mind there; if not, not. Consecutive minds—*vide* multiple personality—may be possible; simultaneous ones are impossible.[12]

---

[12] The alert reader will note that I am hereby committed to denying that Sally, who claimed to exist as a subterranean consciousness during Miss Beauchamp's childhood and indeed after *B2* entered on a fairly normal life, could be said to have, or be, a mind. Further, I would have to deny that 'brains in vats' have minds. I am not entirely happy with this, and so should make a comment or two.

It cannot be adequately stressed that 'mind' is a term of the vernacular, bred to serve everyday occasions. Thus *if* brains in vats or coexisting Sally-type consciousnesses became everyday phenomena, then maybe we might come to ascribe minds here. We would still need *some* behaviour—the brain must be able to communicate somehow, and we need to be able to 'retrieve' Sally from time to time to get *ex post facto* reports on her 'life' since we last saw her. But *if* we found ourselves compelled to ascribe minds even where there is only such vestigial behaviour, note how different the case would still be from the split-brain puzzle. For us to say that Sally is/has a mind, she would have to impress us with the general coherence and consistency of her experience, thoughts,

But why, then, should anyone have thought them possible? In part because of the disastrous over-emphasis on *conscious* mental processes, which has led too many post-Cartesian philosophers to reify minds and identify them with the tip of the iceberg of mentality that is conscious. Since it would be stupid to deny that we indeed find transient conscious disunity in commissurotomy patients, the implication would seem to be that we need to postulate two minds to hold the disunited streams. I have long been drawing attention to this insistence on consciousness, and we shall attack it directly in the next chapter.

There may, however, be another reason, which has more to do with the psychology of philosophers than the philosophy of psychology. When philosophers speculate upon the nature of a person, they give the most honorific status to pure cerebration. Aristotle, and following him many others, have taken the capacity for abstract non-practical thought to be the highest possible characteristic of the human being. This has meant that the activities of the body have been radically downgraded, and 'armchair philosophy' takes on an ironically double meaning. Now this might be predictable; but it is inconclusive. For anyone is likely to find most important the aims and interests which he puts at the top of his hierarchy of ends; philosophizing is, normally, a voluntary activity and in general is chosen primarily for its own sake. Consequently professional philosophers, who may be expected to prefer their own activity to that of others, naturally tend to produce analyses of a person which give pure cerebration pride of place. Given that initial bias, it is easy for them to imagine two independently operating hemispheres (in harmony or not, as the case may be), two centres of mental activity, and the consequent fragmentation of the person. Parfit, for example, does just this, when he imagines [1971] a harassed examination candidate, fortunate enough to have a bisected brain, working on two possible solutions to a problem at once.

But this is grossly undemocratic. Ballet dancers, boxers, painters, pianists would all have entirely different hierarchies of ends, and to a greater or lesser extent will prefer their chosen professions. Whereas the idea of two sedentary philosophers in one body may not on the face of it seem absurd, that of two ballet dancers certainly is. Indeed, it is trivially true that even in the most cerebral of occupations some bodily movement is required often or occasionally; Parfit's split-brained examinee

preferences, memories, attitudes, and the like; so would the bathing brain. We would need to find a 'character' there; and, as I have argued, we do not get splits of character after commissurotomy—the split is too superficial and transient.

could not be one-armed, nor would his unusual ability benefit him in a viva voce examination. All this is trivial—a mere reminder that we have only one pair of hands, feet, eyes, only one mouth—but it does remove all ground for speaking of two concurrently operating minds in a single body: we are not constructed so as to allow for this. To try, desperately, to talk of two qualitatively similar but numerically distinct minds in the same body is an argument in the same vein which is equally vain. For the only way we have of counting minds is by looking at the behaviour manifested by the persons whose minds they are.

11. A FINAL WORD ON THE BRAIN

We can conclude this chapter by making a point about the brain that stands analogous to that made about the mind, and which allows us to pick up a loose end left dangling from Section 3. I have argued that it is dangerously misleading to identify the mind with the *conscious* mind. I have also argued that it is gravely mistaken to identify the brain with the cerebral cortex. It is, of course, only the connections between the left and right cortex that are severed; the rest of the brain operates undivided. Hemispherectomies, too, remove only half of the cortex, not the whole half-brain. We saw some of the consequences of oversimplifying commissurotomy and hemispherectomy back in Chapter 1.

Too little is known about the relation of the cortex to the subcortical tissues. Certainly *far* too little is known for Puccetti's blithe dismissal of what he calls the 'fusion hypothesis' to be acceptable. His argument, the reader may recall, was that there is no evidence for such a hypothesis, and yet, if there is no fusion, consciousness could not span both hemispheres, for if it did we would see *teacup teacup* when confronted with a single presentation of *teacup*. Therefore consciousness does not span the hemispheres, and all of us have two conscious centres, operating independently but perfectly in tune, all the time. But this dismissal of the fusion mechanism is, to put it mildly, premature:

The search for the mechanism of fusion is precisely what the field of visual physiology is all about. Perception is the perceptual integration (fusion) of sensory inputs into unified percepts. Within each hemisphere, the visual world is multiply represented, and the unified percepts of a single isolated hemisphere thus reflect the integration of processing occurring in many cortical and sub-cortical cell groups. Similarly, in the intact brain, unified percepts involving both visual fields reflect the fusion of visual processing in the multiple areas representing the visual world within each hemisphere. The search for the mechanisms that accomplish fusion is thus well under way (LeDoux and Gazzaniga [1981], p. 110).

Whatever else is clear, it is surely just plain fact that the multiple serial and parallel processes in the brain are engaged constantly in fusing this to that. To assume that it *cannot* happen is most bizarre pessimism.

The rest of the brain, the undivided mass of it, is essentially involved in whatever the conscious mind may do; and, of course is responsible also for all psychological activity that it not clearly conscious. It is only if we form the prejudice that consciousness is all, and that the cortex is all, that commissurotomy then seems to present a difficulty for personal identity.

On the other hand, despite its failure as a serious challenge to the notion, it has allowed us to fill out a little bit the 'consciousness' condition.

6

The Coherence of Consciousness

Man, n. An animal so lost in rapturous contemplation of what he thinks
he is as to overlook what he indubitably ought to be.

(Ambrose Bierce, *The Devil's Dictionary*)

1. INTRODUCTION: CONSCIOUSNESS HEAD-ON

In the preceding two chapters, while examining the unity and continuity
of consciousness, we have time and again stumbled up against the
obscurity of the term 'consciousness': against the fact that *this* is an
obscure and perplexing notion. In this chapter, as promised, we shall
look at the concept directly. Thus we will round off the examination of
the sixth 'condition of personhood', the condition that picks on consciousness of some special kind as being something of central
importance to being a person. The main conclusion will be that this is a
misleading condition, which encourages us to look in the wrong places
for what matters about being a person.

We can introduce the obscurities by offering four quotations:

'Consciousness' is the name of a nonentity, and has no right to a place amongst
first principles (James [1912], p. 2);

To anyone but a psychologist, it would seem incredible that textbooks on
thinking can ignore or say little about the stream of consciousness (Pope and
Singer [1978], p. 102);

What is meant by consciousness we need not discuss; it is beyond all doubt
(Freud [1964], p. 70);

Consciousness is like the Trinity; if it is explained so that you understand it, it
hasn't been explained correctly (Joynt [1981], p. 108).

These well illustrate the problem I wish to discuss. James, who affirmed
that 'consciousness' names a nonentity, notoriously went on to write
eloquently about the stream of consciousness, just as Pope and Singer
required. Freud and Joynt look to be too far apart to be able to argue. So
what do we mean by consciousness?

The decline of radical behaviourism has freed psychologists to take the mental seriously once again. Simultaneously, it has made psychology appear to have concerns close to those that interest the philosopher of mind. Both disciplines, after all, discuss such phenomena as memory, emotion, belief, desire, pain, sensation, and so forth, and one would hope that each would benefit from this renewed coexistence.

The apparent legitimation of the study of the mental phenomena just listed is not enough, however, for many psychologists and neuroscientists. As Everest was to mountaineers before 1953, so, for some, consciousness is the yet-to-be-mastered problem. The suggestion is that until this nut is cracked, psychology and the brain sciences remain seriously incomplete. The concern with consciousness is now to be seen wherever you look, but typically in significant places: in the *titles* of collections, in annual Presidential Addresses summarizing in general terms the state of the discipline, or, when textbooks are consulted, usually either in the Preface or in the concluding chapter. The notion crops up rather infrequently in the bread-and-butter reports of work in experimental psychology. Philosophers interested in the work of their laboratory colleagues also display this ambivalent attitude to the problem. Some, like Nagel (see his [1974] and [1979a]), suggest that it is in principle impossible for an objective science to do justice to subjective consciousness; we shall be discussing this argument explicitly in the next chapter. But others, like Dennett [1978b], prod experimental psychologists along by sketching an outline theory of consciousness within which research into the phenomenon might proceed. If some 'special' kind of consciousness is indeed pivotal to the concept of a person, then the manifest obscurity of the notion is worrying.

2. OTHER TIMES, OTHER PLACES

The undeniable interest in consciousness, however, might be somewhat parochial. It can easily be established that other cultures not only can but do manage without anything close to our notion. In this section I shall develop this thought; the argument is meant to be suggestive rather than conclusive, but what it suggests is intriguing enough.

There are two facts to note. First, in English (as in most other European languages) 'conscious' and its cognates are, in their present range of senses, scarcely three centuries old. Second, 'conscious', and 'consciousness' are notoriously difficult to translate into some other languages, and I shall cite ancient Greek, and Chinese, as examples. For some, no doubt, these facts indicate a failure in those other languages and in European self-understanding before the seventeenth century. For the sceptic, they provoke a hard look at the contemporary English terms.

A word on the strategy of this argument. It is important to emphasize that the translation problem, and the relative youth (in English) of the term 'conscious' and its cognates, only *suggest* such an investigation. These features *prove* nothing: the linguistic data are inconclusive. After all, it is boringly and trivially true that every language contains and lacks terms that other languages lack or contain; every language has terms that are more or less hard to translate; and every language enriches itself by acquiring new terms throughout its history. I accept this fully. Language differences of this sort become significant only when the terms in question are (purportedly) those that pick out phenomena that are central to our experience, our forms of life, the way we see and understand the world and our place in it. If 'consciousness' is as central and unavoidable as many seem to suggest, it is then at least prima facie interesting that other languages, and English before the seventeenth century, appear to lack the term, or anything that corresponds more than roughly with it; in other words, that what strikes some of us so forcefully, as being so 'obvious', seems to have left little impression on others.

Well, it made no impression to speak of until the seventeenth century. The *Oxford English Dictionary* finds the first use of 'conscious' to mean 'inwardly sensible or aware' in a sermon of Archbishop Ussher in 1620, who said he was 'so conscious vnto my selfe of my great weakenesse . . .' (*OED*, vol. i [1971], p. 212); but even then Hobbes, as late as 1651, continued to use the term with its etymologically based sense of 'shared knowledge'—*cum* + *scire*: 'When two or more men know of one and the same fact, they are said to be "conscious" of it one to another; which is as much as to know it together' (*Leviathan* [1651], part i, ch. vii; [1946], p. 37). Some early uses of 'conscience'—which also kept in the seventeenth century the idea of *sharing* knowledge—were extended to overlap with some of today's uses of 'conscious', as the immediate continuation of Hobbes's quotation makes clear:

And because such are fittest witnesses of the facts of one another, or of a third: it was, and ever will be, reputed a very evil act, for any man to speak against his 'conscience', or to corrupt or force another so to do: insomuch that the plea of conscience has been always hearkened unto very diligently in all times. *After-wards, men made use of the same word metaphorically, for the knowledge of their own secret facts, and secret thoughts; and therefore it is rhetorically said, that the conscience is a thousand witnesses* (Hobbes [1651/1946], p. 37, italics mine; note the 'metaphorically' here).

Earlier than that, the Middle English term *inwit* had some overlap with today's 'consciousness' too. But the use of the term 'conscious' itself, with a recognizably modern meaning, awaited the first quarter of the seventeenth century. 'Conscious*ness*' did not appear until 1678; 'self-consciousness' not until 1690. (To the extent that the appropriate French and German terms are indeed equivalent, they appeared at roughly the same times; in French perhaps a few years later.)

So for a very long time we managed happily without a term that cor-responds more than roughly with the term as we have it today. So did the ancient Greeks; and yet there we have a great and glorious psychological understanding. (It is not necessary to argue for this: consider Euripides, or Aristophanes.) But there is no term that *even roughly* translates 'conscious(ness)'.[1] Several note this, and are unhappy about it; *vide* Hamlyn [1968], writing about Aristotle's psychology:

there is almost total neglect of any problem arising from psycho-physical dualism and the facts of consciousness. Such problems do not seem to arise for [Aristotle]. The reason appears to be that concepts like that of consciousness do not figure in his conceptual scheme at all; they play no part in his analysis of perception, thought etc. (Nor do they play any significant role in Greek thought in general.) It is this perhaps that gives his definition of the soul itself a certain inadequacy for the modern reader (p. xiii).

Hamlyn is right that Aristotle, and Greek thought in general, ignore 'facts of consciousness' *per se*. But since one of our questions is, pre-cisely, whether 'facts of consciousness' are of central significance to our understanding of ourselves, I shall not linger long in defence of Aristotle; anyway, we shall return to him in the final chapter. Clearly the onus of proof must be Hamlyn's—to spell out what such facts Aristotle neglects (and which Euripides presumably neglects too, in his analysis of Medea's psychology). But we might note briefly what Aris-totle does and does not talk about, to see the difficulty of charging him

---

[1] It should not need saying that of course several Greek terms can occasionally be translated by 'conscious', and that the English term can in different contexts be translated into Greek in several ways. The point is that there are *several* options available; no Greek term provides a systematic translation.

with any clear sin of omission; he seems to be able to talk about almost all the phenomena that we group as 'conscious', and what he admittedly ignores may perhaps deserve neglect.

First, what he does discuss: he writes about sleeping and waking, and dreaming with its *aisthemata* (images). He examines the five senses and their integration, and sensori-motor control. He discusses pains, emotions—thoroughly 'conscious', 'phenomenal', and 'subjective' phenomena, in our terminology. He has a long and intricate analysis of the imagination. Above all he has a great deal to say about practical and theoretical ratiocination and deliberation: these are to him the most central and essential human capacities.

What are the omissions? He is not, it is true, particularly interested in 'introspective self-access', 'privacy', etc. He does indeed comment that we usually perceive *that* we perceive, and are rarely wrong about it; but before we excitedly dub him a closet Cartesian, talking about epistemological privilege in our conscious access to our mental states, we should bear in mind that he sensibly goes on to note that we usually also perceive that we are walking. Another 'omission' is of our alleged *experiences* of seeing, hearing, etc.: phenomenal sensations, 'qualia', 'sense data'. No term in ancient Greek translates these—Aristotle never talks about sensory experience*s* (note the plural; the plural form *aisthemata* occurs only in his treatment of dreaming, never in connection with the senses). Perhaps this is an omission? Later in the chapter we shall examine the validity of the postulate of qualia, sense data, etc. For the moment, simply note that one needs *argument* for the claim that 'visual experience' cannot be understood except in terms of 'visual experience*s*'.

We shall come back to this in another context. For the moment let us pass on to look briefly at Chinese.[2] The term closest to 'consciousness' is *yìshì*, which has two components—*yì*, and *shì*. Originally both *yì* and *shì* had much the same meaning: knowing, or remembering. Furthermore, in ancient Chinese *yì* seems to have been closer to *tacit, implicit* knowledge than to 'conscious', front-of-mind, knowledge. Qiu Renzong gives an intriguing example:

In one of the Chinese classics *Da Dai Li* it was said that 'Wu Wang (the Military King) asked if the Tao of Huang Di and Zhuang Xu existed in *yì*, or could be

2 When I was giving talks in China in 1986 I could not fail to notice the difficulty for the translator in finding the most appropriate Chinese term to render 'conscious', nor for the audience, in understanding what was meant by the English term. I am very grateful to Qiu Renzong and others for helping me understand the reasons for this translation problem.

seen'. Obviously the Tao of ruling the country by Huang Di and Zhuang Xu was supposed to be a kind of tacit, implicit knowledge (Qiu [1984], p. 2).

Today, according to Qiu, *yì* includes (*a*) meaning, or implication; (*b*) wish, desire, or intention; (*c*) conception, idea; (*d*) anticipation or expectation. *Shì* is primarily knowing, or knowledge. Both elements of the combination *yìshì* are thus highly cognitive.

Qiu characterizes three contemporary uses of the combination. The first is 'an opposite concept of matter . . . It covers the various processes or product of psychology and thinking such as sensation, perception, representation, concepts, judgment, inference, abstraction, generalization and even feeling, emotion, will and personality' [1984], p. 1). Second, as a psychological term, it is 'that at the highest level of psychological development which is inseparably connected with language and is supposed to be characteristic of [the] human being' [(1984], p. 1). The third is 'being aware of', 'realizing', etc. ([1984], p. 2).

To put it mildly, the scope of the term *yìshì* is highly *unclear*. The first of the three senses would allow us to include under *yìshì* much that we would *not* in English call 'conscious'; indeed, it seems closer to 'psychological', and includes much more than is suggested by the highly intellectual—cognitive—components *yì* and *shì*. The second sense by contrast *excludes* much that we would probably wish to include: most would wish to argue for non-linguistic, but none the less conscious, states in both humans and other animals. The third sense highlighted does indeed tally with one of our uses, 'being conscious/aware *of*'; but, by tallying with only one such use, gives a narrower meaning than the English term.

If, as I shall argue, the English term 'conscious' does *not* pick on a specific, 'special', psychological state, capacity, or whatever, then it is not surprising that the language lacked a word for it until the seventeenth century, that Greek managed splendidly without it, and that the complex term *yìshì* overlaps 'conscious', but overlaps very loosely and partially.

I now turn to defend the claim that there is no 'thing' which is consciousness—no unitary or special capacity or state of mind.

3. THE HETEROGENEITY OF CONSCIOUSNESS

Nobody, I assume, would wish to argue that 'conscious', or its nominalization 'consciousness', are clear notions. The range of disagreement about the scope of the terms puts that out of the question. For example, we find on the one hand those who liberally expect to ascribe consciousness one day to computers, taking it for granted that human and many non-human animals are indubitably conscious; while on the other are those like Sir John Eccles, or Descartes, who do or might deny consciousness to all artefacts, to the right hemisphere of the human brain, and to non-human animals.

Moreover, 'conscious' as an adjective is ascribed to a pretty heterogeneous bunch of things, and it has at least four distinguishable uses. In one of them 'conscious' is a one-place predicate which takes complete systems (organisms, maybe robots) as subject, as in 'John is conscious again', 'Tom is not yet conscious'. The remaining three uses all treat 'conscious' either as a two-place, relational term—cf. 'John is conscious of Tom's grimace'; or as a one-place predicate taking mental states and events as subject—cf. 'conscious beliefs', 'conscious perceptions'. I shall sketch these four main uses, which I think to be importantly distinct. But it should first be stressed that this is not intended as an exhaustive or exclusive botanization of types of consciousness (indeed, if ways of being conscious were so easily classifiable, the notion would be more tractable than I believe it to be). The intention is rather to underline the heterogeneity of conscious phenomena, to suggest that there are *at least* four interestingly distinguishable kinds of ascription of consciousness.

1. The first of my four kinds of consciousness is the use in which 'conscious' is a one-place predicate used most typically of individuals. Here 'conscious' means, roughly, 'awake', as opposed to being asleep or in a coma. Sometimes the significance of this use of the term is discounted, and it is regarded as merely being an elliptical shorthand for expressions taking the form 'conscious of' or 'conscious that'. According to such a view, when we say of someone 'he's conscious now', what we mean is, really, that he is now capable of being conscious *of* things (us, our voices, the radio). However, this seems wrong. For one of the tasks of the behavioural and brain sciences is to explain the nature of, and the differences between, sleeping and waking states themselves, as such—and also, of course, they have to take on as *explananda* states of dreaming, hypnosis, fugue, epileptic automatism, and the like. So I shall include this use of 'conscious' as a phenomenon with which we should deal.

2. The remaining three forms all admit both a relational use ('*A* is conscious of *x*') and a non-relational use in which 'conscious' is a

predicate of mental states and events (pains, beliefs, perceptions). Of the three, perhaps the most familiar is the one where the mental phenomena to which 'conscious' might be ascribed comprise the set of sensations. Now, sensations have traditionally been picked out in the philosophical literature by various epistemological features that are said to characterize our relationship to them. (Why there is this epistemological emphasis will emerge clearly in the next chapter.) They are argued, for example, to be 'private' to their possessors; we know of them 'by acquaintance'; we know them 'directly' or 'immediately', and 'without inference'; and these facts give us not only asymmetrical access but indeed 'privileged access' to them, so that our judgements about them are alleged to be 'incorrigible'. Most of this could be summarized by saying that the *esse* of sensations is *percipi*.

However, all these epistemological features have been challenged, or indicted as obscure, circular, or misleading. The ground here is adequately familiar. 'Privacy', for example, has itself a number of distinct senses (see Ayer [1959]). One reading collapses 'private' into 'what we are incorrigible about', so adds nothing to the criterion of incorrigibility; another gives it the unconvincing interpretation 'incommunicable', which just seems false—we can communicate a lot about such things as pains; a third is the innocuous 'inalienable', which simply points out that a pain is private rather as haircuts and passports are—I cannot give you mine so that it becomes yours. Knowledge by acquaintance has been attacked by a flourishing tradition which denies that there is awareness or knowledge of anything except under a description (see Shoemaker [1975], although he does not put the point in just these terms). Both the notion of 'immediacy' and that of 'without inference' become dubious when we allow—as we surely should, and as psychologists must—for the existence of tacit knowledge and non-conscious, subdoxastic states: not all that counts as inference need be conscious, so we may be unaware of many of the inferential steps in our thought processes. Incorrigibility about our mental states is either just false, or at least needs to be weakened (in the manner, perhaps, of Rorty [1970a]) to mean something like: 'at present, the testimony of the subject is taken to be authoritative.' All in all, the epistemological 'marks of the mental' look to be both inadequate and unclear. Moreover, it would not in fact be unfair to abandon them; they were, after all, introduced *not* to provide a perspicuous characterization of the mental, but rather to help pick out a class of statements immune to the Cartesian sceptic—as we shall see in the next chapter. These days we tend no longer to attempt to rebut scepticism by appeal to a privileged set of indubitable propositions, but think that we have other means of handling the problem; hence the alleged epistemological properties of some mental phenomena, sensations in particular, may be replaced too.

Fortunately, it is not difficult to delineate the set of sensations in other ways. In particular, we can group them by examining paradigm instances: pains, itches, tingles, twitches, butterflies in the stomach, pins and needles, tickles, shivers down the spine. If we consider these, we can see some properties that are common to them all. For instance, they are occurrent and clockable—they have duration, and we can often count them; they are located, often quite precisely; and they all fit somewhere on one or more of a range of qualitative spectra: from faint to intense, from pleasant to unpleasant, from steady to spasmodic, and so forth. Evidently, we need not ignore the element of truth that *is* captured by the epistemological features listed above, since we can acknowledge that their *esse* is indeed *percipi*—simply because nothing is allowed to count as a sensation unless it is perceived to be such: that is the way our linguistic habits have it. (This is why sensations are the *only* mental phenomena that firmly fit the epistemological criteria, for it is only with these that our linguistic conventions are thus strong.) We should note, though, that it might or might not be convenient for a scientific psychology to adopt the convention that the *esse* of sensations is indeed *percipi*; that is as yet an open question to which we shall return.

3. We turn next to the third use of 'conscious'. Like the second, this is either used relationally ('*A* is conscious of *x*'), or is used as a predicate of mental states and events. This third use is typically, but I believe erroneously, fused or confused with the second. I mean, of course, the employment of the term to characterize our sensory experience: the five senses, and kinaesthesia. The (con)fusion is expressed in, and illustrated by, the fact that philosophical terms of art such as 'quale', 'sense datum', or 'raw feel' are employed both to pick out sensations of pain and to pick out 'the experience' of seeing something red. That such a fusion is mistaken is easy to argue. Sensory experience is not jointed—it does not occur in the manner of beads on a string. It is not locatable (we see *with* our eyes, but that is not thought to be where the seeing *is*). It has no duration, except in the boring sense that we can stop seeing by closing our eyes and start again by opening them—the other senses are harder to suppress. We cannot sensibly count visual or auditory experiences; in other words, it is difficult to make much sense of the

plural of 'experience' where the five senses are concerned. ('Quale', or 'sense datum', purport to be count-nouns.[3] 'Seeing', in its everyday use, is not. Remember too that Aristotle lacked the plural—did not treat 'seeing' as a count-noun.) Further, sensory experience is usually not set on qualitative spectra (such as faint/intense, steady/spasmodic, pleasant/unpleasant) except in a parasitical way—the partially blind or partially deaf may experience clear objects or loud noises as 'faint' or 'indistinct', and certainly looking at a Monet may be a pleasant visual experience. But except in such instances as these, qualitative properties fail to apply.

Moreover, if we resurrect for a moment the epistemological features claimed to hold good of mental phenomena, here too sensory experience is clearly distinguishable from the having of sensations. It is, presumably, no longer possible to neglect the mass of evidence for subliminal perception (visual and auditory); and 'blindsight', a paradoxical condition whereby a subject with a specific lesion is able to discriminate shapes, patterns, and—perhaps—colours, while denying that he sees anything (see Weiskrantz *et al.* [1974], and Weiskrantz [1980] and [1986]), has provided another kind of example. Again, many blind people in fact get around by using a form of echolocation, but generally have absolutely no idea that they are doing so.[4] The *esse* of sensory experience is therefore emphatically not *percipi*, nor are we in any important sense privileged about, or incorrigible with respect to, it. (The alleged incorrigibility of 'I have an *X* experience' is, of course, no counterexample. The content of this is exhausted by 'I seem to see something *X*', and this is an incorrigibility with respect to thought

---

[3] The difference between count-nouns and non-count nouns can be readily illustrated by a word which is both, 'lamb':

> Mary had a little lamb
> Its fleece was white as snow;
> She took it off to Birmingham—
> Just look at the damn thing now!

That is 'lamb' as a count-noun. As a non-count-noun:

> Mary had a little lamb
> She ate it with mint sauce;
> And everywhere that Mary went
> The lamb went too, of course.

'Pain' can be a count-noun. 'Seeing' is not; 'quale', 'sense-datum' seem to purport to be.

[4] If the ears of congenitally blind people are muffled, they become much clumsier and bump into things more than they do when they are hearing normally. This strongly suggests that they learn—although without realizing it—to exploit the echoes resulting from the various noises in their environment.

rather than with respect to sensory experience. We could, after all, play the same game with 'a walking experience'/'seeming to walk'. Thoughts we shall come to shortly.) In sum, sensory experience is in many respects very importantly different from, say, the having of pains.

It is difficult to understand exactly what we are doing when we call some occasions of sensory experience 'conscious' and others not. Presumably we can say that subliminal perception and blindsight count firmly as non-conscious. What is far less clear is whether run-of-the-mill sensory experience, when we successfully get around even if pre-occupied with something other than the immediate environment, should be called conscious.

The test that waits to tempt us is 'ability to report': the suggestion is that we are conscious of the sensory experience that we can describe. But such a test is, as we noted briefly in the last chapter, highly suspect. It favours that subclass of conscious systems which have the ability to use language, leaving us in the dark about how to sort out conscious from non-conscious experience in non-human animals or the right hemisphere; more importantly, perhaps, it delivers results that are tricky to interpret even when language-users are in question. For, if we ask an agent to report upon his contemporaneous visual or auditory experience, then we have to bear in mind that we have significantly changed the phenomenon we seek to describe. Anyone who is asked to tell us about his ongoing sensory input is behaving very differently with respect to it from the man who, preoccupied with his forthcoming dinner party, negotiates obstacles in a supermarket. But if we try not to alter the phenomenon in this way, and rely instead upon the test of whether the agent can give us *ex post facto* reports, then the results become inconclusive. We used in the last chapter the hackneyed example of a car driver driving skilfully while engaged in lively conver-sation. We can use it again to make a slightly different point: such a man may be unable, even after a tiny time lag, to say anything at all about the nature of the road over which he has just driven. Yet evidently his sensory discrimination must have been subtle and refined, certainly not exclusively subliminal. (In fact, we would expect to be able to distinguish both subliminal and non-subliminal processing in the perceptual activity that helps to explain his driving skill.) Much more of our routine sensory experience is like this than we perhaps care to realize; maybe it escapes our attention because when we do stop to consider, and concentrate upon, our sensory experience, we are again altering the very phenomenon we are trying to describe.

At best, it seems, we must make do with clear cases of conscious sensory experience at one extreme—as, for example, when a subject is reporting upon the current contents of his visual field; and clear cases of non-conscious experience at the other—as, for example, in blindsight or in subliminal perception. If we resort to this way of marking the distinction, however, we are admitting that the bulk of our sensory experience (including most of the common and interesting forms), as well as practically all the sensory experience of other animals, elude or resist the dichotomy.

4. The last category of mental phenomena to get prefixed (or not) by the adjective 'conscious' is itself heterogeneous; it includes all the propositional attitudes. Two distinctions need to be made in this large class.

The first distinction is that between occurrent and dispositional attitudes. Turning first to the 'occurrent' side: we know that thoughts can suddenly strike one, tunes may run through the head, even to the point of distraction; one may engage in explicit deliberation, thinking in words; and memories may unexpectedly flood back (consider Proust's experience with the madeleine cake). On the other, the 'dispositional', side, we find the beliefs, desires, memories, emotions, preferences (etc.) which can fairly be ascribed to a sleeping man.

The distinction between occurrent and dispositional propositional attitudes does not of course tally with any conscious/non-conscious division. For although the most familiar instances of occurrent thoughts are typically regarded as conscious, there is no incoherence to the idea that pre-, sub-, or unconscious occurrent thoughts may exist. (I happen to think that this is not a particularly helpful or perspicuous way to talk—but, after all, one of the aims of this chapter is precisely to cast doubt on the utility of any conscious/non-conscious dichotomy.) If we accept certain claims made by psychoanalysts and indeed by psychologists too, there are countless occurrent thoughts that are not conscious. If we believe (we might not) that we are not conscious when dreaming, then, at least under the everyday understanding of what it is to dream, occurrent but non-conscious thoughts are to be found then too. Certainly the test of reportability as a mark of consciousness, which we have already found to be in various respects suspect, cannot be deployed here. For thoughts which we should surely consider to be pre-conscious, or if not pre-conscious then at least not conscious, can be directly reported. A familiar example bears this out: one who stumbles at the top of a flight of stairs may say, as he dusts himself down, 'I thought there was another step' (note that he might instead have said, 'I *must have* thought there was another step')—and his testimony is surely privileged to the same extent (whatever that may be) as would be his report about thoughts that might indeed have been explicitly running through his head.

Conversely, ascriptions of dispositional states are not always ascriptions of non-conscious beliefs, desires, etc. But it just is not clear what we want to say about beliefs that are *not* being pondered by the agent at the time; they are not obviously 'conscious' either. We might find ourselves talking of one of the 'conscious beliefs' of someone who is asleep, or of someone engaged in a task visibly unrelated to the belief we ascribe to him. This might, or might not, mean that we think he has come, after a process of reasoning, to that conclusion. Nor is it obvious that such ascriptions are elliptical: elliptical for a statement of the form, 'If you asked him if he thought that *p*, he would assent.' He need never have thought specifically of the proposition which we say he believes—it may, for instance, be a proposition that follows easily from other propositions we know he holds true, but one which he has never made explicit to himself. (For instance, '13 is the square root of 169'.) Perhaps an ascription of a conscious belief is *occasionally* elliptical for something like 'if you were to ask him whether he thinks that *p*, he would assent'; but here again we are in danger of altering the phenomenon we seek to describe, in that we are asking for the subject's attention to be drawn to the thought in question. Moreover, linguistic behaviour is only one of the many kinds of behaviour that we use to justify our ascriptions of belief, so that it seems somewhat arbitrary to favour it (as well as being useless when we need to consider animals, or the right hemisphere). In general, I think, we do not bother to ask the question 'conscious or not?' about dispositional or tacit beliefs. Still less does the question make much sense when the 'belief' ascribed is a boringly trivial taking-for-granted, the sort of thing one rarely *needs* to state explicitly (for instance, 'Jaruzelski's mother had parents').

The second subdivision we need to make among the propositional attitudes is the distinction between those that take, and those that do not take, the agent himself or his own mental states as their subject-matter. This distinction seems to me to tally reasonably well with that between *self*-conscious thoughts (etc.) and the rest. Only reasonably well: the notion of self-consciousness is a fairly fuzzy one which is unlikely to tally precisely with anything. The distinction is, though, usefully reminiscent of Frankfurt's [1971] dichotomy between second-order and first-order mental states. Curiously enough, self-consciousness (so inter-preted) may be easier to understand than consciousness. One reason for saying this is because self-conscious thoughts, as described above, are relatively clearly picked out by their subject-matter. But consciousness remains as hard as ever to pinpoint. We can see this if we note the paradoxical fact that not all self-conscious thoughts need be conscious. In other words, someone can have beliefs about himself that, intuitively, seem not to be conscious. One example is that of the anorexic, or the obsessed dieter, who appears to have a non-conscious belief that his (more usually her) body is fatter than it evidently is. A second sort of case comes from an ingenious experiment conducted by Holzman, Rousey, and Snyder [1966]. A number of subjects heard a tape of twenty different voices reading the same innocuous sentence. Their own voice was always the twelfth recorded, although they did not know this. Various physiological tests (such as galvanic skin response tests, electromylograms, finger plethysmograms) showed in almost all instances clear autonomic arousal reactions when they heard their own voices, but more than half failed to recognize any voice, let alone the twelfth, as their own. No doubt self-consciousness is in some respects as vexed and obscure a notion as is that of consciousness; however, it seems not unambiguously to be a clear, if sophisticated, kind of consciousness.

To return to our fourth class, the propositional attitudes, generally: while, again, we have clear paradigm cases of admittedly conscious thoughts—e.g. when a sentence runs through the head—and clear paradigm cases of non-conscious ones—e.g. the disavowed beliefs of the self-deceived, or the thoughts in the Freudian System Ucs.—the vast majority once more wander between the poles of the dichotomy.

4. PARENTHESIS: TWO PATHS TO AVOID

From the preceding section, consciousness emerges not only as thoroughly heterogeneous, but also as a prima-facie unpromising, phenomenon for systematic exploration. The majority of psychologically interesting or important events, states, and processes seem not clearly conscious, but are yet not evidently non-conscious. I shall shortly go on to discuss what the brain and behavioural sciences are doing, and can be expected to do, with respect to all four kinds of consciousness listed earlier; and then we can go on to try to draw some conclusions about the actual basis of acription in everyday language. But first I want to mention, in order to reject, two attractive intuitions about the nature of consciousness which, if not expelled, might confuse the argument.

The first such intuition is that consciousness is a kind of internal illumination; a spotlight in the private inner theatre of the mind that picks out some, but not all, of the passing show; a light that may be dimmed or intense, loosely or narrowly focused, but which is unambiguously either on or off. This metaphor just will not suffice—it conflicts with too many common uses of the term 'conscious'. Consider sensory experience. We can and do say that we are conscious of things, but more often than not these are public phenomena: the highlights of a painting, the expression on a face, the rumble of traffic outside. The technique of attending to one's experience *as such*, as phenomenological experience, is a sophisticated and rarely used one: people have to be trained to do it. Nor do sensations fit the 'spotlight' model; we seem to regard it as one and the same thing to have a sensation and to be conscious of that sensation—illumination and illumined coalesce. Similarly, we do not regard conscious thoughts as thoughts about this and that *plus* an inner apprehension of such thoughts; were that to be the case, rather few normal thoughts would be conscious. In fact, the inner spotlight idea, if it grips at all, looks to be more appropriate to conscious *self*-consciousness, where we can make sense of the idea that a conscious thought takes as its object a mental event of some kind. The metaphor here is not wholly misleading, and presumably lies behind the idea of intro*spection*. But, apart from that, the spotlight analogy, deriving as it does from the 'private inner theatre' metaphor, must be rejected along with that powerful, but powerfully misleading picture. (In the next chapter we go into more detail about what is wrong with inner theatres.) However we are to understand the nature of consciousness—if indeed it is the sort of thing that *has* a nature—it will not be in terms of this on/off, yes/no model of an internal illumination.

The second intuition to guard against is closely related to the first, in that spotlights can be focused or unfocused; it is the idea that consciousness is some form of attention. This is a popular view: '[i]n cognitive psychology, consciousness is for the most part equated with attention' (Le Doux [1985], p. 204). However, attention, whatever else may be said of it, is among other things the allocation of our cognitive resources, and such allocating is just as critical when non-conscious states are in question as it is when we are attending consciously. Moreover, 'any problem-solving or game-playing computer pays attention . . . first to one candidate course of action and then to another, and presumably it would not on this ground be deemed conscious' (Dennett [1978*b*], p. 209). In fact, even if consciousness were helpfully to be understood in terms of attention, we would not thereby get much forrader. This is because the same problems would plague the ascription of attention in the examples discussed earlier: to what, if anything, is the man in the supermarket, preoccupied with his forth-coming dinner party, attending? To what extent must we uninter-ruptedly attend to our pains if we are truly to have them? No; some attention is conscious, and some consciousness is attentive, and more than that we cannot usefully say. The main point to note, though, is that since attending can be clearly non-conscious, we cannot hope to understand consciousness by assimilating it to attention.

5. CONSCIOUSNESS AND THE SCIENCES

I return now to the rough list of four types of conscious phenomena, to see what help we might get from psychology and the neurosciences in understanding each of them; and to see what they have to contribute to the concept of a person. The point of turning to these sciences is that, as we saw back in Chapter 1, as far as we know all actual persons are human beings; so we can expect to get some insights into what is special about persons by consulting scientific theories about *homo sapiens*. At the start of this chapter we noted how ambivalent contemporary psychology is about consciousness *per se*; but now we have subdivided it into four distinguishable phenomena. If any of the four kinds of con-sciousness is 'special' to being a person, then science's contribution might shed light on it. If none of them seem particularly significant or crucial to the sciences, then our scepticism about consciousness is somewhat reinforced.

1. The first category I mentioned above was consciousness as a waking, as distinct from non-consciousness as a sleeping or comatose, state. It goes without saying that this distinction constitutes one *explanandum* for the sciences, and it is indeed a lively field of study; nevertheless, this is only one element of a more exhaustive investigation of these and a variety of other states. After all, sleeping itself divides into rapid eye movement (REM) sleep and four different levels of non-rapid eye movement (NREM) sleep, and a typical sleeper during an uninterrupted night will pass through a 70-90 minute cycle of these five

or six times. Physiological considerations suggest that some at least of the various sleeping states should for theoretical purposes be assimilated more closely to the waking state than to other sleeping states. REM sleep is tied to the dreaming process (although some rather fragmentary dreams seem to occur occasionally during NREM periods), and dreams evidently present a major topic for systematic examination—yet the conscious/non-conscious dichotomy breaks down completely here. To some, dreaming seems a way of being conscious, and there are clear reasons for saying this; after all, one has thoughts, perceptions, plans, and surprises in dreams (or so it seems). To others, on the other hand, dreaming is patently a form of non-consciousness, and there are clear reasons for that too; the dreamer usually lies placidly, immune to the environment—the very epitome of unconsciousness. I shall later suggest that there is no fact of the matter here at all, no true answer to whether the dreamer is conscious or not.

Meanwhile, however, we should note that dreaming is not the only difficult sleeping state for the conscious/non-conscious dichotomy to grip: sleep-walking and sleep-talking also present problems for it. Both of these typically occur primarily during NREM sleep (sleep-walking always does, since during REM sleep the main postural muscles are fully relaxed), but each also indicates mental processing of a highly sophisticated kind. The sleep-talker talks, after all, and his words are often coherent and meaningful; and linguistic behaviour is usually, as we have seen, taken to be the most reliable sign of consciousness that we have. The somnambulist negotiates obstacles and engages in activity that is often reasonable and well-directed activity. More complex behaviour yet can be seen with those in states of epileptic automatism. I have already mentioned in Chapter 4 the doctor who, while in such a state, conducted a reasonably efficient examination of a patient, even making notes in his case-book; the question of whether he was or was not conscious at the time surely just does not arise—*that* is not what is interesting about the case. It is just as well that it is not; for we have no idea what to say in those terms. Presumably fugue states qualify as conscious, if only because they may last months or years and would escape the notice of most observers. The Revd Ansel Bourne, also cited in Chapter 4, had to weigh the groceries, count the change, converse with his customers, and would be considered conscious by anyone. Hypnotic states, though, may be much harder to classify. There are several depths of hypnotic trance, as we saw when discussing the case of Miss Beauchamp in Chapter 3; all have some features in common with the waking state, with REM sleep, or with one of the various stages of NREM sleep, as both behavioural and physiological evidence would testify. In sum, classification in terms of consciousness or its absence is simply too crude to cope with all this diversity. Profitable research into these and other phenomena will require a theoretical classification determined along different, and probably more fine-grained, principles.

This sort of attribution of consciousness, moreover, tells us nothing about the nature of the person. Non-persons can be awake, as distinct from being asleep (whether dreaming or not), or they can be in a coma. We cannot look to find what is special about persons from this source.

2. If we turn now to the second form of consciousness, namely the experiencing of sensations, much the same holds here too. I shall run the argument in terms of the sensation of pain (as do most when discussing sensations; pain is certainly one of the most important and striking of the class, and it is doubtful whether the discussion would differ significantly if thirst, say, or tickling were to be examined instead). Now it is indeed important to insist that in humans at least most paradigm instances of pain are inseparable from the knowledge or belief that the subject is in pain. This feature, which cast in different terms just is the consciousness of pain, is thus certainly something which any adequate account of pain must accept as an *explanandum*. Will this shed light on one aspect of consciousness?

There seems no reason of principle why psychology and the neuro-sciences should be debarred from taking this kind of consciousness into account. It may, however, not be *qua* consciousness that they do so. Consider this: the line of research that looks at present to be one of the most profitable treats pain as a phenomenon with a causal–functional role in the psycho-physical economy of the organism. The occupant of this causal role cannot, despite the hand-waving abbreviations of some philosophers, be sensibly regarded as a single state (e.g. 'C-fibre firing'). It needs rather to be treated as a set of states, running both sequentially and in parallel, of which set the stimulation of C-fibres in the brain stem is usually an early member. The states themselves may be described in functional or—as our knowledge permits—in structural terms as well; this does not matter for our present purposes.[5] The sequences of states initiated by C-fibre activity are considered, by some contemporary theoreticians, to be series of information-processing states, and the

---

[5] In fact the structure–function distinction is a highly purpose-relative one, and is certainly not absolute (no more is the hardware–software distinction). I do not defend this here; the point is well argued in Kalke [1969].

processing of such information may require the postulation of (*inter alia*) hierarchically ordered sets of processors. Thus it may implicate not only the paleocortical aversive-motivational system, but also a hierarchy of stages in the neocortical, more cognitive, system (cf. Melzack and Wall [1965, 1982]). These complex sequences of processes may have familiar behavioural outcomes: the sufferer, for instance, typically resiles from the source of pain, tends the injured area, hunts for bandages and iodine, telephones a doctor. Usually the complexity of the behavioural response appropriate to the pain for that sufferer will presuppose a corresponding complexity in the psycho-physical processes postulated by the theory. For example, if an adult human is to take proper care of a burn or cut he must have beliefs and desires about the pain, its intensity, and its extent—that is, the higher cognitive functions must be in play. But note that they are not always needed; there are times when we find that we have snatched a hand from a source of pain *before* we knew what was going on, before, that is, the relevant information was assimilated by these 'higher' processors. The explicit recognition of pain will, of course, speedily follow, but appropriate action can be taken before we are aware of any pain.

This last observation—that we sometimes react to pain *before* we experience it consciously—allows us to introduce a much-neglected but abundantly familiar, and highly relevant, phenomenon. This is a phenomenon which, I shall argue, should be considered to be pain even though it is not 'experienced' at all. I have in mind the mild and unnoticed discomfort of a slightly overstrained muscle, for instance, or of low degrees of strain, pinching, or pressure. Throughout the day, and indeed throughout the night too, we make hundreds of minute postural adjustments to alleviate or prevent such discomfort, and we are usually not aware of doing so: when we are asleep we are emphatically *not* aware of doing so. That such states belong on the same spectrum with paradigm instances of pain is something readily discovered by anyone who is for some reason prevented from making the tiny shifts of position required for their elimination; they grow steadily into experienced pain. Seen in this light, the congenitally pain-insensitive are not merely individuals who do not *feel* pain consciously, but are rather people who do not *have* pain, who do not have even these mild and unnoticed forms: there is nothing with the relevant causal-functional role going on in them. This is born out by the fact that it is not only cuts and burns to which they fail to respond, but also strains and pressures to which normal people adjust non-consciously. Thus they are not only in danger from untreated burns, breaks, and cuts, but also tend to end up warped and lamed because they cannot compensate for muscular strain. (The proper care of such individuals requires that they be regularly moved about when they are in bed, and encouraged to shift position frequently when awake.) This gives us excellent reason to talk of unnoticed pain. The response appropriate to deal with minor strain and pressure is so easy—uncrossing a leg, shifting slightly the orientation of the head—that there is no reason for the strain or pressure to be consciously recognized as such; we can, that is, manage without consciousness, higher control, here.

One of the pressing problems for the brain and behavioural sciences is the construction of a taxonomy of *explananda*. It is evident that pain, under some description (or descriptions; 'pain' covers a heterogeneous variety of things) must feature in such a taxonomy. However, what counts as pain for the purposes of the sciences will prove to be in part at least a product of what kinds of phenomena the *explanantia* serve to unify. (This is a wholly general point about scientific classifications: classes are picked out, defined, or redefined, in large part by the laws that serve to explain them.) Thus a scientific category of 'pain' may diverge from the extension of the class of phenomena picked out by the vernacular term. I am suggesting that examination of the functional description of pain may, and probably will, require that such instances of unnoticed pain as those discussed above count, properly and equally, as pain discrimination by the organism; and this despite the fact that we need not be aware either of the painful stimulus or of the compensatory response. Hence the sciences may for principled reasons refuse to agree with the vernacular that the *esse* of pain is *percipi*. If so, there would be nothing incoherent in the study of pain discrimination in non-human animals by someone who is as agnostic as is Eccles about the question of their consciousness; pain would no longer *presuppose* the transparency of immediate awareness.

None the less, pain research so conceived need omit nothing, for it will remain a fact that the most interesting and important cases of pain in humans (and *I* would say in the higher non-human animals as well) indeed implicate the higher cognitive processes, without which appropriate responses to noxious stimuli would often be difficult or impossible. These processes then need to be described and explained; although there are of course colossal difficulties in practice, there seems no bar in principle to such a psycho-physical endeavour. It would be perfectly legitimate to describe such a project as research into the consciousness of pain; legitimate, but not particularly helpful, since the most perspicuous level of description would count it as research into the highest of a series of stages of processing of a certain range of stimuli.

Furthermore, discussion in terms of consciousness often obfuscates and confuses one's ability to describe and explain other sorts of pain. Let us consider hypnotic anaesthesia, already mentioned in Chapter 3. The dissociation that is shown by subjects who, while *saying* that they feel no pain, simultaneously *indicate* that they are experiencing quite intense pain, makes nonsense of the attempt to describe what is going on in terms of consciousness or its absence. In fact there does not seem to be a fact of the matter about whether the hypnotized subject is really in pain or not. After all, the vernacular concept of pain is a pretty crude notion which includes a heterogeneous diversity of sensations (few sensations are less similar than a dull stomach ache and the prick of a pin). It is only to be expected that a scientific taxonomy should delineate the extension rather less crudely and—perhaps—in accordance with theoretical demands of its own which may include both unnoticed and dissociated pain as legitimate kinds.

As before, we get no help in discovering what it is to be a person from this second form of consciousness. Non-humans experience pain too (it is the denial of this claim that needs argument, to put it mildly). Anaesthetics work with animals; and they too make the slight postural adjustments that compensate for slight strain or pressure. This cannot be the special form of consciousness for which we are looking.

3. *Mutatis mutandis*, the argument adjusts readily to fit our third category, that of sensory experience. Indeed, it will fit more easily, inasmuch as we seem far less firm in our intuition that sensory experience must always or even primarily mean *conscious* experience. Here too, I suggest, consciousness as such will not figure as a unique *explanandum* for the brain and behavioural sciences, even though what we are trying to do with the prefix 'conscious' should get adequately acknowledged in the scientific account. For example, we should expect any psychophysiological account (and in this field the information-theoretic account, mentioned above, is fairly popular) to provide an explanation of the differences between subliminal perception and the perception of well-lit objects in the centre of the visual field. Now, as we have already noted, the distinction between subliminal perception and 'centre-field' perception does not tally well with any distinction we may want to draw between non-conscious and conscious perception. Nevertheless, there is some overlap between the two distinctions; so to

the extent that there is this overlap, a scientific explanation of the differnces between the two kinds of perception will represent an explanation of the differences between non-conscious and conscious perception.

The vexed problem of qualia—if one takes seriously the existence of sensory qualia, sense-data or 'raw feels', as I admit I find it hard to do; I have as yet found no coherent or consistent description of what is meant to be picked out by these alleged count-nouns, and the ancient Greeks as we have seen managed splendidly without them—is entirely irrelevant to the argument. That it is irrelevant is surely shown by the fact that qualia, if they are to be postulated at all, must equally be postulated at a non-conscious level. For one role that they are assigned is to assist in the explanation of how we distinguish objects on the basis of their colour (and other sensory) qualities; but subliminal perception too involves colour discrimination. Moreover D.B., Weiskrant's most famous blindsighted patient, seemed able to report the colours of stimuli flashed to the blindsighted part of his visual field—although, of course, he thought that he was guessing randomly. (See Weiskrantz *et al.* [1974].)[6] Hence, *if* qualia are brought in to explain colour discrimination, we would need them at the level of non-conscious perception too. One could of course stipulate that qualia can be ascribed only when conscious (or at least not subliminal or blindsighted) perception is the subject of discussion. '*Quale*', after all, is a term of art that can be legislated to mean whatever one wants. But even then no particular or novel problems arise. For we shall still need to investigate the psycho-physical processes involved in ordinary ('conscious') perceiving, in subliminal perception, and in blindsight—*inter*, of course, much *alia*—and whatever characterizes the first but not the last two forms of perception we can, if the fancy strikes us, call the functional basis of qualia.

Anyway, let us ignore qualia for now; although they are much-discussed (but *only* by philosophers, which should make one wonder whether there is a genuine issue here), there is no acceptable account of them (and see Dennett [forthcoming]). Leaving them aside, then, it seems wholly plausible to suppose that the postulation and study of more or less complex and hierarchically ordered levels of information-processing should be expected to explain, among other things, our ability to recognize explicitly objects of perception (which, approximately,

---

[6] Weiskrantz *et al.*'s [1974] paper was non-committal about the extent to which D.B. indeed succeeded in identifying correctly the colours of stimuli flashed into his 'blind' field. Weiskrantz has since told me (in conversation) that subsequent research seems to bear out the view that colours too can indeed be 'blindsightedly' identified.

means our ability to be conscious of things we see). However difficult—and the understanding of higher-order cognitive processing is at present extremely sketchy—the problem is one of difficulty rather than of principle.

Yet again, there is no help from this third form of consciousness for the concept of a person. Non-human animals have a sensory apparatus too, and their senses are often far more acute than ours. To explain animal perception we shall need, just as we do with humans, to distinguish between what is perceived normally and what is perceived subliminally, or blindsightedly—in fact everything said above will hold of most of the higher animals at least.

4. We shall return to some of this in a slightly different context. For the moment, let us turn briefly to the fourth class of candidate conscious phenomena, that of the propositional attitudes. These, of course, are among the main topics of study for much of cognitive psychology. For whether we call beliefs and their like conscious, pre-conscious, subconscious, unconscious, or simply non-conscious, whether we talk in terms of beliefs, of representations, or of information processing, here is the stuff of which post-behaviourist psychologies are made. I have already suggested that in everyday life (in our common-sense descriptions and explanations) we are inconsistent and vague—or, more accurately, we simply do not bother—about the applicability of the adjective 'conscious' to the majority of the propositional attitudes. It is thus prima facie implausible to suppose that a blurred, shifting conscious/non-conscious dichotomy, which is neither exhaustive, nor exclusive, nor clear, could hold much promise for systematic study.

A fashionable theoretical notion currently dominating the cognitive psychological scene is that of a 'representation'; crudely, to postulate a representation is to postulate a psychological state which has content. The content of states is something to which other states have, or do not have, access. This is supposed to hold true right along the line—from subdoxastic states (for instance, those representing the texture gradient of visual input) all the way to the most sophisticated and cognitive states (which may perhaps be identified with something like our familiar beliefs, expectations, and the like). Some want to postulate proposition-like representations, while others insist that we need not only these but also image-type representations;[7] this is irrelevant for our purposes,

---

[7] A taste of this hard-fought debate is readily accessible in Block (ed.) [1981], vol. ii, part 2. This debate is only one of the many disputes about what representations are; further argument rages about 'explicit', 'tacit', and 'implicit' representations, 'hardware'

because in either case the postulated entities are characterized in such a way as to cut across any distinction we may hope to draw between conscious and non-conscious forms of representation. The varieties and various roles of representations, the types of processing to which we must assume they are subject—these are the topics that seem to constitute the *explananda* for systematic study. So we find again what we found before, that the question of consciousness simply drops out; anything that we needed the term 'conscious' to do can be handled more efficiently without it.

However, it is the category of 'the propositional attitudes', whether or not we deem them 'conscious', that seems to hold what we are looking for when examining the concept of a person. For there can be little doubt but that here there is a marked difference—albeit of degree rather than kind—between human and non-human animals. This is close to what Aristotle was getting at, when he claimed that the capacity for reason, both practical and theoretical, was the defining and distinctive characteristic of man. The sorts of thoughts, beliefs, desires, etc. that humans can be said to have (whether consciously or not) vastly outrun those ascribable to other sorts of animals. Moreover, the capacity to have thoughts, desires, etc., *about* oneself and about one's other thoughts and desires etc., which seems to be roughly what we mean by *self*-consciousness, is a capacity that we rarely, if ever, see fit to ascribe to members of other species. Sometimes we may need to; for example, the chimpanzee is one of the few non-human animals which can recognize itself in a mirror, an achievement which tempts one to ascribe a 'sense of self' (see Gallup [1977]).[8] But the question is a difficult and an open one, and it is unclear what experimental evidence might settle it; mirrors, after all, are highly artificial objects and so may set an unfair test to most animals. Dolphins, to take a different example (their brain-to-body ratio is greater than ours, so we might expect a powerful intelligence),[9] may be highly self-conscious; but they inhabit a

---

and 'software' representations, and so on. That 'representation' is an obscure notion is scarcely surprising, since it is nothing more than a long-winded modern synonym for the Cartesian and post-Cartesian term 'idea', and thus inevitably inherits all the ambiguities of that vexed term.

[8] Very few non-humans seem able to recognize themselves in mirrors. Apart from chimpanzees, orang-utans can; gorillas, gibbons, and macaque monkeys cannot. It is interesting that some retarded humans do not recognize themselves in mirrors (see Harris [1977]).

[9] Admittedly the brain-to-body ratio is not necessarily significant: after all, the squirrel monkey, the marmoset, and the lowly mouse would on this showing beat both man and dolphin. The criterion that gives the 'right' answer—where 'right' is interpreted

world so alien to us that testing them with mirrors may be comparable with testing our ability to echolocate. These tests must evidently exploit the capacities and environment of the organism in question (man included), and with other animals we may simply not have found the appropriate ones yet.

We shall return to self-consciousness in the concluding section of this chapter. Leaving self-consciousness on one side for the moment, then, and considering just the other propositional attitudes called conscious, it seems rather to be the sophistication and the complexity of these attitudes that distinguishes human animals from the rest, and not their consciousness as such. This sophistication and complexity may be due to the fact that we but not they have language (and so can have thoughts about Mondays, or Shakespeare's plays); or to the fact that we have a more extensive intelligence and rationality—as Hume put it, our minds may be simply 'larger'. But, in any case, what is right about the condition of consciousness would seem to be exhausted by the other conditions (of rationality, of the capacity to use language, and of being a subject of suitably complex Intentional ascriptions). Perhaps the Chinese *yìshì*, more centrally focused upon cognition than is 'consciousness', would be a superior notion.

6. 'CONSCIOUSNESS' IN THE VERNACULAR

Scientific research, it would seem, can manage best if it ignores the notion of consciousness. If it did so, it would not thereby leave out anything either important or crucial. We are thus thrown back on the unsurprising thought that 'conscious' and 'consciousness' are terms of the vernacular, which not only need not but should not figure in the conceptual apparatus of psychology or the neurosciences even when 'consciousness *per se*' is subdivided into the four main forms of consciousness I have outlined; for the concepts required in those theories will need to group phenomena along different, more systematic, principles. Put another way, 'consciousness' does not pick out a natural kind, does not refer to the sort of thing that has a 'nature' appropriate

as putting man top, with chimpanzees, dolphins, etc. not far behind, and keeping the mouse in its place—is the 'encephalization quotient'. This is measured by the formula $E = kP^a$, where E is brain weight, P body weight, k is a constant estimated at 0.12, and a is another constant variously estimated as 0.655, 0.66, and 0.69. This brings man out with an encephalization quotient of 7.44, the dolphin at 5.31, and the chimp at 2.49; the mouse scores 0.5033.

for scientific study, or which can constitute a 'joint' into which nature is to be carved by the sciences. (Nor do 'carpet' or 'calendar', and for precisely analogous reasons.) So there may be no helpful or substantial generalizations about human consciousness wherewith to aid our study of the person via the study of *homo sapiens*; so we must look next at how we use the term in everyday language, in the hope that from this source we can discover how, or if, it is crucial to the notion of personhood.

Qua term of ordinary language, it is wholly unsurprising that 'consciousness' has no precise definition. Very few such terms do—it is rather the sciences that need to aim for crisp definitions—and this is as true of non-psychological terms of the vernacular (e.g. 'chair') as it is for psychological terms. Moreover, as with all our other everyday mental terms, our ascriptions of consciousness are based on a thoroughly anthropocentric prejudice. We 'spread' mentality across infrahuman species to the extent that their appearance and behaviour approximate to ours, and to the extent that we can relate to or interact with them. As noted earlier, the rather stupid koala bear (which looks a little bit like us), or the cuddly puppy (which lives with us), are anthropomorphized much more than is the intelligent pig. Now a scientific psychology cannot work from a basis of anthropocentricity. What it says about organisms must hold, or fail to hold, quite independently of what is said about the species *homo sapiens*. But our use of the vernacular is subject to no such objectifying constraints. Thus the fact of anthropocentricity in our everyday mental ascriptions means that there is little concern with an alleged rightness or wrongness, truth or falsity, in our attributions either of consciousness or indeed of many other mental states. We will call a pig, or a bat, conscious if its behaviour and activities make it seem convenient and appropriate to do so.

It seems—as I have suggested elsewhere (Wilkes [1978*b*], pp. 111 f.) —that 'consciousness' should be regarded as what we might call a 'second-order concept'. This needs explanation. 'Intelligent', which certainly is so regarded, will provide a useful analogy.

Nothing is called intelligent if it can perform just one, or a very few, tasks well, even if it does them with extreme efficiency and sophistication. As we saw in a different context in Chapter 1, we do not call spiders, despite their ability to create intricate webs, intelligent; nor the fish and birds that travel, unerringly, thousands of miles to an exact location; nor chess-playing computers, nor the computers that can beat the world backgammon champion, nor expert systems used in medical diagnosis, nor pocket calculators; nor the *idiots savants* who can juggle

numbers with lightning speed. None of these is intelligent, and, as we
have already noted (Chapter 1, p. 32), the estimate in 1979 of the IQ
level of the best computers of the day brought them out roughly level to
the earwig. Intelligence is ascribed as a function of the degrees of skill
and flexibility *and* originality with which a number of tasks of a range of
diverse sorts can be performed. (Remember Descartes: 'Reason is a
universal instrument that can serve for all contingencies.') Put another
way, in a deliberately paradoxical way, to highlight the point: IQ tests
do not test intelligence. At least, they do not test for intelligence directly.
They test performance at a set of first-order tasks (mathematical,
spatial, verbal, practical, etc.), and intelligence is parasitically ascribed
to the extent that enough of these are well done. So it is a 'second-order'
predicate in the sense that its ascription rides pick-a-back upon the
ascribability of a number of directly testable predicates. That it has a
healthy adverbial form ('intelligent*ly*') bears out the claim that it is not a
first-order ascription, since first-order ascriptions by and large lack the
adverbial cognate.

'Consciousness' is in many ways rather like 'intelligence'. The term
has a familiar adverbial form; it too is parasitic for its ascription upon
the applicability of an assortment of other, more directly ascribable,
predicates. In other words, we presuppose a healthy subset of a whole
slew of psychological ascriptions—to do with perception, motivation, belief and desire, misperception, illusion, recognition, and so on
and so forth—when an ascription of consciousness is to make sense.
Conversely, where some set of first-order mental statements can
appropriately be ascribed, then the 'fact' of consciousness follows
automatically: there is no further question to ask.

Now, of course, the ascription of these first-order psychological
predicates, upon which ascriptions of consciousness are parasitical, is
itself a highly complex business. It requires us (*inter alia*) to take into
account the holism of the mental—to look at the complex role that these
attributes are taken to play in the system's cognitive and motivational
economy. As Gunderson nicely puts this general point, most psychological terms are 'like members of a linguistic clan that romp around
together in the same connotative-denotative heather of semantic space'
(Gunderson [1971/1985], p. 208). We can see this in the case of perception, when we ask ourselves what would be required if a robot were to be
said to perceive. The causal-functional role which paradigm instances of
perception display (both in ourselves and other animals) and which
determines what it is to be a state of perceiving, is vastly richer than that

open to any robot, existing or contemplated. When *we* see things we can describe them, paint them, or write poems about them; ignore, avoid, move, or eat them; sit on them, fear them, drop bombs on them. Non-human animals have a somewhat more restricted, but still extensive, 'heather' in which to romp: a range of ways of interacting with perceived objects. But the computer, like some of the lower animals, is severely restricted in what it can do with 'seen' objects—hence, of course, the legitimation of the scare-quotes around the term 'seen'. Computer 'perception' is not part of this rich network of (loosely or tightly) associated capacities, a network we take for granted, and which characterizes human and animal perception; so we cannot justify removal of the scare-quotes (and, although the difference may be one of degree rather than kind, the degree is very considerable and may be wellnigh insurmountable: see Chapter 1 and Dreyfus [1979], pp. 1-66). For the same reason, 'blindsight' is a good name for the condition so labelled, even though Weiskrantz in his [1983] remarked that coining the term had led to misunderstanding; the name reveals that this form of residual vision is *paradoxical*, in some ways like, but in several ways unlike, normal vision. We cannot quite say that D.B.'s residual vision is seeing without 'raised eyebrow', or 'scare'-quotes: this 'seeing' has lost its normal connections with other capacities—in particular, with that of believing that one is seeing. This holism, found even in prima-facie straightforward psychological predicates, complicates any and every ascription of each of them, as is well seen by the mess we get in to when, in everyday psychologizing, we try to make sense of the behaviour of brain-lesioned patients; their abilities and disabilities cut across the holistic connections that we are accustomed to expect. We saw just this in Chapter 5, when discussing people with pure alexia. Within the framework of common-sense, or everyday, psychology we could not make sense of their combination of abilities and disabilities.

Nevertheless, if we cleave to the example of perception, we find one necessary (but not sufficient) condition for its ascription: the subject must have a visual apparatus enabling it to detect objects by that apparatus; i.e. without direct bodily contact and in terms of light waves carrying information about the object's shape and colour. (So a tele-vision camera, for example, meets the necessary, but not the sufficient condition.) With consciousness, and intelligence, there is no such necessary condition, and it is partly for this reason that I call both 'second-order' predicates. There will naturally be a number of psychological predicates that are dubiously classifiable.

There are, then, no necessary and sufficient conditions for the ascribability of mental terms like 'see', 'hear', 'want', 'is afraid', and so on through a long list, any more than there are for 'is conscious'. None the less, the legitimacy of ascribing consciousness will be a function of what other mental predicates we want to ascribe; and the legitimacy of ascribing these is a function of what are the range of behaviours open to the agent, the range of stimuli to which he can react discriminatingly, as well as the necessary conditions (if any) required for the ascription of that term—and, perhaps above all, of our attitude to him or it: a robot candidate for consciousness would stand a better chance if it resembled a 'Sleeper' sort of humanoid than if it were a Dalek.

'Consciousness', it has been argued, is a term that groups a thoroughly heterogeneous bunch of psychological phenomena. This suggests that it is one of those vernacular terms that is unsuited *per se* for scientific or theoretical purposes. That does not, of course, impinge upon its utility in the vernacular idiom; there are many such terms, as we have already noted (cf. 'chair', 'carpet', 'ashtray'). But for our purposes here we should note that we cannot count on the notion to tell us much about the concept of a person. The ascription of consciousness is, as we have seen, parasitic upon the ascription of other psychological predicates, the ascription of which, in turn, is *in part* a function of what is true of the subject, but which is in part also a matter of what we know, believe, think, and feel about the subject. We will ascribe the 'special' sort of consciousness that is suggested by the sixth 'condition of personhood' if (*a*) we have reason to call the individual awake, sentient, a subject of experience, and capable of certain advanced propositional attitudes, and if (*b*) we *already* regard him as a person—have already included him in the privileged category. The point is that there is nothing else; nothing left over or left out, nothing that we can be right or wrong about.

If this seems a surprising or a counterintuitive conclusion, one should remember the terminology of the ancient Greeks; and in the next chapter we shall be looking at the Greek notion of mind in some detail. Here, especially with Aristotle, we find a sophisticated and detailed conceptual apparatus for describing the behaviour and character of man; and yet there are no terms that consistently translate—even roughly—as 'conscious' or 'consciousness'. (The same goes for 'qualia', and 'experiences'—note the plural—as we have seen; and for 'mind'.) Yet it would be rash to allege that Aristotle missed anything; everything he (and the great psychological dramatists like Euripides and Aristophanes) wanted to say about the person, they could say. And to recall: the modern term *is* modern—only three centuries old in its present sense.

The word entered European languages at a time when psychology and ordinary thought were under the influence of theories of the mind, stemming largely from Descartes and from the ideology of the Reformation, according to which the contents of a person's mind can be known and judged by that person alone . . . Unfortunately the whole drift of modern psychology is against this assumption (Morton [1983], p. 114).

We have seen some of the reasons why modern psychology might be thus opposed. Soon we shall look at the 'influence of theories of the mind' that helps explain the domination of the notion of consciousness.

7. SELF-CONSCIOUSNESS

We are thus left with the thought that consciousness, and/or 'a special kind of consciousness', is an unreliable and unhelpful 'condition of personhood'. It has proved virtually impossible to spell out what is intended by the condition. All we can find on the positive side is the idea that the *complexity* of cognitive attitudes matters (but we noted that not all such complex attitudes need be conscious) and that *self*-consciousness may—possibly—be what distinguishes our paradigm persons (human beings) from other animals.

Self-consciousness I described as the ability of the individual to take himself, or some of his mental states, as subject of his thoughts. If we combine this with the principle that persons are rational agents, then we can see why the 'unity' and 'continuity' of consciousness have seemed important:if one is aware of one's thoughts, beliefs, and desires then one will be better able, particularly in complicated situations, to discover and weed out incongruities, decide between rival strategies for attaining some goal, choose between incompatible ends, and achieve a degree of consistency between thought and action. The person will thus be 'a thinking intelligent being, that has reason and reflection, and can consider itself as itself, the same thinking thing, in different times and places'. In the light, however, of this chapter and the two preceding chapters we can insist that (1) unity and continuity are needed, and found, at levels that nobody would wish to call 'conscious'; and (2), that all of us tolerate a substantial amount of disunity and discontinuity without wanting to withdraw the title 'person'.

7

Models of Mind

If one is drawn by unassailable scientific argument to the
conclusion that man is a cockroach, rat or dog, *that* makes a
difference. It also makes a difference when one achieves ultimate
certitude that man is a telephone exchange, a servo-mechanism,
a binary digital computer, a reward-seeking vector, a hyphen
between an *S* and *R* process, a stimulation-maximiser, a food,
sex, or libido energy-converter, a 'utilities' maximising game-
player, a status-seeker, a mutual ego-titillator, a mutual
emotional (or actual) masturbator, or a hollow cocoon seeking
ecstasy through the liquidation of its boundaries in the company
of other cocoons similarly seeking ecstasy.

(Koch [1974], p. 7)

1. INTRODUCTION: 'MODELS'

In this penultimate chapter I shall stand back a bit. Leaving at last
discussion of specific 'conditions of personhood', we shall look at the
past history of the topic, at least in the European tradition. We have
already seen that the content of the term 'person' is, in part at least, a
function of what we think (rightly or wrongly) people actually are. It is
equally, in part, normative: a function of what we think (rightly or
wrongly) people should be. It would therefore be interesting to see how,
and to what extent, it might have changed over the centuries; for surely
opinions of what people are and should be have changed. Furthermore,
there have been substantially diverse conceptual frameworks by means
of which different civilizations have approached the subject, reflecting
incongruent views about how best to characterize our psychological life;
if, for instance, a culture has no term corresponding to our notion
'mind', can it have anything like our understanding of a person? As
against this cultural diversity, though, there is the gravitational pull of
common human needs, a common environment, a common biology: to
what extent do these work to hold relatively stable the content of the
term 'person'—despite all the theoretical flights of science and
philosophy?

I shall take three, or rather three and a half, pictures or models of what it is to be a person. These look, at least at first sight, fundamentally dissimilar. They are, first, the ancient Greek—which will divide into two; second, the post-Cartesian; and, finally, the contemporary picture, which is perhaps becoming dominated by the computer metaphor. We have already touched to some extent on all of these. Now we will compare them as ways of looking at the person. Of necessity the discussion will be broad and sweeping, perhaps too much so. But even then the results are of interest.

By talking of a 'model' or 'picture' I mean something like this. There are background assumptions and presuppositions that colour our thinking about all sorts of subjects, leading us to see the world under certain interpretations. These background assumptions need not be consistent with other things we hold. For example, few are not compelled to experience the earth as stable and the sun as the object that circles it, despite our knowledge that this is false (and despite the splendid attempts by such as Churchland [1979], pp. 30-4, to get us to drop the naïve geocentric picture). Nor need these beliefs be held explicitly, although they may be. They form the backing ground against which we create our explicit theories; and, as we know from *Gestalt* theory, the ground helps determine the nature of the figure which stands against it.

The relation between such a background of assumptions and presuppositions on the one hand, and the beliefs we form and hold on the other, is not unrelated to the relationship between 'theory' and 'observation': to the claim that observation is theory laden, so that what our theories tell us determines, or at least colours, what we see to be the case. But it is perhaps closer to the relationship between what we might call the *Zeitgeist* within which scientific theories emerge, and those theories themselves. A couple of examples would make this claim more concrete. It was the (explicitly held) belief in atomism, deriving from Newton, which made it more or less inevitable that the British empiricists when studying the mind would assume that the mental ontology was also atomistic. Later, it was the continuing hold of atomistic physics that ensured that early psychologists such as Wundt and Titchener would liken their 'simples' to physical atoms (see Wilkes [forthcoming]). Or, to take a more fundamental instance, the assumption that the world had a supreme, omniscient, and omnipotent Intelligence as its Creator, who worked according to rational general principles, was in large part responsible for the determinism of such as Laplace, and helped make possible the discovery of Newtonian mechanics (see Lelas [1985]). What I am calling the *Zeitgeist*, the metaphysical or metatheoretical background, may not be explicitly recognized or spelled out, and so its impact may be underestimated. It is perhaps most easily acknowledged *ex post facto*, if and when it gets replaced by a new set of presuppositions—when, for instance, atomism gets challenged by field theory. One thing seems certain: this background is not the sort of thing to be overthrown by direct experimental test. If it succumbs at all, it succumbs to a new set of presuppositions and assumptions; to a rival metaphysical picture.

In fact, though, the distinction drawn here between 'background *Zeitgeist*' and 'theory' is not one that is very significant for our present context, where the two will be found to merge. For, as I have argued elsewhere (Wilkes [1984]), the common-sense psychological vocabulary (which is what we are examining: 'person', as we have seen, is an every-day term rather than a natural-kind term of science) does not constitute anything that resembles a scientific theory. Thus in common sense there is no relatively clean distinction to be drawn between a metatheoretical *Zeitgeist* and the theories which arise out of it. There is only the continuum, stretching all the way from more or less unchanging metaphysical assumptions at one end, to new beliefs plucked from exciting or fashionable new theories (such as those of Darwin, or Freud) at the other, beliefs which may change with comparative speed as newer theories take their place. The term 'model', then, is trying to absorb and to merge *both* what is true about the claim that 'theory determines observations' *and* what is true about the broader assertion that theories can only arise within the context of particular metaphysical or metatheoretical assumptions and presuppositions.

Let us look at the first of the three models.

2. MAN IN THE *ILIAD*

This we have met already, in Chapter 4. There I discussed briefly the Homeric (specifically the Iliadic) picture of man as an aggregate, both physical and psychological. Now, at the cost of some slight repetition, we shall go into more detail.

'[T]he parts appear more frequently than the whole, the relation to the whole is not clear, and there is no word for the whole, apart from the implications of the personal pronouns' (Adkins [1970], p. 22). Adkins illustrates this claim by examining the use of *psuche* in the

Iliad—the *psuche* being a somewhat inactive affair as far as agency was concerned—and the role of the more energetic action-initiating parts: the *thumos* (approximately: 'spirit'), *kradie, etor, ker* (all three approximately: 'heart'), *phrenes* (approximately: 'lungs', 'midriff', or 'liver', generally credited with emotion-laden thoughts), *noos* (approximately: 'intuition', or 'insight'). *Thumos* is sometimes an organ, sometimes rather a 'spirited thought'—one can have more than one *thumos*. What is more, hands and feet can have a say in the matter as well: 'And my *thumos* in my chest is zealous to fight . . . and my feet below and my hands above are eager' (*Iliad*, xiii. 73 ff.; quoted by Adkins [1970], p. 21). The parts, rather than the whole, take over the decision-making role: the Greek heroes seemed not to make decisions themselves, but acted in accordance with, for example, 'what my *thumos* told me to do', or 'what seemed to his *kradie* to be the best plan'. These parts were substantially anthropomorphized, too. The *thumos* can be called 'great-hearted': not only is it a heart, it has one. (Maybe this was a cliché; but all fossils were alive once.) We often see, too, the Iliadic heroes conversing with their *kradie* or *etor*.

The approximate nature of the translations offered above is important to note. Adkins offers 'mind' as a translation for both *phrenes* and *noos*; I have not, for reasons that will soon emerge. *Psuche* Adkins sensibly leaves alone. Nor are these the only important psychological terms for which translation fails, or becomes approximate at best; there are others, both psychological and moral, some of which have been noted from time to time in preceding chapters. There was, as I described in the last chapter (Section 2) no term that translates smoothly as 'conscious' or 'consciousness'; although the Greeks talked of sensory experience, they had no term of art corresponding to the Cartesian and post-Cartesian 'idea', 'qualia', 'sense-datum', or 'sensory experiences' (note the plural); and we can add to these that there was no term for 'will', none for 'rights' or 'duties'; none even for 'moral'.

Another features we saw in Chapter 4 was that the picture of man-as-aggregate was not restricted to the psychological domain, but extended also to the physical. Just as there was no term that translates readily as 'mind' in ancient Greek, so there was no term for 'body' in the sense of 'living human body': *soma* means 'corpse' while *chros* or *sarx* are 'skin'. To get closer to the modern notion of body we need either of two terms that pick out aggregates: *melea* or *guia*—'limbs'. Thus:

[N]ot surprisingly, the early Greek art of Mycenae and its period shows man as an assembly of strangely articulated limbs, the joints underdrawn, and the torso almost separated from the hips. It is graphically what we find again and again in Homer, who speaks of hands, lower arms, upper arms, feet, calves and thighs as being fleet, sinewy, in speedy motion, etc., with no mention of the body as a whole (Jaynes [1976], p. 71).

Or, as Feyerabend puts it: 'All we get is a puppet put together from more or less articulated parts' (Feyerabend [1975], p. 243).

No mind; and no body either? This picture is beginning to look very alien. Jaynes reaches a startling conclusion:

> [T]he soldiers [of the *Iliad*] were not at all like us. They were noble automatons who knew not what they did. . . . We cannot approach these heroes by inventing mind-spaces behind their fierce eyes as we do with each other. Iliadic man did not have subjectivity as do we; he had no awareness of his awareness of the world, no internal mind-space to introspect upon ([1976], p. 75).

Such individuals lack a mind; and would of course lack the 'special kind of consciousness' (difficult as it is to make solid sense of that idea) which was the last of the six conditions mentioned in the first chapter. Man-as-aggregate, man-as-puppet, would fail to qualify as a person. Where there then then no people at this period of European history?

However, we should slow down. We are in danger of accepting without quibble the sort of claim illustrated by Snell ([1953], p. 5) in his comment: 'if they had no word for it, it follows that as far as they were concerned it did not exist.' Any argument that rests even in part upon a move from 'they had no word for X' to 'you cannot ascribe X to them' needs careful defence. It requires first and foremost the reificatory—and indeed self-congratulatory—move: that we, by having a term 'X', have now hit on something real and important, so that any culture which lacks the term has failed to notice or discover something real and important. Yet that reificatory claim cannot be made about the terms we are now considering. It cannot be made because it is not just among the Greeks of the Homeric period that there were no terms for 'mind', 'will', 'sensory experiences', or 'consciousness'; as we saw in the last chapter Aristotle, and the great psychological dramatists like Euripides and Aristophanes, managed happily without them too, and so it is manifestly obvious that in the classical Greek period we have a great, and comprehensive, psychological understanding. It is thus surely impossible to deny, as we read those plays with understanding, amusement, or sympathy, that the dramatists are dealing with 'real people'.

Let us look, moreover, more sceptically at the notions we employ today. I have argued already, in the preceding chapter, that 'consciousness' is a term which cannot easily be construed as referring to a particular property of the human mind. It is used to pick out rather fuzzily a large and very heterogeneous variety of psychological phenomena; and we have as yet to be shown that for any one of these phenomena the Greeks were unable to describe and examine features that we would regard as central or important. The Chinese seem to cope with a notion that overlaps only very roughly. I shall not add here to the earlier discussion, except to remind the reader of the history of the term itself. Etymologically the word 'conscious' comes from *cum-scire*, to share knowledge with another; and this was the use to which Hobbes put it (in 1651) in the extract quoted (p. 170). The sense of 'inwardly sensible or aware' was not found until 1620. The term 'conscious*ness*' appears first in 1678, and 'self-consciousness' in 1690. Thus 'conscious' and its cognates, in the contemporary sense of the terms, are relative newcomers to the psychological vocabulary: we managed without them for centuries. All this was argued more fully in Chapter 6; but it bears summary repetition because we shall shortly examine the background conditions that help to explain the elevation, in the seventeenth century, of 'the conscious mind' to the centre of the stage.

Since many might be unconvinced by the discussion in the last chapter, though, let us consider some different examples drawn from both the moral and the psychological spheres. For instance, many would want to argue that what we now say in terms of 'rights' and 'duties' could be said equally well—I would myself say better, more perspicuously—without them. In all serious discussions of rights today, greater progress is made if we abandon the terminology of 'rights' and appeal directly to the underlying considerations which support claims to possess them; 'rights talk' is best seen as (useful) shorthand for the arguments upon which it is parasitic. If so, we would *lose* nothing substantial if, like the Greeks, we lacked the terms. Take another example, on a more general level. Aristotle's ethical writings are arguably the greatest written in any language; yet his phrase *ethike arete*, invariably translated as 'moral virtue', does not mean that at all: it means 'excellence of character/disposition', and does not draw any important or significant distinction between self-regarding (= 'prudential') and other-regarding (= 'moral') excellences.[1]

---

[1] To be accurate, there is exactly one place where Aristotle talks of 'moral virtue' in the sense of 'other regarding' activities. This is in *Nicomachean Ethics*, v. 1. 1129^{b}25–7, where he describes 'universal justice' as 'complete excellence, *but not absolutely, but in relation to others*'. The excellences ('absolutely') are characteristics that can be exercised in relation to one's own good or in relation to that of others, or of course a bit of both.

Above all, our term 'mind' is not a sacrosanct given. This claim was argued at length in Chapter 5. The term itself has no clear or agreed extension; and, to exploit one more time comparisons with other languages, it is worth noting that Croatians fluent in English disagree about whether *duh*, or *um*—two words with very different meanings in Croation—better translate 'mind', so it again looks as though *our* term is dispensable.[2] Perhaps, as we saw, the least tendentious description that could be given of 'mind' would be something like: 'the most general term for the subject-matter of all non-behaviourist psychologies, scientific or everyday'. Descartes persuaded subsequent generations that *consciousness* was the most significant fact about the mind, and we shall shortly see why; but today it is becoming generally accepted that the conscious part of the mind is but the tip of an iceberg, and that many or most mental phenomena are not conscious. If we try to use the term 'mind' to include all *mental* states, events, and processes in contradistinction to *physical* events, states, and processes, we are no better off: for the mental/physical distinction, in turn, is hopelessly fuzzy.[3] Where, for example, should we put 'sleepy', 'dizzy', or 'having a toothache'? Should we assign to the mental, or to the physical, camp some of the conjectured functions of neuropsychology (ascribed to regions of the brain) such as 'expectancy generators', 'comparators', or 'stimulus analysers'? Just as there are no interesting or non-arbitrary distinctions between psychology and neuropsychology, or between neuropsychology and neurophysiology, so also, and for precisely the same reasons, there is no interesting or sharp distinction between what counts as 'mental' and what as 'physical'.

Returning to the Greeks: we can certainly agree that the nearest rival to 'mind', *psuche*, was not a superior notion at the time when the *Iliad* was written. Its role was always unclear and somewhat marginal in that epic, and it played little part in the description of thought and action. One sense it maintained throughout its development, before and after

[2] *Um* seemed to some a little too intellectual, focusing rather on rationality, wisdom, the controlled emotions, and thus inapt to capture the irrational, uncontrolled, irresponsible thoughts and feelings that 'mind' allows for; but *duh* smacked rather too much of 'spiritual' to translate 'mind' smoothly. These seemed to be the two main contenders.

[3] In fact there are two main traditions for characterizing 'the mental'; first the Cartesian criteria of immediacy, incorrigibility, privileged access, etc., and second the medieval criterion of 'intentionality' (often spelled 'intensionality': roughly, the idea that mental states are 'about' things). The former of course neglects all non-conscious mental phenomena; the latter is arguably too hospitable—if it is thought over-hospitable to ascribe 'mental states' to chess-playing computers or to areas of the brain such as the amygdala or hippocampus.

the *Iliad*, was simply that which distinguishes living and active, from non-living or inactive, things. Hence Thales is said to have held that lodestones with their magnetic properties had *psuche* and were therefore alive. But in the *Iliad* it also appears as that which survives death and descends to have a rather bleak existence in Hades: its *esse* would be *superesse*. There is no coherent account, covering magnets and men, that can be given of it. Indeed, even in the sophisticated hands of Plato the ambiguities of the notion remain; it is notoriously difficult to read the *Phaedo* and find the term used in a theoretically consistent way. Even if we could remove the ambivalence from the treatment in the *Phaedo*, though, it is doubtful that we would want to accept Plato's notion of *psuche* for discussion of personal identity: it is far too intellectual, and firmly restricts its scope to abstract, not even practical, thinking. Maybe Socrates' *psuche* survived death; what we are left wondering after reading the *Phaedo* is whether *Socrates*—humour, warts, and all—so survived. Anyway, reverting to the *Iliad*, there is admittedly no term, apart from proper names and the personal pronouns, that succeeds in doing what the term 'mind' is *trying* to do: provide something a bit more unified than the aggregated sum of the individual's psychological parts. But the point I want to make is that 'mind' is not a notion that is *obviously* superior—it is far from clear that if Homer had deployed a term equivalent to 'mind' in his vocabulary, he would then have described heroes without the apparent psychological disorder that intrigues Jaynes so much.

We shall soon turn to contrast 'mind' with a clarified and improved notion of the *psuche*; let us first look at some of the other terms in contention. Consider responsibility, decision, and purposiveness, which are usually singled out as marking a great gulf between the self-conception of the Homeric Greeks and the self-conception we have today. If a culture sees purposive actions not as stemming from 'volition', 'intention', 'decision' or 'purpose' but rather as stemming from 'what my *thumos* tells me', or from 'what my *etor* debates'; if it has numerous words—*menos, sthenos, bie, kikus, is, krator, alke, dunamis*—for the various 'forces' that can compel an individual to action; does this not suggest that the individuals lack a sense of free action, of autonomous choice? No; none of this by any means entails that its members do not have full agency and responsibility, consciousness and self-consciousness, even if they would not so describe themselves. Not everyone, by any manner of means, wants to be a realist about such alleged spurs to action as 'the will', 'an intention' (etc.), so any preference for the way we describe the origins of purposive behaviour can scarcely be due to the belief that the Greeks got some *facts* wrong. Many of our own idioms are in fact not so very different: consider 'it seemed to me that . . .', 'it struck me that . . .', 'it occurred to me that . . .', 'I was suddenly hit by the realization that . . .', 'I was pulled in two directions at once by the conflicting arguments that . . .', 'I was moved by the thought that . . .', 'I was driven to . . .', 'what possessed me to . . .', 'what got in to me to make me . . .', 'the force of argument', 'a powerful argument'. Or consider the definition of 'decide' given by Ambrose Bierce in *The Devil's Dictionary* (1906): 'Decide, *v.i.* To succumb to the preponderance of one set of influences over another set.'

Moreover, and trivially, if what it is to be me *is* to be an aggregate of the kind illustrated, then actions initiated by part of the aggregate are indeed actions initiated by me. The result may surprise me; cf. *Iliad*, xi. 407: 'But why did my *thumos* say these things to me?' On the other hand, we should be used to that: we can find ourselves thinking along strange lines (as we would now say; cf. 'whatever put that thought into my head?'). We even occasionally give desires to bits of the body, just like the Iliadic heroes, when we say, for instance, 'my hands itched to slap him'. Furthermore, as we have seen throughout the earlier chapters of this book, we are steadily being forced into admitting that we are *not* always as unified as we might fondly like to believe; even if the Iliadic aggregate picture seems to us to go too far, our insistence on the 'unity of consciousness' exaggerates in the opposite direction. However that may be, responsibility ('moral responsibility') is accepted by the Iliadic heroes just so long as the chain of action–causation stays inside the aggregate that constitutes, say, Achilles or Hector.

A different argument, though, can be used to drive a wedge between the ancient Greek and the modern notion of a person. If we examine not so much ascriptions of responsibility and purpose as those actions for which we do *not* claim responsibility, then we indeed discover a most interesting and significant gulf between the way the Greeks of the *Iliad* saw themselves and the way we now do. When the Greek hero behaved abnormally or irrationally, responsibility was very firmly externalized and handed over to the gods. To take just one example: Adkins quotes Agamemnon at *Iliad*, xix. 86 ff., trying to explain 'what possessed him' to steal Achilles' prize, the slave-girl Briseis:

But I am not the cause. No; Zeus and *moira* and the Fury that walks in darkness are the cause, who cast fierce blindness, *ate*, into my *phrenes* on that day when I myself took away Achilles' prize. But what could I do? The goddess brings all things to pass. *Ate*, the eldest daughter of Zeus, who blinds all mankind, baneful one.

There are countless further examples that could be cited. The gods took sides in the Trojan war, and each had protégés whom they protected, if necessary by giving them unpredictable strength or fleetness of foot, or by making their opponents behave stupidly or irrationally. Now, is not a culture that sees men as so essentially and intimately related to gods surely one that has a very different idea of what it is to be a person?

It should not now be found surprising or paradoxical that to discover so marked a difference we have to resort to considerations of *irrationality*. In Chapter 3 it was argued that the notional 'purely rational' man would not be recognizable as a person at all. Perhaps the six conditions—seven, if we include the creation and use of tools—listed in the first chapter should be increased by one: the contemporary concept of a person is of a being who is capable of certain specific forms of madness or aberration. Certainly it seems true that we do include that in our picture of the person; and, apparently, the ancient Greeks, at least in the Homeric period, did not.

None the less, this argument cannot be pressed too far, and for two reasons. First, whenever the divine intrudes into the philosophical picture, we get trouble. Today, too, millions see themselves as having essential and intimate relationships with a god; and that god is often regarded (and explicitly so in prayers and hymns) as active and effective in inspiring or checking action. Such a faith, for those who hold the creed, somehow coexists with the belief that individuals can themselves be deemed wholly responsible, and punished, for their actions. The Iliadic Greeks claimed responsibility for most of their rational behaviour, but handed over to gods responsibility for the aberrant and abnormal. They handed over the responsibility, but *also* accepted agency themselves—remember that Agammemnon blames the gods for the occasion on which, as he put it, '*I myself* took away Achilles' prize'. This may be striking to us, but it is no harder to understand than is contemporary Christian sharing of responsibility between God and man; at least it escapes the conflict between reason and faith which makes it wellnigh impossible to understand how much Christian thinking sees purposive activity. However, the philosophy of religion is fortunately not here my concern.

The second reason why the argument above cannot be pressed too far is closer to our subject; whenever the *irrational* intrudes into the picture, we get trouble. We have seen this already; in Chapter 5 I argued that the common-sense framework for explaining behaviour, inasmuch as it starts with a presupposition that explanation is a matter of showing how something is rationally intelligible, *ex hypothesi* has problems with irrational and abnormal behaviour. It inevitably has problems, because all its attempts (as we saw to some extent in Chapter 3 when discussing Freud) must rely upon our normal 'rational' pattern of psychological explanation. They all try to show how something apparently abnormal or mad is in fact, if seen in a certain light and given certain background assumptions, rationally intelligible.

Therefore, not surprisingly, attempts to explain irrationality have throughout history been feeble; often they are wildly imaginative and even beautiful, but as explanations they are generally feeble. The Greeks deferred the responsibility for their abnormal behaviour to the gods, but the gods had their reasons: if this hero-protégé is to be saved, then it would be thoroughly sensible to blind his opponent temporarily, or to give him a sudden access of speed or strength. In later eras, such as the early medieval period or nineteenth-century America, the responsibility for unpredictable, abnormal, irrational, or aberrant behaviour was assigned to witches, warlocks, demons—but they too had their (malign or benign) reasons for using their spells, charms and potions. Today we have Freud, and perhaps that is an improvement. It is an improvement at least in the sense that the origins of abnormal behaviour remain in the mind—or at least the head—rather than being externalized completely. But, as became clear in Chapter 3, Freud relies essentially on the 'rational' model of explanation. He needs of course to set out, using a mainly non-rational, causal-mechanistic description, the *genesis* of the ideas in the System Ucs. This is where he ropes in the full-blooded theory: of infantile sexuality, of repression, condensation, distortion, sublimation, displacement, overdetermination; where, in short, he is at his most abstract and even abstruse. But then—given those ideas, having swallowed the theory—we revert to familiar rational explanation: the patient's strange behaviour is shown to be *rationally* intelligible after all. ('*Obviously* someone in such a position would do that.') Better some explanation than no explanation; and we would not today find an explanation that went via gods or witches satisfactory. But to say that Freud's theory gives us a good explanation of abnormal behaviour would be regarded by many as the grossest of exaggerations.

In short, then, the Homeric Greeks found irrationality puzzling, and so do we. They opted for an uneasy relationship with a bunch of gods whose behaviour they could understand as essentially rather like theirs. We are equally puzzled, and some have opted for an uneasy relationship with a bunch of theoretically postulated internal systems whose behaviour is essentially rather like ours: remember the anthropomorphism noted earlier in the descriptions given of 'those shady Middle European refugees—the Ego, the Super Ego and the Id' (Asher [1972], p. 36). Plato too ascribed a triadic structure to the *psuche*, and equally personified his three internal agents; the ancient Greek picture of the person is perhaps in this respect not so very different from ours after all.

Thus the 'argument from vocabulary' does not *by itself* suggest that the Iliadic Greek notion of the person differed seriously or significantly from ours. *Of course* there were centrally significant differences: the values deemed important by that ancient Greek society are often quite alien to the values of the Judaeo-Christian tradition. In particular, at least until Socrates, Greek ethics were an ethics of success, and the implications a 'results culture' held for the way they saw themselves and the world around them were substantial; Adkins (in the work cited [1970], and also in his [1960]) brings this out excellently. The 'competitive' excellences were rated higher than the 'co-operative' ones: that alone would suggest that 'unity' and 'integration' were not what success most required. But that they were persons by our standards, and that we would be so regarded by theirs, is not, *pace* Jaynes, in doubt.

3. ARISTOTLE'S MAN

I turn now to another strand in the ancient Greek picture.[4] Here we find the *psuche* grown into something of enormous theoretical import—something that can indeed carry the personality and personal identity, in a way we can recognize, along with it. This is Aristotle's picture; inevitably, I shall shuffle some problems under the carpet and oversimplify many details, but I am here concerned only with the broad sweep of his account. (I make no apology for highlighting Aristotle so consistently throughout this book. The justification, as I see it, is that contemporary psychologists, whether they realize it or not, are in fact returning to a picture of the human agent that is distinctively Aristotelian—and to my mind are rightly so doing.)

[4] The content of this and the following section is treated more fully in my [1978*b*], ch. 7. I have changed my mind in some respects, but stand by the bulk of those earlier arguments.

For Aristotle, the *psuche* was the form of an organism. The form of any and every X tells us 'what it is to be' an X; thus the form of a statue is primarily its shape, the form of a dog is primarily a description of its characteristic activity, that of a corkscrew is primarily its function; that of a threshold is primarily its location, of a road its direction, and of breakfast, its timing. (The qualifier 'primarily' will be explained shortly.) *Psuchai* are thus members of a subclass of forms, being forms of living organisms. To be an organism is to have a form which is a *psuche*; to have a form which is a *psuche* is to be an organism. Thus, the form of an eye is sight, a form which is not a *psuche*; but '*if* the eye were an animal, sight *would be* its *psuche*' (Aristotle, *De Anima*, ii. 1. 412^{b}18-19). So we find maintained the traditional core of the notion, as that which marks off living from non-living things.

Thus maple trees have *psuche*, as do mosquitoes, mice, and men. Evidently, though, 'what it is to be' a maple tree will be different from 'what it is to be' a mosquito or a mouse. Yet the *psuchai* of all these constitute an ordered hierarchy. To be a maple tree is to have certain capacities for growth, taking nourishment, metabolism, etc. Mosquitoes need all that; but they also have capacities for movement and some forms of sensory perception; and having sense perception brings with it some degree of desire, pleasure, and pain. The mouse, to be a mouse, must be able to grow, take nourishment, see, desire, move—but it also has forms of locomotion and perception that are more flexible than are those of the mosquito. The higher animals show increased diversity and range in their sensory, desiderative, and locomotive abilities, and have some capacity for imagination. Finally the human enjoys all the lower *psuche* functions, but at the top of the pyramid has the capacity for rational thought, both practical and theoretical. The result is a human *psuche* which is immensely rich and many-layered: 'A problem arises immediately: in what way we should speak of the parts of the *psuche*, and how many there are. For there are in a sense an indefinite number, and not only those parts which some mention when distinguishing them ... (*De Anima*, iii. 9. 432^{a}22 ff.). We have to look and see.

Understanding anything presupposes studying its form; thus, to understand an organism presupposes studying its *psuche*, running *seriatim* through its diverse parts and their connections and interplay. We find here—and this I want to underline—the analysis proceeding from and presupposing an empirical study of what these objects, organs, and organisms are. I suggested in the first chapter that the philosophical account of persons and the scientific account of the species *homo sapiens* ought to converge, simply because humans are the only real people we have around to look at. That philosophy and science must thus converge is, by Aristotle, taken for granted.

Note next that this insistence upon examining the *psuche*, the aspect that tells us 'what it is to be' this organism, does not embroil Aristotle in dualism. There are several reasons for this. (*a*) were we to detect here a dualism of *psuche* and body, and attempt to compare it to our mind-body dualism, we would have the problem that such a 'dualism' must be equally imposed on maple trees and mosquitoes. Indeed, since digestive functions are part of the *psuche* too, we would have a dualism not only for the mind, but also for the stomach. Worse yet: since the supposed dualism appeals to an alleged duality between form and matter (and not only between *psuchai*-type forms and matter) we would have to be 'dualist' about everything: about, say, buildings and houses, for the matter of a house is a building and its form is its capacity to shelter property and living beings. (*b*) in order for anything to be *one* thing at all, a single substance, that thing must be enmattered form (or in-formed matter); there is no such thing as 'bare' matter. Things are not *combinations* of form and matter. A human body minus its *psuche* is still one thing, but is now simply a corpse; it still of course has a form, but that is a different one, a form which is not a *psuche*: a corpse's form is a matter of its shape and structure. Whatever else dualism may be, it is not a mind-*corpse* dualism. (*c*) form and matter constrain each other and cannot be understood separately. For instance, one cannot have a corkscrew made of wool. Conversely honey-water, the stuff, determines the form of the drink, honey-water. In this last case—the case of a fairly low-level substance—it may be hard to tell whether one is studying it *qua* form or *qua* matter. Indeed, the mutual constraining of form and matter explain the qualifier 'primarily' in the list of forms given above: the form of a threshold is not *only* its location. A threshold must also be hard, resistant—a large oblong soufflé would not do. (*d*) above all, the distinction is not an absolute one: there is a carefully crafted hierarchy here. Straw and mud are matter for bricks, the shape and function of which 'forms' them into the substance, a brick; bricks are matter for the different substance, a wall; this in turn is part of the matter of another substance, a building; buildings are the matter of houses. Aristotle is very clear about this, saying, for instance, that 'anger' can be studied *either* as 'the boiling of the blood and the hot stuff about the heart' *or* as 'a desire for revenge' (*De Anima*, i. 1. 403^{a}29-^{b}3). The form-matter distinction, which can profitably be compared with the contemporary function-structure distinction, is no more a hard-and-fast one than is the latter, and for much the same reasons.

The complex structure of the human *psuche*, with the base of the pyramid rooted in metabolic functions and its tip constituted by reason, gives us a picture of the individual with far more unity, in one important sense of that troubled term, than does 'mind'. For it presupposes the unity and continuity of biology and psychology—indeed, the difference emerges as theoretically insignificant. The capacity to digest food is as fully a part of the *psuche* as is the capacity to solve mathematical theorems. Hence we find in Aristotle's writings discussions of breathing, moving, sleeping and dreaming, sensation, imagination, and reasoning. None the less, the *psuche* functions of most significance for studying *this particular kind of organism* are those that distinguish it from others; and in man this is of course his (practical and theoretical) reasoning. Further, we cannot pretend that the individual is not a part of society; and so social psychology, sociology, language, culture, and co-operative activities must all take their places on the continuum of concern. For Aristotle, as we have seen, notes the brute empirical fact that 'man is by nature [*phusei*: essentially] a social animal' (*Nicomachean Ethics*, i. 7. 1097^{b}11), and so an indispensable part of any full investigation will be, indeed must be, to see how he applies his practical reason to his social engagements. The theory of the individual is thus at every point rooted in the sciences of man, from biology to anthropology. Aristotle would have found remarkable the proportion of philosphical ink spilt on capacities like sense perception and the capacity for pain: these are important, certainly, and fully part of the human *psuche*; but even the lowest animals have them too.

Moreover, the hierarchical organization of the *psuche* ensures another sort of unity as well. The capacities—again diverse—of the tip of the pyramid unite the rest. Consider a dog. Its *psuche* has the omnipresent digestive and nutritive functions: why? These help to render possible its highest faculties, its active running-barking-chasing life. But, just as important, there is evidently feedback from above too: since running, chasing rabbits, resting, and the like foster its digestion and metabolism. The point is that in the healthy dog the lower *psuche* functions contribute towards making the higher functions possible, and the higher functions loop back on to the healthy regulation of the lower. It is just the same in the human *psuche*. The human individual requires the lowest *psuche* functions (of digestion, metabolism) to function well if he is to engage in his characteristic activity of purposive intelligent action; and that activity also presupposes essentially the proper working of his sensory, desiderative, and locomotive abilities, the 'middle-level' *psuche* capacities. These are 'bottom-up' contributions, from lower *psuche* capacities to the exercise of the highest ones. But there is feedback 'from above', too. He needs to work out how to grow his food, how to find shelter, how to avoid an enemy; and as we have seen, he lives in a complex social world, so that if he is to stay healthy and happy, able to exercise his senses and exploit his mobility, he must arrange personal and social matters appropriately. This requires him to exercise his practical reason to ensure that his material, social, economic, and political environment is well suited for his health, his particular projects, and for his human flourishing in general. As with the dog, there is full-blooded feedback from man's highest to his lowest capacities, but the highest faculties dominate just because these are the *characteristic* features of human existence, telling us what differentiates man from all else. So 'the part which chooses' is the *ruling* element (*Nicomachean Ethics*, iii. 4. 1113ᵃ4-6). When this is exercising its powers to the full, it ensures that there is a balanced and healthy physical and psychological 'unity'; and, just as essential to a rational organism which is by nature social, it aims to promote social and political 'unity'—security and stability—as well.

We saw in the last chapter that although Aristotle 'lacked' a term that systematically translated 'conscious' this proved to be rather an advantage than a disadvantage. 'Consciousness' is too elastic and elusive; and anything said in terms of it is probably better said without. Now it begins to look as though he has a second advantage: *psuche* seems theoretically superior to 'mind', which is of course another term Aristotle 'lacks'. We can add to these two a third virtue of his account: that Aristotle's man is *active*, an agent. His highest good (*eudaimonia*, roughly translatable as 'flourishing') is glossed in terms of activity: living well, and doing well. 'A man seems to be a source of actions' (*Nicomachean Ethics*, iii. 3. 1112ᵇ31-2); and consider this; 'choice is either desiderative reason or ratiocinative desire, *and such a source of action is a man*', (*Nicomachean Ethics*, vi. 2. 1139ᵇ4-5). We become the people that we are by choosing, deciding, acting; we have the responsibility for shaping ourselves, our characters, and our lives. This stress on agency and activity, man *in* the world and not just an observer of it, is one of the most attractive features of his general theory—a feature which, we shall see, was jettisoned in the seventeenth century.

Aristotle's picture of the individual, like so much else of his, largely dominated successive generations. His Christian followers found embarrassing the fact that the form-matter relation excluded personal survival after death,[5] and so wrestled with the impossibility of trying to inject into the picture a *psuche* that was a *separable* form; but we find *precisely* Aristotle's account, contaminated only by the accretion of a stuff-like soul, confronting Descartes. It is now time to look at the transition—because it is, exactly, a transition from Aristotle's view that we see taking place before our eyes, in only three paragraphs, in Descartes's *Second Meditation*.

4. FROM *PSUCHE* TO MIND

Descartes writes, near the beginning of the *Second Meditation:*

In the first place, then, I considered myself as having a face, arms, and all that system of bones and flesh as seen in a corpse which I designated by the name of body. In addition to this I considered that I was nourished, that I walked, that I felt, and that I thought, and I referred all these actions to the soul; but I did not stop to consider what the soul was, or if I did stop, I imagined that it was something extremely rare and subtle like a wind, a flame, or an ether, which was spread through my grosser parts (Descartes [1641]; Haldane and Ross [1967], vol. i, p. 151).

This is almost all pure Aristotle. ('Almost', because the 'wind, flame or ether' are Christian accretions, albeit borrowed from early Greek—Presocratic—philosophers.) We start with the matter: the body. Then we find, listed in the correct hierarchical order, many of the functions of the human *psuche* discussed by Aristotle: desire, pleasure and pain, and imagination are among those missing. This, then, is how Descartes used to consider himself—as an Aristotelian man.

But then:

Let us pass to the attributes of soul and see if there is any one which is in me. What of nutrition and walking (the first mentioned)? But if it is so that I have no

---

[5] It is true that Aristotle, embarrassingly, allows (at *De Anima*, iii. 5. 430ª10-25) for a form of dualism; the active intellect is 'distinct, unaffected, unmixed . . . immortal and eternal'. It would be fair to say that nobody has made satisfactory sense of this chapter. There must be some connection with his theological views, because this active intellect, like a god, is 'in essence activity'. Theological overtones can help explain, even if not excuse, much philosophical incoherence. What survives is anyway extremely puzzling; it is not thought itself, but something that stands to thought in the way that light stands to colours, making them visible.

body it is also true that I can neither walk nor take nourishment. Another attribute is sensation. But one cannot feel without body, and besides I have thought I perceived many things during sleep that I recognised in my waking moments as not having been experienced at all. What of thinking? I find here that thought is an attribute that belongs to me; it alone cannot be separated from me . . . to speak accurately I am not more than a thing which thinks, that is to say a mind or a soul (Descartes [1641]; Haldane and Ross [1967], vol. i, p. 151).

Here he runs through, still in the proper order, the functions that Aristotle assigned to the *psuche*, omitting again the capacities he omitted earlier. Now, though, he has cut off and given a special place to the tip of the pyramid, the capacity for thought. Note that sensation (sense perception and pain perception) has been thrown out.

However, it is soon salvaged. It is salvaged thus: although one can be deceived about whether or not one is really seeing something, one cannot be deceived about the proposition that one seems to see something. So, construing 'sees' as 'seems to see', sensation gets to be a kind of thought process:

But it will be said that these phenomena are false [seeing light, hearing noises, feeling heat] and that I am dreaming. Let it be so; still it is at least quite certain that *it seems to me that* I see light, that I hear noise, and that I feel heat. That cannot be false; properly speaking it is what is in me called feeling [sentire]; and used in this precise sense that is no other thing than thinking (Descartes [1641]; Haldane and Ross [1967], vol. i, p. 153).

If seeing gets back in so easily, why not walking? Perhaps even Descartes would jib at calling 'seeming to walk' the *proper* sense of the term 'walk'; but conversely Aristotle would baulk at describing 'seeming to see' as the *precise* sense of the term 'see'. (He notes, in *De Anima*, ii. 5. 417^{b}20-1, that 'the things that produce the activity of sense perception are external, for instance the objects seen and heard, and so also for the rest of the senses'; see too *De Anima*, ii. 8. 420^a 17-18: 'but a sound is something public rather than private.') Anyhow, Descartes makes his new, generous use of the term 'thought' completely explicit elsewhere:

Thought is a word that covers everything that exists in us in such a way that we are immediately conscious of it. Thus all the operations of will, intellect, imagination, and of the senses are thoughts (Descartes [1641]; Haldane and Ross [1967], vol. ii, p. 52).

Given this bit of sleight of hand, the mind can finally replace the *psuche*:

But what then am I? A thing which thinks. What is a thing that thinks? It is a thing which doubts, understands, conceives, affirms, denies, wills, refuses, which also imagines and feels (Descartes [1641]; Haldane and Ross [1967], vol. i, p. 153).

And to cap it all, in a letter to Mersenne:

As to [the proposition] . . . *that nothing can be in me, that is, in my mind, of which I am not conscious*, I have proved it in the *Meditations*, and it follows from the fact that the soul is distinct from the body and that its essence is to think (Descartes [1641]; Kenny [1970], p. 90).

The mind, *qua* the conscious mind, is thus conjured into existence—a product of purely epistemological considerations. Descartes sought in the *Meditations* to evade scepticism, and the birth of the conscious mind was the key to his solution. Incorrigibility can be found only in the current contents of the conscious mind: thoughts, ideas, *cogitationes*. These then had to take on the role of unshakeable foundation-stones for the rebuilding of our structure of empirical knowledge.

The British Empiricists followed suit in emphasizing the epistemological weight of a conscious mind. Locke, for instance, talks of 'that consciousness which is inseparable from thinking, and, as it seems to me, essential to it; it being impossible for any one to perceive without perceiving that he does perceive . . . consciousness always accompanies thinking . . .' (Locke, *Essay* [1690], Book ii, ch. xxvii, para. 11; [1959], vol. i, pp. 448-9). Or consider Hume, who comments economically that 'the perceptions of the mind are perfectly known' (*Treatise* [1739], Book ii, part ii, s. vi; [1965], p. 366); and '[c]onsciousness never deceives' (*Enquiry* [1748], s. vii, part 1, para. 52; [1963], p. 66). Aristotle's interests, by contrast, were not epistemological but scientific: biology and psychology. Yet it is Descartes who had dominated subsequent scientific psychology, to the exasperation of Thorndike in 1898:

[Descartes's] physiological theories have all been sloughed off by science long ago. No one ever quotes him as an authority in morphology or physiology . . . Yet his theory of the nature of the mind is still upheld by not a few, and the differences between his doctrines of imagination, memory, and of the emotions, and those of many present-day psychological books, are comparatively unimportant (Thorndike [1898], p. 1).[6]

---

[6] And not only in 1898. Some think that the Cartesian influence still holds too much sway today; *vide* Hayes (1986): 'Why should psychologists be reluctant to accept that humans can learn in this way? [i.e. that task-relevant information need not be represented in a form that is open to conscious inspection—K.V.W.] An obvious can-

Rorty [1970*b*] has a most attractive explanation that can be adapted to show what has gone wrong here—wrong, that is, as far as scientists like Thorndike are concerned. He points out that if 'ontology' was a subject which we left to scientists to determine (which is what the man in the street does: there are electrons, there are no longer any dodos; science has told us so) then there is nothing left for a separate discipline, philosophy, to say about it. Ontology *per se* is an empirical matter. The excuse for philosophers to investigate ontology lies with their further preoccupations and motivations. For instance, Rorty suggests, one such excuse is the desire to find out what there would *have* to be if we are to have the knowledge that we apparently do have:

To say that we need better answers to the question 'What is there?' than either science or common sense gives us makes sense only if we see some . . . principle endangered by either science or common sense. If to be a philosopher who does ontology is to be something different from an armchair scientist, the difference will only appear by isolating the questions which impelled him to become an ontologist. What sets apart the ontologies of professional philosophers is that they are created in response to questions arising in other areas—specifically, epistemology, ethics, logic and semantics ([1970*b*], p. 276).

Descartes, in the *Meditations*, was a pure philosopher; Aristotle, throughout, was a scientist. He put epistemology firmly in its place, secondary to ontology *per se*, when he said—speaking from a scientific point of view: 'there is knowledge of something only when we have grasped its essence' (*Metaphysics*, vii. 6. 1031^{b}6-7). No wonder Thorndike finds the psychological theories deriving from Descartes's epistemology so frustrating *for the scientist*. It may be now clear, from the preceding chapters and from the above, why I find the Aristotelian *psuche* so manifestly superior to the Cartesian *mens*—since what we are trying to do is to describe the person.

5. THE DOMINATION OF THE MIND

So Descartes was the person primarily responsible for introducing the *conscious* mind, or at least for making it the central and dominating strand in the philosophers' notion of what it was to be a person. That

didate is an allegiance (explicitly or implicitly held) to the Cartesian model of mind. According to this view, a system which learns without the products of its learning being available to processes which can inspect, report, and if necessary modify them is essentially out of control' (pp. 4-5).

picture has determined discussion of the subject ever since. To Descartes a person was a *res cogitans*, a 'thinking thing', where 'thinking' was interpreted in the way we saw in the last section: essentially conscious. Locke, of course, picked up the theme, and we may as well remind ourselves again of the famous quotation; 'person' stands for:

a thinking intelligent being, that has reason and reflection, and can consider itself as itself, the same thinking thing, in different times and places; which it does only by that consciousness which is inseparable from thinking, and, as it seems to me, essential to it (*An Essay Concerning Human Understanding* [1690], Book II, ch. xxvii, para. 11; [1959], vol. i, pp. 448 f.).

This is all far too familiar to need elaboration. What is important for our purposes is that not only consciousness but also *unity and continuity*—a unity and continuity of consciousness—now takes centre stage. The person is an inner eye, an inner conscious self or ego: a 'ghost in the machine'.

Thinking is modelled on perception. Now this of course was often true also in the ancient Greek period, as the roots of the term *theoria* well indicate; but the differences are what concern us here. In the Greek period there had not been:

the conception of the human mind as an inner space in which both pains and clear and distinct ideas passed in review before a single Inner Eye. There were, to be sure, the notions of taking tacit thought, forming resolutions *in foro interno*, and the like. The novelty was the notion of a single inner space in which bodily and perceptual sensations ('confused ideas of sense and imagination' in Descartes' phrase), mathematical truths, moral rules, the idea of God, moods of depression, and all the rest of what we now call 'mental' were objects of quasi-observation (Rorty [1980], p. 50).

There is only one spectator, one Inner Eye, having the whole 'mental' domain to scrutinize; and so no question about unity.

Whatever the alleged epistemological gains, the costs of this transformation are high. Part of the cost, of course, is that we have thereby lost entirely the Aristotelian insight into the multiple *heterogeneity* of the elements of human psychology (remember *De Anima*, iii. 9. 432^{a}24, 'there seem to be indefinitely many parts of the human *psuche*'). Now, though, bodily sensations and the idea of God trip hand in hand through the mental theatre. A further cost is that we now have dualism thrust upon us: there is an inner realm, and an outer, and we must devise theories to get them back together again. A third, and expensive, cost is that we have swapped activity for passivity—we have swapped man acting *in* the world for man as a private observer of it; or rather, as an observer of what he takes his world to be. Put another way, study of man's capacities, of what he *does*, has been traded for study of the mental events that take place inside him. (Indeed, we still see the impact of this today, in the idea that 'cognition', or 'perception', can be studied in isolation from sensori-motor control—e.g. by computer modelling.) Finally, the Inner Eye metaphor of course sets the post-Cartesians a most uncomfortable paradox. Sensation, as we saw in the preceding section, was rescued from the 'physical' pit into which Descartes had consigned nutrition and locomotion precisely by being redescribed as a kind of thinking. But thinking is hard to think about without the metaphor of sight—of *ordinary* sight. The viciousness of this circle is impossible to exaggerate. Ordinary sight has objects to look at. Hence, it seems, thought must have objects, and objects analogous to public objects of sight in the real world, mental *entities:* 'ideas', 'impressions', 'sense data', 'qualia'; these are soon to be construed as 'mental atoms' by parallel with Newtonian atoms. Thus we get the second domain of the mental, and a double ontology. That foists on us the dualism of the inner and outer realms; and we now cannot understand either thinking or perception.

Hume was the first to see— although not to solve—the incoherence of this picture for understanding the self. It in fact leaves no room for the essential spectator or Inner Eye, no room for the idea of one thing continuing uninterruptedly through the succession of ideas and impressions that constitute the mind:

The mind is a kind of theatre, where several perceptions successively make their appearance; pass, re-pass, glide away, and mingle in an infinite variety of postures and situations. There is properly no *simplicity* in it at one time, nor *identity* in different; whatever natural propension we may have to imagine that simplicity and identity. The comparison of the theatre must not mislead us. They are the successive perceptions only, that constitute the mind; nor have we the most distant notion of the place where these scenes are represented, or of the materials, of which it is compos'd (*Treatise on Human Nature* [1739], Book I, part iv, s. vi; [1965], p. 253).

The only way out—or back—would prove to be the Kantian one: the unitary transcendental ego.

The inconsistencies, and the detail, of this model are not our concern here. That a picture cannot be made coherent does not prevent it from dominating our theoretical understanding of ourselves. What is relevant to our purposes is the impact it had upon that understanding, for this was colossal.

Descartes could 'see clearly that there is nothing which is easier for me to know than my mind' (*Meditation* II [1641]; [1967], vol. i, p. 157). We can sit, in our dressing-gowns before a fire, observing ourselves (not acting, note). But this leads swiftly to solitude. I and I alone have privileged access to my thoughts and feelings—only I can 'see' them in the focus of the spotlight of consciousness—and hence I am incorrigible about them. However much I may tell you about what is going on in me, this you can never fully understand; because to know those thoughts and feelings would require you to have them, and that you cannot do. The mind, like the grave, becomes a fine and private place. The solitude in which I find myself is irredeemable, for the sceptical problems that the 'mind as inner theatre' model poses cannot be resolved: there is now no adequate resting-place between solipsism on the one hand and the rejection of myself entirely in crude behaviourism on the other.

Worse, solitude destroys me. I become opaque to myself. My mind—which started off with Descartes as the paradigm of what could be fully, completely surveyed and understood—now turns into something I do not understand at all. The best-known arguments for this, stemming mainly from the later writings of Wittgenstein and from Strawson [1958], are of course those that display the internal incoherence of the solipsist standpoint. Here, though, I want to bring to bear a rather different strand of thought, one which we have met before. For what the Cartesian and post-Cartesian model cannot tolerate is evidence of disunity, of a stream of consciousness with gaps in it: and the disunity, and the gaps, cannot be overlooked. We have seen many of these gaps already; but we can add to the number such trivial everyday phenomena as slips of the tongue, puns, lapses of memory—these exemplify more gaps, because we cannot discover by introspection where they originate: the associations are not conscious. (Indeed, according to Lashley, '*no* activity of mind is ever conscious'.) Where there are gaps, I cannot provide an intelligible explanation of my thoughts and actions. Alienation from others ends up in alienation myself. If I cannot understand myself, and since nobody else can, then I am wholly unintelligible. The Greeks had difficulty with problems like weakness of will and self-deception because these showed that man was not fully rational, that he could sometimes act against what he knew to be his own best interests. Post-Cartesian philosophy in the British tradition shared those problems; but the failure of rationality displayed was not so worrying as was the failure of unity, the failure of the conflicting thoughts and desires to resolve their disharmony in the allegedly all-embracing focus of conscious attention.

The brute fact of gaps in consciousness and of disunity led inevitably to a weakening of the 'I', if 'I' was seen as the unified consciousness, for this could no longer claim to be coextensive with the mind. The mind contains, and must be recognized to contain, depths to which such an 'I' has no access.

Now this split is a *far* more fundamental one than is the dichotomy with which philosophers in the analytic tradition have been mainly concerned, the so-called mind–body problem. For this latter problem (until relatively recently), presupposing that 'mind' was equivalent to 'conscious mind', therefore in general treated only of *conscious* mental states and events and their relation to physical processes. (Never before had *sensations* been so exhaustively discussed; I commented earlier on how this would have surprised Aristotle.) Thus philosophy served to reinforce with relatively little criticism the Cartesian model of the mind, and it was left to literature (and Continental philosophy) to explore the interplay between conscious and non-conscious psychological states and events, thus giving a far richer picture both of the mind and of the person. Put another way, English-language philosophy continued to attempt a rational reconstruction of personal identity as a matter of a 'unity of consciousness', leaving to literature the exploration of what is in fact far more compelling and important. Both of course accepted the centrality of consciousness—philosophy by virtually ignoring anything else, literature by its fascination with the interrelations between the conscious and the non-conscious—that much of the Cartesian heritage is dominant yet. But the philosophical discussions of personal identity frolicked for a long time in a cul-de-sac of irrelevance.

6. THE PERSON AS A COMPUTER

If Simon is right about the imminence of artificial intelligence, [computers] are on the verge of creating an even greater conceptual revolution—a change in our understanding of man. Everyone senses the importance of this revolution, but we are so near the events that it is difficult to discern their significance. This much, however, is clear. Aristotle defined man as a rational animal, and since then reason has been held to be the essence of man. If we are on the threshold of creating artificial intelligence we are about to see the triumph of a very special conception of reason. Indeed, if reason can be programmed into a computer, this will confirm an understanding of man as an object, which Western thinkers have been groping toward for two thousand years but which they only now have the tools to express and implement. The incarnation of this intuition will drastically change our understanding of ourselves. If, on the other hand, artificial intelligence should turn out to be impossible, then we will have to distinguish human from artificial reason, and this too will radically change our view of ourselves (Dreyfus [1979], pp. 78 f.).

In the first chapter I argued that computers themselves do not, and will not, challenge our monopoly of personhood; no full or rich form of reason can be programmed into a computer. But that does not by itself prevent us from being caught up by a *model* of the individual as an unimaginably complex computer. The imagination can easily extrapolate from the fact that computers can do many things that we do to the conclusion that we are all really no more than immensely complicated computers. As Hobbes proclaimed, 'reason is but reckoning'. This may be thought to transform our self-understanding; by altering the *Zeitgeist* against which we frame and develop our theories.

The merits of such a model are evident. In terms of the computer analogy we get free of the idea that there must be a 'ghost in the machine'; there is no immaterial computer inside the familiar object sitting on the desk, and no temptation to postulate one. Or, to put it another way, we can postulate all the ghosts, or homunculi, that we need because '[h]omunculi are *bogeymen* only if they duplicate *entire* the talents they are rung in to explain' (Dennett [1979], p. 123). They are 'bogeymen', that is, if we try to explain, say, our ability to see things in terms of a little man in the brain who looks at mental pictures; that 'explanation' smuggles the *explanandum* back into the *explanans*. They are not bothersome if they are assigned subordinate tasks—reacting to colour contrasts, texture gradients, vertical lines. So on the basis of the computer metaphor we need postulate no Lockean ghost, no Cartesian thinker; all we need is rather an organized hierarchy of subsystems (homunculi) each of which has a function to fulfil, a nested hierarchy which ultimately helps to explain some psychological capacity like perceiving or calculating. Unity and disunity too start to look far less problematic, as we see writ large in the ordinary computers of today the variety of routines and subroutines that indeed interlock, but which may interlock more or less efficiently. And part at least of the mystique of consciousness is mitigated by familiarity with this hierarchy of information-processing routines and with scanning and self-scanning devices. Indeed, without recognizing what they are doing, contemporary cognitive scientists have been reverting to the Aristotelian picture; for this systematic examination of hierarchically organized structures and functions is exactly what Aristotle's *psuche*, and the form–matter terminology, allow them.

The demerits of the analogy are equally obvious. As with so many analogies, it is easy both to forget that it is one, and to neglect the disanalogous elements. The computers we now have, albeit triumphs of technology and ingenuity, are not intelligent, cannot be ascribed any psychological terms in any full-blooded sense, are *manifestly* mindless. I argued in Chapter 1 that there are strong reasons, even if they are not reasons 'of principle', for supposing that they will stay that way. There we saw that the differences between people and computers are perhaps as great, in many respects, as are those between people and earwigs (see Chapter 1, pp. 32 f.). Even if future progress sees computers achieving the intellectual level of the lower mammals—which would be a very large jump from the earwig, and which would certainly require robots rather than 'bedridden' computers—we are yet a very long way from interesting *intelligence*. If it is forgotten that what we have is an *analogy*, and hence by definition something that must have more or less significant *disanalogous* elements, then to say 'we are no more than computers' evidently reduces us—reduces us, because that with which we compare ourselves is so primitive or simple (relatively speaking). But to say 'we are no more than immensely sophisticated and flexible computers' is not helpful, because then we do not have any instances of that with which we are comparing ourselves, and do not know what this means. In particular we do not know what the put-down phrase 'no more than' means. In fact, the only 'immensely sophisticated and flexible computers' around would just be: people; and *all* that the claim can amount to then is the expression of an allegiance to some version of monism or materialism.

So the computer analogy can do this much at least: it can make materialism look far more plausible. *If* we are immensely complicated and sophisticated computers, then we are like computers in that we are 'only' physical systems. Artificial intelligence can show us how states of a purely physical system can have content, can be 'about' something; and it can provide *rough, partial* analogies for *very primitive* versions of the mental phenomena (the ascriptions of which to computers are typically protected by 'raised eyebrow', or 'scare'-quotes) that have vexed the mind–body debate for centuries. Throughout the history of that debate, the materialist has been on the defensive: struggling to ward off the challenges from dualists. If the burden of argument had been the other way around—with dualism challenged to defend the coherence of that position—the history would look very different: it is appallingly difficult to describe a coherent or intellectually attractive form of dualism. The computer analogy now gives materialism prima-facie probability. And it is the materialism that shocks. Robinson has recently expressed the horror most passionately:

James called materialism a tough-minded theory. . . . That picture is hypnotising but terrifying: the world as a machine of which we are all insignificant parts. . . . But reason joins with every other constructive human instinct in telling us that it is false and that only a parochial and servile attitude towards physical science can mislead anyone into believing it. To opt for materialism is to choose to believe something obnoxious, against the guidance of reason. This is not tough-mindedness, but a wilful preference for a certain form of soulless, false and destructive modernism (Robinson [1982], p. 125).

Little can be done to combat this very powerful sort of reaction to the materialist claim; it requires therapy rather than argument. Much depends on one's attitude to the physical sciences. To those of us who believe that physics is entering regions that compel, stretch, and defeat the imagination, the charge of 'soulless, false and destructive modernism' scarcely sticks. It rests on a false equation of contemporary physics with mechanical engineering (note that Robinson accuses materialism of regarding 'the world as a *machine*'). Some, with Shelley, find modern science liberating rather than restrictive:

> All things are void of terror; man has lost
> His desolating privilege, and stands
> An equal amidst equals: happiness
> And science dawn though late upon the earth.
> (Shelley, *The Daemon of the World*)

Much of the distaste for the idea that man is 'no more than' a computer derives from the fact that the computers with which we are familiar are indeed mindless (and, if you like, 'soulless'). The mysteries of physics, however, are no less wonderful than are those of the mind. If man is 'only' a computer, we have some astonishing computers.

One way of expressing what might be left out by materialism, what might be inadequate in the computer analogy, what might be 'obnoxious' to our self-image, is given by Nagel's now familiar challenge: is there anything that it is like (for this X) to be an X? There is, the suggestion runs, something that it is like to be a person, or a bat[7],

---

[7] *Quaere*: how do we know that the bat's echolocation is not 'blindsighted'; i.e., that there is *nothing* that it is like for a bat to echolocate?

and nothing that it is like to be a hamburger or an IBM computer. The subjective character of experience, which is essentially connected with a single point of view, must be lost by objective science. (Little man in the brain, where are you when we need you most?)

If we acknowledge that a physical theory of mind must account for the subjective character of experience, we must admit that no presently available conception gives us a clue how this could be done. The problem is unique. If mental processes are indeed physical processes, then there is something it is like, intrinsically, to undergo certain physical processes. What it is for such a thing to be the case remains a mystery (Nagel [1974], p. 445).

There is little doubt that Nagel's discussion is the single best attempt to capture the residual X-factor that apparently eludes systematic study by the behavioural and brain sciences, and hence stands in the way of saying that people just are incredibly complex computers. The notion of a subjective point of view, ineffable and inexpressible but sharp, complex, and known to the subject, seems to be something that materialism cannot handle.

There are a number of related points in such a challenge, but none are easy to state sharply. One, however, we can get out of the way at the outset: we simply *do not know* whether there would be 'anything that it is like to be' an artefact whose capacities rivalled those of the human. I do not think, though, that this ignorance matters; we are such a distance away from confronting intelligent artefacts like Hal in *2001* that the speculation is pretty pointless—inconclusive science fantasy. Without even committing oneself to any strong form of verificationism the question itself seems not to be a sensible one; we are not going to get artefacts like that, and have no idea what we would say about them if (*per impossible*) we did. It might indeed be 'a mystery' that there is something that it is like to undergo certain physical processes—but physics is full of mysteries. Quantum mechanics is an obvious example; and, to the layman, the equation of matter with energy is pretty 'mysterious'; this last oddity was in fact exploited by Nagel [1965]. Mysteriousness is to a large extent a function of what we do and do not know. There is no viable argument leading to the conclusion that *no* artefact could ever have, in the relevant sense, an 'inside', and hence that we are not relevantly analogous to computers.

The intuitively appealing idea of 'what it is like to be an X' is in fact a deeply puzzling one. One rather blank argument—blank, because there seems to be little that can be done with it—is to object that one does not share Nagel's intuitions. That is, I would deny that I know what it is like, except in a highly boring and unproblematic sense, to be me, or human, or a little bit Scottish, or female. Consider Wittgenstein's challenge:

Can you imagine absolute pitch, if you have not got it?—Can you imagine it *if* you have it?—Can a blind man imagine seeing? Can *I* imagine it?—Can I imagine spontaneously reacting thus and so, if I don't do it? Can I imagine it any better, if I do do it? (Wittgenstein [1967], para. 266, p. 49ᵉ).

(Substituting 'know what . . . is like' for 'imagine' brings out the point clearly.) There is of course a harmless sense in which I know what it is like to be me: I can describe myself to myself and equally to others. But I am aware of nothing that qualifies as *knowledge* over and above that—nothing as significant as Nagel claims. Put another way, a psychiatrist who has remained sane throughout a life devoted to the study of schizophrenia knows more, and better, about what it is like for the schizophrenic to be schizophrenic than does the lay sufferer; put in the form of an objection to Hume, it seems to my intuition that a congenitally deaf scientist who (improbably) had devoted his career to the phenomenology and psychophysiology of auditory perception would know far more than I do about hearing.

These are *just* conflicting intuitions (and perhaps more share Nagel's than share mine: an informal and unscientific survey of students and colleagues over several years brings Nagel out ahead, but not by much). Little more can be done than simply to state them. However blank the point, though, the clash of intuitions is not worthless; it reminds us of the metaphilosophical point raised in Chapter 1 that intuition is often an indecisive or unreliable tool. Although the mere affirmation of a conflicting intuition cannot of course overturn Nagel's case, it can weaken it to the extent that it questions the trustworthiness of a premiss: that there is something precise, particular, but ineffable about what it is like for an X to be an X, facts which do not consist in the truth of propositions expressible in any objectifying language.

A more direct objection is to query the coherence of the postulation of such puzzling facts. Thus to object would require one to marshal some of the familiar arguments against 'the myth of the given', or against the view that there can indeed be knowledge by acquaintance which is not knowledge by (or under) a description. It challenges the idea that facts can be ineffable even though non-conceptually effed by an alleged knower. If the Wittgensteinian and Strawsonian arguments against the presuppositions of a private language go through, the subject cannot create *a novo* a subjective phenomenology for himself; and it seems to me that the arguments do go through—at least, I do not see where Nagel would fault them. A more direct way of putting the point is to object that 'having A' need not entail 'knowing (about) A'—I can be the last to know about the inkblot on my face. It is true that having A does sometimes put me in a privileged epistemological position about it, and this I enjoy *vis-à-vis* a great many mental phenomena (although not all). But the knowledge thus possessed is public (or publicizable) enough, so cannot be what Nagel is after; and I find it hard sensibly to characterize what he *is* after: knowledge that is a priori restricted to acquaintance gives us no way of characterizing 'facts' or 'knowledge', still less particular facts and precise knowledge.

Evidently the sciences, seeking to transcend the individual (and indeed to transcend the human) point of view, will not themselves say much that is directly enlightening about subjective points of view. However, they have no need to worry about this omission; the complaint misunderstands their job. Just as a map of the London underground system often helpfully has an ancillary arrow stating 'YOU ARE HERE', so the notional, complete, psychophysiological-physical picture of the world could be supplemented for its users: 'THIS IS YOU', from which the way things are experienced from that position may be inferred. The addition 'YOU ARE HERE' to a map is, evidently, not the cartographer's business, and such maps could not be sold at bookstores; similarly, the addendum 'THIS IS YOU' to a complete psycho-physical account is not a proper part of the scientist's concern. But a fixed map in an underground station on which the station-master could stick his arrow, or an objective psycho-physical description to which one could *give* the subjective 'fix'—and both would be heuristics, assisting the user to interpret the maps—could each supply the point of view: from here, Victoria is four stops east on the Circle line, from this perspective, red and green would be indistinguishable (i.e. the viewpoint of a colour-blind man). Psychologists and neuroscientists, like cartographers, must first frame their representations; then, if they want to be helpful, they will show us how to interpret and use them—will show us how to find 'the subjective point of view'.

To sum up, sciences do not and need not explain every phenomenon under every description. No science, as I have mentioned already, explains what it is to be an ornament. Thus there seems no reason to suppose that science has, or fails to grapple with, the question of 'what it is like to be a person'—especially if this is said to be inexpressible and ineffable even within the far richer conceptual resources of the vernacular. The sciences may one day give us a full and systematic account of what it is to be human beings, though: the only real persons we have.

7. CONCLUSION

The three models we have been discussing are not part of any explicit theory of 'Mind and its Place in Nature'. They cannot even be described as 'paradigms' in anything close to Kuhn's sense of that term. They supply background strands in terms of which we build our scientific and philosophical theories and conjectures about human motivation and behaviour.

We see that the *theories* have diverged significantly over the last 2,000 years. Descartes could scarcely be further from Aristotle. These theories, as I have tried to illustrate, are in part determined by under- lying background (epistemological, scientific, metaphysical, and metatheoretical) presuppositions. Yet despite all that, we—as laymen in the street—can read and learn from Aristotle and Descartes alike; we can appreciate the plays of Euripides as much as Proust's novel. We have added a few presuppositions, perhaps ('Oedipal complexes'?) and dropped a few too. But the layman of the twentieth century AD would be much more at home with his fellow layman 2,400 years before than Aristotle would be with Descartes, or Locke with Skinner, or vice versa.

Why is this? In general, I would claim, because the everyday understanding of real people is only marginally contaminated (temporarily, or perhaps to some slight extent permanently) by scient- ific and philosophical theories. The layman does not go in for 'theories', and the *Zeitgeist* behind his attitudes to others is based firmly in the reality of human social life. Whatever the theoreticians get up to, people have to coexist, to survive, to provide for their family, to pursue the diverse ends—diverse, but characteristically theirs—which make life worth living. Our needs are fundamentally the same as those of Homer's heroes; our brains are no bigger than Aristotle's. 'There is a massive central core of human thinking which has no history . . . there are categories and concepts which, in their most fundamental character, change not at all' (Strawson [1959], p. 10). The practical demand, posed to a specific and fragile biological organism, for coping in various physical and social environments remains generally constant whatever details may change in those environments. So when new (scientific or philosophical) theories come along, the everyday understanding might, *or might not*, be affected. Not being a paradigm, not being explicit, not being—I would claim—realistically construed, this understanding cannot be ousted by a successor-model. It is far too tolerant of, and welcoming towards, the grossest apparent inconsistencies: everything is grist to its mill. For instance: practically everything upon which Descartes's model of the mind rested has long since been rejected; we now construct our theory of knowledge without his search for 'foundations', and we are perhaps less inclined to take epistemological *desiderata* to be ontological presuppositions. None the less, as Thorndike complained, we cleave to the 'theatre model' of the mind; or at least, we stick by it much of the time—in our idioms, that is to say in our language. At the same time we are picking up bits of the computational picture; quite neglecting the incompatibility of the model of the brain-as-computer with that of the mind-as-naked-consciousness, we happily exploit the resources of both models, whenever it suits us to exploit either—or to exploit both in the same sentence, if necessary. We have already displayed this carefree tolerance when combining mangled bits of Freudian theory, whenever we felt it useful to do so, with the Cartesian conscious *mens*—a marriage that any realist must think to be doomed from the outset. It is my guess that the infinite tolerance of ordinary language (a tolerance that has never ever been worried by inconsistencies that should perplex the realist) inevitably raises philosophical problems *for philosophers*. The unholy mix of bits of Cartesianism, bits of Freud, bits of Skinner, bits of computer terminology, makes it impossible to impose rational sense on the resulting hotchpotch. Philosophers are constantly creating mysteries which the layman finds uncompelling: but it was after all the philosopher, not the man in the street, who was the fly that Wittgenstein wanted to release from the fly-bottle.

It may be true that the computer analogy transforms, for some, their self-understanding. If so, it will be due to intellectual confusion: we are no more like *these* computers than we are like earwigs. The analogy is of some help in enabling us to come to terms with the difficult (but Aristotelian) idea that the person is a rational and sentient *physical* object which—under some descriptions although not all—can in principle be systematically understood by the psychological and the physical sciences. Difficult as it may be, what else is compatible with evolutionary theory?

Whatever you may be sure of, be sure of this: that you are dreadfully like other people (James Russell Lowell, *My Study Windows*, 1871).

EPILOGUE

We have seen that all persons so far are human beings. This has been our excuse and justification for deploying what we know and believe about *homo sapiens* to cast light on our examination of the concept of a person.

When we consider a person *qua* member of the natural species we can see that what Locke got right in part was part of what Aristotle got right: both would insist that a person is a thinking and intelligent being, with capacities to reason and reflect, and capable of memory and foresight. What Aristotle would want to add and emphasize is something which Locke, with his Cartesian and solipsistic heritage, was unable to highlight adequately: that a person is a thinking, intelligent, *and social, and active*, being (not a Cartesian *mens*, a Lockean soul, nor a brain in a vat). Aristotle took these 'extra' features for granted because he concentrated upon what human beings really are. The characteristic features of the kind *homo sapiens* are rationality, activity, social preoccupations. Rationality requires *inter alia* long-term planning and long-term memory, so the human animal is indeed something that considers itself as a being lasting through time; the complexity of the rationality that humans possess and the demands made on it in their equally complex environments help explain the development of language; and the expression of rationality is purposive agency. Human activity presupposes rational engagement in the world, and denies the significance of a split between 'the mental'—whatever that may be—and 'the physical'; it insists that 'cognition', and 'sensori-motor control', are facets of one and the same whole; it explains why the 'seventh' condition (mentioned but not emphasized in the first chapter) of toolmaking and use might prove as central and as important as the ability to use language, for it is with and through tools that man's rational activity has expressed itself most conclusively. (This does not debunk allegedly 'purely intellectual' activity: the alphabet, the abacus, the Latin primer, and the PC are as much human artefacts as are the bulldozer and the Mir space station.) The social nature of *homo sapiens* provides the dimension within which the human animal primarily exercises his rational activity: that is why the psychopath is as maimed in his own way as is the mentally retarded. Social life presupposes more than 'mere cognition': to be social entails sentience as well as sapience—entails love and resentment, pain and pleasure. According to Aristotle, anyone who can or does survive in isolation is 'either a beast or a god', or, we might add, a computer or a psychopath.

This gives us a fully-fledged and substantial depiction of what matters about being human. It incorporates most of what the 'six conditions', outlined in Chapter 1, were trying to isolate, but adds to and deepens them. To see this, let us run briefly through them. The first was rationality: now we can see more clearly how and where that rationality is most characteristically expressed—in social, and/or goal-directed, activity. The second was a matter of being the subject of Intentional ascriptions; this, as we have seen, is rather trivial—lots of non-human animals are such subjects. The third and fourth, the 'stance' and 'reciprocation' conditions, arise inevitably from the sort of social arrangements within which the human animal typically operates. The fifth, use of language (and, let us now add, of other human artefacts too) again depends upon and contributes to the characteristic rational activities of the human. The sixth, some 'special form of consciousness', seemed to be a mess: it is true that much of our reasoning can be called 'conscious' and much of our purposive activity 'consciously controlled', but the content of this assertion seems to be exhausted by a consideration of the depth and complexity of our capacity for rational reflection. The 'unity' and 'continuity' that the condition of consciousness was *inter alia* trying to supply was, in so far as we do enjoy such unity and continuity, adequately explained by the requirements of rational and purposive activity in a complex social environment, and by the interplay of the many faculties of the human organism.

It is perfectly possible to leave the matter there. In contemporary English 'man' and 'person' are used as if they were synonymous. Many languages have terms that can be translated as either or both; the ancient Greek terms *aner* and *anthropos* are examples. Not all languages, to put the point another way, would find it easy to capture Locke's distinction between 'man' and 'person'. But the philosophical discussion of the topic of personhood wants to examine the possibility that, even if 'man' is *de facto* coextensive with 'person' (bating the borderline cases we have considered) it is not essentially so. It is not science fantasy but rather science fact to note that many stars are known to have planetary systems; and it would seem plausible to conjecture that many millions do. Therefore the assumption that none of these could provide conditions suitable for the emergence of intelligent life forms should strain credulity to its limits; and some such intelligent entities may well—if we ever come across them—strike us as being real people. If the English term 'person' is only contingently coextensive with 'man', this leaves open the possibility that non-humans might one day be counted as persons, that men are a subclass of persons.

Unlike *homo sapiens*, however, 'person' is not a natural-kind term. We have seen throughout the book that when unsure about whether or not some abnormal or impaired human was a person, our attitude to it made a considerable difference. There was no 'right' or 'wrong' answer to the question whether Miss Beauchamp, or a microcephalic infant, was or was not a person. So we should now look back over some of the reasons, other than those deriving from 'what it is to be' *human*, that there might be for including, or excluding, non-humans from the category of persons.

The most important, since our attitude to the entity in question is so often decisive in determining our conclusion, is whether we can make its behaviour intelligible to ourselves, and in our terms. Rational and social creatures from radically different environments may be well-nigh impossible to understand (cf. 'if a lion could talk, we could not understand him' (Wittgenstein [1963], p. 223[e]). To take an actual case: many speculate about the intellectual abilities of dolphins, whose encephalization quotient is closest to ours, and which are undeniably social animals. A dolphin's world, though, is so dramatically different from ours that its forms and modes of socialization, the manner in which it exercises practical reason, the stance which it is appropriate to take to it, and its ability and manner of reciprocating such a stance, may be something with which we cannot get to grips. Just so, perhaps, with aliens from other planets.

Now, we have seen that making behaviour rationally intelligible requires showing that it can be understood in terms of our common-sense psychological framework. Self-deception and weakness of will are philosophical problems precisely because we cannot satisfactorily do this. Pure alexia is not a philosophical problem, just because we have abandoned the attempt to show the syndrome of retained and lost abilities to be rationally intelligible (that is, in psychological terms): we have a satisfactory, but non-rational, explanation instead (in neuroscientific terms). The planets, rivers, rainbows, and so on were once explained on 'our' rational model; physical explanations eventually ousted them, and so rivers and rainbows, although once 'personified' seriously, are now no longer so. It is essentially to stress that for any success in seeing behaviour as *rationally* intelligible, we need both to know, and to take into account, the background against which the behaviour is set—the environment, the beliefs and needs, the abilities, and often the history, of the organism whose behaviour is under scrutiny. Psychoanalytic explanations are satisfactory (to the extent that they are found so) inasmuch and in so far as they show how the peculiar behaviour is rationally intelligible—once we have discovered and accepted some bizarre set of background conditions due to non-rational features such as infantile sexuality, repression, resistance, and the like. With knowledge of his history, and informed and sympathetic use of the imagination, we can sometimes see why the schizophrenic rationally behaves and reacts as he does. At present, and for the reasons given in Chapter 3, it is well-nigh impossible with a psychopath. Anthropologists at first found tribes such as the Ik or the Hopi virtually unintelligible, because too little was known about their background preoccupations and beliefs; sustained and sympathetic attempts to find out more about this background increased our ability to explain and understand that rational activity.

Our common-sense psychological framework has developed against and in accordance with our environment, needs, concerns, preoccupations, abilities. It is irreducibly and centrally anthropocentric, but is powerful even so: knowledge of others, and indeed of other animals, allow us to explain, sometimes, such phenomena as compulsive handwashing; why a dog is excited; why a chimpanzee is sulking. In so far as we regard the behaviour we try to explain as purposive and goal directed (and of course not all behaviour is, solely or even primarily), then the model is always '*if* all that were true of an entity with some share of rationality—of which human rationality is the paradigm and the starting-point—then in such circumstances it would be reasonable for that entity to act thus and so'. If it had an unconscious fear of x, if it were deprived of a meal when hungry, if it were ten years old, if its history at the hands of its parents had been thus and so . . . We start from ourselves, modifying our expectations as we turn to other animals, or as we go down the age scale; and we 'spread' mentality on to other systems to the extent that we can. The flexibility of the common-sense framework—the fact that we can, given a sensitive grasp of the multifarious background conditions, succeed in making intelligible so much of the purposive behaviour of other humans of many non-human animals, shows just how far the 'principle of humanity' and the 'principle of charity' can take us. Erroneously sometimes, of course: it is wrong to approach rivers, or the phenomenon of pure alexia, with the common-sense psychological framework. It may be misguided to treat some forms of depression as psychologically intelligible—maybe, for instance, we should look rather for causal explanations concerning limbic system deficiencies in catecholamine. But the overall success vastly outruns the occasional failures, and we are entitled to expect that such success will increase.

Some animals are harder to understand than others, and the dolphin is here the best example. Its behaviour and indeed its high encephalization quotient indicate advanced intelligence. But its watery environment and its abilities are so very far from our own that the basis from which rational explanation starts is largely mysterious. The 'background' against which it exercises its agency is further from us than that of the schizophrenic, or the Hopi Indian. Even there, those who have spent large amounts of time with dolphins—entering in to, and getting to understand, their background—can predict and understand their behaviour to some extent. All the same, the dolphin illustrates the difficulties we might have if we came across intelligent beings from other planets—with different abilities, environments, preoccupations.

We can see, though, that we would not call them 'persons' unless they proved to be intelligible to the (extended) framework of our self-understanding. We might conclude they were extremely intelligent—maybe their artefacts would suggest that they were in some ways more so than are we. But persons have to be entities to which we can react, to which we take a specific 'stance'; and to do that presupposes that we know enough about them to understand their goals and fears, abilities and limitations, and the structure of their social arrangements, so that we know how they will 'reciprocate'. The reason for taking humans as the paradigms of persons, then, is that to be a person is to possess the features characteristic of humans.

> It were no slight attainment could we merely fulfil what the nature of man implies.
>
> (Epictetus)

BIBLIOGRAPHY

Adkins, A. W. H. [1960], *Merit and Responsibility* (Clarendon Press, Oxford).
— [1970], *From the Many to the One* (Clarendon Press, Oxford).
Aristotle, *Nicomachean Ethics*.
— *De Anima*.
Asher, R. [1972], *Talking Sense* (Pitman Books Ltd., London).
Austin, J. L. [1962], *How to Do Things with Words* (Clarendon Press, Oxford).
Ayer, A. J. [1959], 'Privacy', *Proceedings of the British Academy* (Oxford University Press, Oxford).
Barnes, J. [1987], 'Four Legs Bad', *The Observer*, 21 June, p. 25.
Bennett, J. [1964], *Rationality* (Routledge and Kegan Paul, London).
Benson, D. F., and Geschwind, N. [1969a], 'Developmental Gerstmann Syndrome', *Neurology*, 20: 203–8.
— — [1969a], [1969b], 'The Alexias', in *Handbook of Clinical Neurology*, ed. P. J. Vinken and G. W. Bruyn (North-Holland, Amsterdam), iv. 112–40.
Bentham, J. [1780, 1789], *A Fragment on Government and an Introduction to the Principles of Morals and Legislation*, ed. W. Harrison [1948] (Basil Blackwell, Oxford).
Berry, A. [1979], 'When the Issues of Peace and War Lie with the Computer', *Daily Telegraph*, 21 November, p. 17.
Bierce, A. G. [1972], *The Devil's Dictionary* (Limited Editions Club, New York).
Bloch, S., and Chodoff, P. (eds.) [1981], *Psychiatric Ethics* (Oxford University Press, Oxford).
Block, N. (ed.) [1981], *Readings in Philosophy of Psychology* (Methuen, London), ii.
Bogen, J. E., Fisher, E. D., and Vogel, P. J. [1965], 'Cerebral Commissurotomy: a Second Case Report', *Journal of the American Medical Association*, 194: 1328–9.
Bohr, N. [1959], 'Discussion with Einstein on Epistemological Problems in Atomic Physics', in P. A. Schilpp (ed.), *Albert Einstein: Philosopher–Scientist*, (Harper Torchbooks, New York), i. 199–241.
Bouwsma, O. K. [1942], 'The Mystery of Time', in Bouwsma, *Philosophical Essays* (University of Nebraska Press, Lincoln), 99–127.
Boyle, R. [1672], *The Works of the Honourable Robert Boyle* [1772] (printed for J. and F. Rivington, L. Davies, and W. Johnston, London), 6 vols.
Brown, J. R. [1986], 'The Structure of Thought Experiments', *International Studies in the Philosophy of Science: the Dubrovnik Papers*, i. 1–15.

Cheek, D. B., and LeCron, L. M. [1968], *Clinical Hypnotherapy* (Grune and Stratton, New York).

Churchland, P. M. [1979], *Scientific Realism and the Plasticity of Mind* (Cambridge University Press, Cambridge).

—— [1984], *Matter and Consciousness* (The MIT Press, Cambridge, Mass.).

Churchland, P. S. [1986], *Neurophilosophy* (The MIT Press, Cambridge, Mass.).

Clark, A. [1980], *Psychological Models and Neural Mechanisms* (Clarendon Press, Oxford).

Condon, W. S., Ogston, W. D., and Pacoe, L. V. [1969], 'Three Faces of Eve Revisited: A Study of Transient Microstrabismus', *Journal of Abnormal Psychology*, 74: 618-20.

Confer, W. N., and Ables, B. S. [1983], *Multiple Personality: Etiology, Diagnosis, and Treatment* (Human Sciences Press, New York).

Congdon, M. H., Hain, J., and Stevenson, I. [1961], 'A Case of Multiple Personality Illustrating the Transition from Role-Playing', *Journal of Nervous and Mental Disease*, 32: 497-504.

Corkin, S., Sullivan, E., Twitchell, T., and Grove, E. [1981], 'The Amnesic Patient H. M.: Clinical Observations and Test Performance 28 Years after Operation', *Abstracts of the Society of Neuroscience*, 80: 12-35.

Davidson, D. [1970], 'Mental Events', in *Experience and Theory*, ed. L. Foster and J. W. Swanson (University of Massachusetts Press), 79-101.

Dennett, D. C. [1971], 'Intentional Systems', *Journal of Philosophy*, 68: 87-106.

—— [1976], 'Conditions of Personhood', in *The Identities of Persons*, ed. A. O. Rorty (University of California Press, Berkeley), 175-96.

—— [1978*a*], 'Why You Can't Make a Computer that Feels Pain', *Synthèse*, 38: 415-56.

—— [1978*b*], 'Towards a Cognitive Theory of Consciousness', in *Minnesota Studies in the Philosophy of Science*, 9, ed. C. Wade Savage (University of Minnesota Press, Minneapolis), 201-28.

—— [1979], 'Artificial Intelligence as Philosophy and as Philosophy', in Dennett, *Brainstorms* (Harvester Press, Hassocks), 109-26.

—— [1988], 'Quining Qualia', in *Consciousness in Contemporary Science*, ed. A. Marcel and E. Bisiach (Oxford University Press, Oxford), 42-77.

Descartes, R. [1637/41], *The Philosophical Works of Descartes*, ed. and trans. E. S. Haldane and G. R. T. Ross [1967] (Cambridge University Press, Cambridge), i, ii.

—— [1641], *Descartes: Philosophical Letters*, ed. and trans. A. J. P. Kenny [1970] (Clarendon Press, Oxford).

Diels, H., and Kranz, W. [1968], *Die Fragmente der Vorsokratiker* (Weidmann, Dublin/Zurich), 3 vols.

Dimond, S. J. [1980], *Neuropsychology* (Butterworth, London).

Dreyfus, H. L. [1979], *What Computers Can't Do* (Harper and Row, New York), rev. edn.

Evans, E. P. [1906], *The Criminal Prosecution and Capital Punishment of Animals* (Bungary Press, London); rep. [1987] (Faber, London).

Farrell, B. A. [1981], *The Standing of Psychoanalysis* (Oxford University Press, Oxford).

Feyerabend, P. [1975], *Against Method* (Verso, London).

Fingarette, H. [1969], *Self-Deception* (Humanities Press, New York).

Frankfurt, H. [1971], 'Freedom of the Will and the Concept of a Person', *Journal of Philosophy*, 68: 5–20.

Freud, S. [1963], *The Standard Edition of the Complete Psychological Works of Sigmund Freud*, ed. and trans. J. Strachey and A. Freud (Hogarth Press, London).

—— [1964], *New Introductory Lectures in Psychoanalysis*, ed. and trans. J. Strachey (W. W. Norton, New York).

—— [1965], *The Interpretation of Dreams*, ed. and trans. J. Strachey (Avon Books, New York).

—— [1969], *An Outline of Psycho-Analysis*, ed. and trans. J. Strachey (W. W. Norton, New York).

Gallup, G. G. [1977], 'Self-Recognition in Primates: A Comparative Approach to the Bi-Directional Properties of Consciousness', *American Psychologist*, 32: 329–38.

Gazzaniga, M. S., and LeDoux, J. E. [1978], *The Integrated Mind* (Plenum Press, New York).

Gerstmann, J. [1931], 'Zur Symptomatologie der Hirnläsionen im Uebergangsgebiet der unteren Parietal- und mittleren Occipitalwindung', *Nervenarzt*, 3: 691–5.

Geschwind, N. [1964], 'The Development of the Brain and the Evolution of Language', in *Monograph Series on Languages and Linguistics*, 17, ed. C. I. J. M. Stuart (Georgetown University Press, Washington), 155–69.

—— [1974], *Selected Papers on Language and the Brain. Boston Studies in the Philosophy of Science*, 16, ed. R. S. Cohen and M. W. Wartofsky (Reidel, Dordrecht-Holland).

—— and Fusillo, M. [1966], 'Color-Naming Defects in Association with Alexia', *Archives of Neurology*, 15: 137–46.

Glover, J. C. B. [1970], *Responsibility* (Routledge and Kegan Paul, London).

Goffman, E. [1961], *Asylums. Essays on the Social Situation of Mental Patients and Other Inmates* (Doubleday-Anchor Books, New York).

Greaves, G. B. [1980], 'Multiple Personality 165 Years after Mary Reynolds', *Journal of Nervous and Mental Disease*, 168: 577–96.

Gruenewald, D. [1971], 'Hypnotic Techniques without Hypnosis in the Treatment of Dual Personality', *Journal of Nervous and Mental Disease*, 153: 41–6.

Gunderson, K. [1971], *Mentality and Machines* (Doubleday, New York); 2nd edn. [1985] (Croom Helm, London).

Hamlyn, D. W. [1968], *Aristotle's De Anima Books II, III* (Clarendon Press, Oxford).

Hampshire, S. [1962], 'Disposition and Memory', *International Journal of Psychoanalysis*, 43: 59-68.

Hare, R. M. [1981], *Moral Thinking* (Clarendon Press, Oxford).

Harré, R., and Lamb, R. (eds.) [1983], *The Encyclopedic Dictionary of Psychology* (Basil Blackwell, Oxford).

Harriman, P. L. [1943], 'A New Approach to Multiple Personalities', *American Journal of Orthopsychiatry*, 13: 638-43.

Harris, L. P. [1977], 'Self-Recognition Among Institutionalized, Profoundly Retarded Males: A Replication', *Bulletin of the Psychonomic Society*, 9: 43-4.

Hayes, N. A. [1986], 'Consciousness and Modes of Learning' (MS, Department of Experimental Psychology, Oxford).

Hilgard, E. R. [1977], *Divided Consciousness: Multiple Controls in Human Thought and Action* (Harcourt, New York).

Hobbes, T. [1651], *Leviathan*, ed. H. Morley [1946] (George Routledge and Sons, London).

Hofstadter, D. R., and Dennett, D. C. [1981], *The Mind's I* (Harvester Press, Hassocks).

Holzman, P. S., Rousey, C., and Snyder, C. [1966], 'On Listening to One's Own Voice: Effects on Psychophysiological Responses and Free Associations', *Journal of Personality and Social Psychology*, 4: 432-41.

Howland, J. S. [1975], 'The Use of Hypnosis in the Treatment of a Case of Multiple Personality', *Journal of Nervous and Mental Disease*, 161: 138-42.

Hume, D. [1748], *An Enquiry Concerning Human Understanding*, ed. L. A. Selby-Bigge [1963] (Clarendon Press, Oxford).

—— [1739-40], *A Treatise of Human Nature*, ed. L. A. Selby-Bigge [1965] (Clarendon Press, Oxford).

Humphrey, N. [1983], *Consciousness Regained: Chapters in the Development of Mind* (Oxford University Press, Oxford).

James, W. [1890], *Principles of Psychology* (Dover Press, New York), ii.

—— [1912], *Essays in Radical Empiricism*, ed. R. B. Perry (Longmans, Green, London).

Jaynes, J. [1976], *The Origin of Consciousness in the Breakdown of the Bicameral Mind* (Houghton Mifflin, Boston).

Joynt, R. J. [1981], 'Are Two Heads Better than One?', *The Behavioral and Brain Sciences*, 4: 108-9.

Julier, D. L. [1983], 'Sociopathic Personality', in *The Encyclopedic Dictionary of Psychology*, ed. R. Harré and R. Lamb (Basil Blackwell, Oxford), 600.

Kalke, W. [1969], 'What is Wrong with Fodor and Putnam's Functionalism', *Nous*, 3: 83-94.

Kinsbourne, M., and Hicks, R. E. [1978], 'Mapping Cerebral Functional Space: Competition and Collaboration in Human Performance', in *Asymmetrical Function of the Brain*, ed. M. Kinsbourne (Cambridge University Press, Cambridge), 267-73.

Kleinig, J. [1985], *Ethical Issues in Psychosurgery* (George Allen and Unwin, London).

Koch, S. [1974], 'Psychology as Science', in *Philosophy of Psychology*, ed. S. C. Brown (Macmillan, London), 3–40.

Kripke, S. [1972], 'Naming and Necessity', in *Semantics of Natural Language*, ed. G. Harman and D. Davidson (Reidel, Dordrecht-Holland), 253–355.

Laing, R. D. [1960], *The Divided Self* (Tavistock Publications, London).

—— [1967], *The Politics of Experience and the Bird of Paradise* (Penguin Books, London).

Larmore, C. [1980], 'Descartes' Empirical Epistemology', in S. Gaukroger (ed.), *Descartes: Philosophy, Mathematics, and Physics* (Harvester Press, Brighton), 6–22.

LeDoux, J. E. [1985], 'Brain, Mind and Language', in *Brain and Mind*, ed. D. A. Oakley (Methuen, London), 197–216.

—— Wilson, D. H., and Gazzaniga, M. S. [1977], 'A Divided Mind: Observation on the Conscious Properties of the Separated Hemispheres', *Annals of Neurology*, 2: 417–21.

—— and Gazzaniga, M. S. [1981], 'The Brain and the Split Brain: A Duel with Duality as a Model of Mind', *The Behavioral and Brain Sciences*, 4: 109–10.

Lelas, S. [1985], 'Topology of Internal and External Factors in the Development of Knowledge', *Ratio*, 27: 58–70.

Levy, J. [1969], 'Information Processing and Higher Psychological Functions in the Disconnected Hemispheres of Human Commissurotomy Patients' (unpublished doctoral dissertation, California Institute of Technology).

—— Trevarthen, C., and Sperry, R. W. [1972], 'Perception of Bilateral Chimeric Figures following Hemispheric Deconnection', *Brain*, 95: 61–78.

Locke, J. [1690], *An Essay Concerning Human Understanding*, ed. A. C. Fraser [1959] (Constable, London), i, ii.

Ludwig, A. M., Brandsma, J. M., Wilbur, C. B., Bendfeldt, F., and Jameson, D. H. [1972], 'The Objective Study of a Multiple Personality: Or, are Four Heads Better than One?', *Archives of General Psychiatry*, 26: 298–310.

MacPhail, E. M. [1982], *Brain and Intelligence in Vertebrates* (Clarendon Press, Oxford).

—— [1986], 'Vertebrate Intelligence: the Null Hypothesis', in *Animal Intelligence*, ed. L. Weiskrantz (Clarendon Press, Oxford), 37–50.

Mayou, R. A. [1983], 'Personality Disorders', in *The Encyclopedic Dictionary of Psychology*, ed. H. R. Harré and R. Lamb (Basil Blackwell, Oxford), 461–3.

Melzack, R., and Wall, P. D. [1965], 'Pain Mechanisms: A New Theory', *Science*, 150: 971–9.

—— [1982], *The Challenge of Pain* (Penguin Books, Harmondsworth).

Mill, J. S. [1861], *Utilitarianism*, ed. O. Piest [1957] (Liberal Arts Press, New York).

Morton, A. [1982], 'Freudian Commonsense', in *Philosophical Essays on Freud*, ed. R. Wollheim and J. Hopkins (Cambridge University Press, Cambridge), 60-74.

—— [1983], 'Consciousness', in *The Encyclopedic Dictionary of Psychology*, ed. R. Harré and R. Lamb (Basil Blackwell, Oxford), 114-15.

Nagel, T. [1965], 'Physicalism', *Philosophical Review*, 74: 339-56.

—— [1970], 'Death', *Nous*, 4: 73-80; repr. in Nagel [1979*b*], 1-10.

—— [1971], 'Brain Bisection and the Unity of Consciousness, *Synthèse*, 22: 396-413; repr. in Nagel [1987*b*], 147-64.

—— [1974], 'What is it Like to be a Bat?', *Philosophical Review*, 83: 435-50; repr. in Nagel [1987*b*], 165-80.

—— [1979*a*], 'Subjective and Objective', in Nagel [1979*b*], 198-213.

—— [1979*b*], *Mortal Questions* (Cambridge University Press, Cambridge).

Oxford English Dictionary, compact edn. [1971] (Oxford University Press, Oxford).

Parfit, D. [1971], 'Personal Identity', *Philosophical Review*, 80: 3-27.

—— [1984], *Reasons and Persons* (Clarendon Press, Oxford).

Pascal, B. [1960], *Pensées: Notes on Religion and Other Subjects*, trans. J. Warrington (J. M. Dent and Sons, Everyman's Library, London).

Pope, K. S., and Singer, J. L. [1978], 'Regulation of the Stream of Consciousness: Towards a Theory of Ongoing Thought', in *Consciousness and Self-Regulation: Advances in Research and Theory*, ed. G. E. Schwartz and D. Shapiro (Plenum Press, New York), 101-37.

Prince, M. [1905], *The Dissociation of a Personality* (Longmans, Green, London); repr. [1968] (Johnson Reprint Corporation, New York).

Proust, M. *A la recherche du temps perdu*, vol. xi: *Albertine disparue*, trans. C. K. Scott-Moncrieff [1969] (Chatto and Windus, London).

Puccetti, R. [1973], 'Brain Bisection and Personal Identity', *British Journal for the Philosophy of Science*, 24: 339-55.

—— [1981], 'The Case for Mental Duality' and 'Author's Response', *The Behavioral and Brain Sciences*, 4: 93-9, 116-22.

Putnam, H. [1962], 'The Analytic and the Synthetic', in *Minnesota Studies in the Philosophy of Science*, 3, ed. H. Feigl and G. Maxwell (University of Minnesota Press, Minneapolis), 358-97.

—— [1975], 'Is Semantics Possible?', in *Mind, Language, and Reality, Philosophical Papers* (Cambridge University Press, Cambridge), i. 139-52.

Qiu Renzong [1984], 'The Vocabulary of "Consciousness" in Chinese Language' (MS, Chinese Academy of Social Science, Beijing).

Quine, W. V. O. [1972], 'Review of M. K. Munitz (ed.), *Identity and Individuation*', *Journal of Philosophy*, 69: 488-97.

Reich, W. [1981], 'Psychiatric Diagnosis as an Ethical Problem', in *Psychiatric Ethics*, ed. S. Bloch and P. Chodoff (Oxford University Press, Oxford), 61-88.

Robinson, H. [1982], *Matter and Sense* (Cambridge University Press, Cambridge).

Rorty, A. O. (ed.) [1976], *The Identities of Persons* (University of California Press, Berkeley).

Rorty, R. [1970a], 'Incorrigibility as the Mark of the Mental', *Journal of Philosophy*, 67: 399–424.

—— [1970b], 'Cartesian Epistemology and Changes in Ontology', in *Contemporary American Philosophy*, ed. J. E. Smith (George Allen and Unwin, London), 273–92.

—— [1980], *Philosophy and the Mirror of Nature* (Basil Blackwell, Oxford).

Sackheim, H. A., Greenberg, M. S., Weiman, A. L., Gur, R. C., Hungerbuhler, J. P., and Geschwind, N. [1982], 'Hemispheric Asymmetry in the Expression of Positive and Negative Emotions: Neurological Evidence', *Archives of Neurology*, 39: 210–18.

Schreiber, F. R. [1975], *Sybil* (Penguin Books, Harmondsworth).

Seddon, G. [1972], 'Logical Possibility', *Mind*, 81: 481–94.

Shoemaker, S. [1975], 'Functionalism and Qualia', *Philosophical Studies*, 27: 291–315.

Snell, B. [1953], *The Discovery of the Mind*, trans. T. G. Rosenmeyer (Harvard University Press, Harvard).

Sperry, R. W. [1961], 'Cerebral Organization and Behavior', *Science*, 133: 1749–57.

—— [1970], 'Perception in the Absence of the Neocortical Commissure', in *Perception and Its Disorders* (Association for Research into Nervous and Mental Diseases, New York), 123–38.

Squires, R. [1971], 'On One's Mind', *Philosophical Quarterly* 20: 347–56.

Steele Russell, I. [1979], 'Brain Size and Intelligence: A Comparative Perspective', in *Brain, Behaviour and Evolution*, ed. D. A. Oakley and H. C. Plotkin (Methuen, London), 126–53.

Strawson, P. F. [1958], 'Persons', in *Minnesota Studies in the Philosophy of Science*, 2, ed. H. Feigl, M. Scriven, and G. Maxwell (University of Minnesota Press, Minneapolis), 330–53.

—— [1959], *Individuals* (Methuen, London).

Sutcliffe, J. P., and Jones, J. [1962], 'Personal Identity, Multiple Personality, and Hypnosis', *The International Journal of Clinical and Experimental Hypnosis*, 10: 231–69.

Szasz, T. S. [1962], *The Myth of Mental Illness* (Harper and Row, London).

Taylor, W. S., and Martin, M. F. [1944], 'Multiple Personality', *Journal of Abnormal and Social Psychology*, 39: 281–300.

Thigpen, C. H., and Cleckley, H. M. [1957], *The Three Faces of Eve* (Popular Library, New York).

Thorndike, E. L. [1898], 'The Psychology of Descartes', The Columbia University Seminar in Philosophy 1897-8, handwritten MS (Thorndike MSS, Columbia University).

Trevarthen, C. [1964], 'Functional Interactions between the Cerebral Hemispheres of the Split-Brain Monkey', in *Functions of the Corpus Callosum*

(Ciba Foundation Study Group no. 20), ed. E. G. Ettlinger (Churchill, London), 24-40.

Ullmann, L. P., and Krasner, L. [1969], *A Psychological Approach to Abnormal Behavior* (Prentice-Hall, Englewood Cliffs).

Washburn, S. L., and Harding, R. S. [1972], 'Evolution of Primate Behavior', in *Primate Patterns*, ed. P. Dolhonow (Holt, Reinhart and Winston, New York).

Weiskrantz, L. [1980], 'Varieties of Residual Experience', *Quarterly Journal of Experimental Psychology*, 32: 365-86.

—— [1983], 'Evidence and Scotomata', *The Behavioral and Brain Sciences*, 6: 464-7.

—— [1986], *Blindsight: A Case Study and Implications* (Clarendon Press, Oxford).

—— Warrington, E. K., Sanders, M. D., and Marshall, J. [1974], 'Visual Capacity in the Hemianopic Field following a Restricted Occipital Ablation', *Brain*, 99: 709-28.

Whyte, L. L. [1962], *The Unconscious Before Freud* (Tavistock Publications, London).

Wilkes, K. V. [1978*a*], 'The Good Man and the Good for Man in Aristotle's Ethics', *Mind*, 87: 553-71.

—— [1978*b*], *Physicalism* (Routledge and Kegan Paul, London).

—— [1980], 'More Brain Lesions', *Philosophy*, 55: 455-70.

—— [1981], 'Functionalism, Psychology, and the Philosophy of Mind', *Philosophical Topics*, 12: 147-67.

—— [1983*a*], 'Realizam i Antirealizam u Psihologiji', *Filozofska Istraživanja*, 7: 101-16.

—— [1983*b*], 'Mind', in *The Encyclopedic Dictionary of Psychology*, ed. R. Harré and R. Lamb (Basil Blackwell, Oxford), 194-5.

—— [1984], 'Pragmatics in Science and Theory in Common Sense', *Inquiry*, 27: 339-61.

—— [1986], 'Nemo Psychologus Nisi Physiologus', *Inquiry*, 29: 165-85.

—— [1987], 'Describing the Child's Mind', in J. Russell, ed., *Philosophical Perspectives on Developmental Psychology* (Basil Blackwell, Oxford), 3-16.

—— [forthcoming], ' "External" Factors in the Development of Psychology in the West', *Boston Studies in the Philosophy of Science*, ed. R. S. Cohen and M. W. Wartofsky (Reidel, Dordrecht-Holland).

Williams, B. A. D. [1966], 'Imagination and the Self', British Academy Annual Philosophical lecture, 1966; repr. in *Problems of the Self* [1973] (Cambridge University Press, Cambridge), 26-45.

Wittgenstein, L. [1963], *Philosophical Investigations*, trans. G. E. M. Anscombe (Basil Blackwell, Oxford).

—— [1967], *Zettel*, ed. G. E. M. Anscombe and G. H. von Wright, trans. G. E. M. Anscombe (Basil Blackwell, Oxford).

INDEX